The Cultural Politics of Veterans' Narratives

Series Editors: Victoria M. Basham and Sarah Bulmer

The Critical Military Studies series welcomes original thinking on the ways in which military power works within different societies and geopolitical arenas

Militaries are central to the production and dissemination of force globally but the enduring legacies of military intervention are increasingly apparent at the societal and personal bodily levels as well, demonstrating that violence and war-making function on multiple scales. At the same time, the notion that violence is as an appropriate response to wider social and political problems transcends militaries: from private security, to seemingly 'non-military' settings such as fitness training and schooling, the legitimisation and normalisation of authoritarianism and military power occurs in various sites. This series seeks original, high-quality manuscripts and edited volumes that engage with such questions of how militaries, militarism and militarisation assemble and disassemble worlds touched and shaped by violence in these multiple ways. It will showcase innovative and interdisciplinary work that engages critically with the operation and effects of military power and provokes original questions for researchers and students alike.

Available Titles:

Resisting Militarism: Direct Action and the Politics of Subversion
Chris Rossdale

Making War on Bodies: Militarisation, Aesthetics and Embodiment in International Politics
Catherine Baker

Disordered Violence: How Gender, Race and Heteronormativity Structure Terrorism
Caron Gentry

Sex and the Nazi Soldier: Violent, Commercial and Consensual Contacts during the War in the Soviet Union, 1941–1945
Regina Mühlhäuser (translated by Jessica Spengler)

The Military–Peace Complex: Gender and Materiality in Afghanistan
Hannah Partis-Jennings

Politics of Impunity: Torture, The Armed Forces and the Failure of Transitional Justice in Brazil
Henrique Tavares Furtado

Conscientious Objection in Turkey: A Socio-legal Analysis of the Right to Refuse Military Service
Demet Çaltekin

Poetic Prosthetics: Trauma and Language in Contemporary Veteran Writing
Ron Ben-Tovim

The Gendered and Colonial Lives of Gurkhas in Private Security: From Military to Market
Amanda Chisholm

Martialling Peace: How the Peacekeeper Myth Legitimises Warfare
Nicole Wegner

Inhabiting No-Man's-Land: Army Wives, Gender and Militarisation
Alexandra Hyde

Settler Military Politics: Militarisation and the Aesthetics of War Commemoration
Federica Caso

Mobilising China's One-Child Generation: Education, Nationalism and Youth Militarisation
Orna Naftali

The Cultural Politics of Veterans' Narratives: Beyond the Wire
Nick Caddick

Forthcoming:

War and Militarisation: The British, Canadian and Dutch Invasion of Southern Afghanistan
Paul Dixon

The Militarisation of British Democracy: The Iraq and Afghan Wars and the Rise of Authoritarianism
Paul Dixon

The Cultural Politics of Veterans' Narratives

Beyond the Wire

NICK CADDICK

EDINBURGH
University Press

Edinburgh University Press is one of the leading university presses in the UK. We publish academic books and journals in our selected subject areas across the humanities and social sciences, combining cutting-edge scholarship with high editorial and production values to produce academic works of lasting importance. For more information visit our website: edinburghuniversitypress.com

© Nick Caddick, 2024, 2026

First published in hardback by Edinburgh University Press 2024

Edinburgh University Press Ltd
13 Infirmary Street
Edinburgh EH1 1LT

Typeset in 10/13 ITC Giovanni Std by
IDSUK (DataConnection) Ltd, and
printed and bound by CPI Group (UK) Ltd,
Croydon, CR0 4YY

A CIP record for this book is available from the British Library

ISBN 978 1 4744 9279 9 (hardback)
ISBN 978 1 4744 9280 5 (paperback)
ISBN 978 1 4744 9281 2 (webready PDF)
ISBN 978 1 4744 9282 9 (epub)

The right of Nick Caddick to be identified as the author of this work has been asserted in accordance with the Copyright, Designs and Patents Act 1988, and the Copyright and Related Rights Regulations 2003 (SI No. 2498).

CONTENTS

Acknowledgements	vi
Introduction	1
1. The Cultural Politics of Veterans' Narratives	18
2. Britain and 'Her Veterans': Narrating the Veteran Figure	44
3. The 'Super-Citizen' Character: Veteran Cultures and Identities	69
4. In Failure and Success: The Politics of Transition Narratives	95
5. Narrative Politics and the Militarised Academy	114
6. Intertextual Narratives and the War in Afghanistan	135
7. Trauma Stories, Surfing and Undoing the Residue of Militarism	157
Conclusion	177
References	184
Index	203

ACKNOWLEDGEMENTS

During the period in which this book was being written, we lost a dear friend, my father-in-law David Ellis, to whom I dedicate this work. He would certainly have read it, and we'd have had great discussions about its content. We miss him.

There are numerous people to whom I owe my heartfelt thanks for their support during the writing of this book. The Veterans and Families Institute at Anglia Ruskin University has been my academic home for over eight years. My colleagues there are a wonderful bunch, full of care and conviviality, and I'm proud of the environment we've created there together. This book began life over six years ago with the vague notion that I could write about the various aspects of veterans' narratives I've worked on for so long. For supporting the idea during its initial stages, and for invaluable feedback and encouragement throughout the writing process, sincere thanks are due to the series editors Sarah Bulmer and Victoria Basham. I have very much enjoyed working with my editors Sarah Foyle, Ersev Ersoy and Sam Johnson at Edinburgh University Press, and I thank them for their support of this project. Several people read chapter drafts and were kind enough to offer supportive and critical feedback. They include Alice Cree, Katy Parry, Lauren Godier-McBard, Abbie Wood, Katie Davies and Matt Fossey. None of them are to be held responsible for any flaws that remain in the final product. The following people also kindly listened and provided advice and a sounding board for my anxieties and concerns about various aspects of the work-in-progress: thank you to Brett Smith, Harriet Gray and Nivi Manchanda. Further thanks to the audience members and co-panellists at the panel on 'Confronting the militarised academy' at the BISA annual conference in Newcastle in June 2022, for engaged discussion and feedback on an early version of chapter five.

I owe an enormous debt of gratitude to my wife Kristy, and my children Olivia and George. They have supported and patiently endured my work on this book for as long as I have been writing it. Well, except George, who arrived halfway through it, in the early months of the pandemic, at home, with no midwife present for the actual birth. His arrival was a pleasant distraction from the writing, for a while. Thank you, finally, to my parents and my wider family. Your support and encouragement over so many years made it possible for me to write a book in the first place.

Introduction

It is September 2017 and I'm sitting in an enormous, air-conditioned conference hall in Toronto, waiting for the VIP guest speaker to arrive. I'm here for a conference on veteran health, which coincides with the third 'Invictus Games' sporting event – a paralympic-style competition featuring veterans traumatically injured in the recent wars in the Middle East. The people seated around banquet-style tables are a mixture of veterans, serving military personnel, and academics, all waiting silently, patiently, but thrumming with anticipation. The dense chatter of the last half hour was quickly hushed when the emcee announced that our speaker was poised to make his entrance. This conference session is unlike any I've attended before, where a handful of casually dressed academics might saunter into the room after a night on the town. Security is tight, and bags were searched on entry to the venue. Most of the people are wearing formal dresses or suits. A door opens at the back of the hall. 'Please rise, if you are able', the emcee announces. The sound of shuffling chairs briefly fills the room, before a man in Scottish traditional dress enters playing the bagpipes. Behind him walks a young prince, invited here to officially open our proceedings, along with several conference dignitaries. All around the room, smart-phones – including mine – are held aloft to capture this surreal moment on video, and to record a glimpse of the prince up close in real life. The speaker takes the stage, and the bagpipes fade away:

> I'm sure it will come as no surprise to anyone in this room that I am hugely passionate about the Invictus Games. I am passionate about the role that sport can play in the recovery of body and mind. I am passionate about the men and women of our armed forces who have served their countries. And, I am passionate in my

support and admiration for the families of those men and women, because they too have served. In 2013 I visited the Warrior Games in Colorado. It was there that I first saw the impact which sport can play in recovery of these men and women. I was amazed seeing the fiercest competition turn into respect, understanding and friendship the moment that the finish line was crossed. I saw people giving it their all on the court, or in the pool, but then hugging their opponents as brothers-in-arms. Seeing this for myself convinced me that we had to enable more injured and ill servicemen and women to benefit from the power of competition. And we had to find a way to stage a competition that would attract the attention of the world and inspire millions. The idea for the Invictus Games was born. The journey to the first Games was by no means easy. I gave my team nine months to deliver a concept which few people had heard of, and even fewer had seen for their own eyes. But as you know, we succeeded, and here we are at the third Invictus Games. In that first year, what we had hoped, but that none of us could have predicted, was the way in which the public embraced the competitors and the spirit of the games. The support was unbelievable, and the guys and girls responded by putting on a spectacle unlike anything ever seen before. For the competitors, we know that the journey to the Invictus Games is often not an easy one. We are dangling a carrot of sporting glory to help reignite qualities which have been worn-down by months and often years of fighting. Fighting to find purpose, fighting to reconnect with family. Fighting to get fit again, fighting to leave the house, and in some cases fighting to stay alive . . .

Addressing the conference, His Royal Highness Prince Henry ('Harry') of Wales – now Prince Harry, the Duke of Sussex – extols the exemplary human virtues of our servicemen and women, and of sport's redemptive power to heal the wounds of war – wounds which are only indirectly mentioned in his speech. His address tells the story of the birth of the Invictus Games movement, the narrative arc of which mirrors the symbolic re-birth of veterans through competition. The speech itself forms part of a much larger tapestry of narratives about wars, the reasons they are fought, the people who fight in them, and what happens to these people when these wars are 'over'. Just as all narratives select, evaluate and interpret events in order to highlight specific meanings while foreclosing others, Prince Harry's speech emphasises personal and collective resilience, while avoiding the circumstances that brought these 'guys and girls' to Toronto and to the Invictus Games. Notably, the speech is also a minor episode in the romantic story of a young prince, once seen as the rebellious misfit of the British Royal Family, now owning his place at the top of British establishment life through the symbolic virtue of his own military service and coming into his own as the international champion of veterans' wellbeing.[1] This is a cause to which the prince brings his powerful celebrity cachet, which one cannot help but be caught up in when exposed to it, as I was that day in Toronto.

The events I recount above comprise one small moment in what I am calling 'the cultural politics of veterans' narratives', which examines the stories told both *by* and *about* military veterans, and what these stories *do* in our collective moral, social, and political life. This is a politics which directly influences how militarism plays out within and beyond British society, including our understanding of the wars Britain fights and the international legacy of these wars. In twenty-first-century post-COVID, post-Brexit Britain, it also touches important debates about empire, national belonging and identity, patriotism, migration and the welfare state, not to mention the raucous and divisive affairs of electoral politics. Furthermore, the cultural politics of veterans' narratives form an influential battleground for broader social struggles around class, race and gender, which, as Howell argues,[2] take on an 'always, already' martial character. In short, veterans' stories *matter* in all sorts of ways in our contemporary public life. From Prince Harry's depoliticised sporting project masking the impact of war's devastation, to the myriad 'everyday' stories of veterans trying to survive in 'Civvy Street', veterans' stories are shaping not only their own and others' lives, but also our society, our politics and our values. This book's ambition is to unpick the moral and political purpose served by different modes of veteran storytelling, and to suggest better ways of responding and relating to these stories.

For me, the cultural politics of veterans' narratives has been an integral part of my work and life for over a decade, ever since I began researching for my PhD exploring the impact of surfing for veterans diagnosed with post-traumatic stress disorder (PTSD). It was during that project I developed a long-standing interest in veterans' stories – in understanding how the social and embodied legacies of war and military service transformed lives, and the creative responses veterans took towards negotiating these legacies. Through my deepening involvement in the field of critical military studies, I began to understand these stories in a wider political context, including the forms of violence they sometimes obscure, and the contradictory ways in which their stories animate processes of militarism, nationalism and the like. Not wishing to pretend that my own work stands outside the politics I critique, part of the narrative I develop in this book is about how I situate this project as an intervention in cultural politics, and the critical agenda I hope it will support. This will involve reflecting on the tensions I have encountered between different strands of my work on veterans; from the policy-driven research I have undertaken with the Ministry of Defence, co-opted into supporting a retention-focused agenda of reform,[3] to my critical work informed by an entirely different logic of critique and opposition to militarism.[4] There is a personal story here, about how I aim to balance these competing logics in my work, which, insofar as it illuminates the complexities of cultural and academic politics, warrants inclusion in this book.

Veterans' Stories and British Militarism

Veterans move 'beyond the wire', bringing stories from the military realm into civilian life and exposing the illusion of separation created by those barbed-wire fences. My overarching fascination in researching this book has been to question what veterans' stories tell us about the morality and the politics of war and military life. I wish to consider the *political* figure of the British veteran and to critically examine his or her place in sustaining British militarism. My aim is to displace the deeply 'moral' and idealised sense in which veterans are held in the public imagination, for it is this which enables their stories to do so much work on behalf of British militarism. Most people I speak to (both in and outside of academia) seem reluctant to view the veteran figure as political, preferring to think of him or her as a benign heroic figure or dutiful public servant – a figure who *transcends* politics. This is itself a political viewpoint. Likewise, whereas a great many people might feel ambivalent or opposed to *war* (and perhaps even other state-centred manifestations of militarism such as military spending or nuclear weapons), those who fight the wars – as can be clearly seen in 'support the troops' rhetoric – are resoundingly popular.[5] The connection between the 'troop', or the veteran, and militarism itself is never quite made. I will discuss the character of British militarism further in Chapter 2. For now, it is simply worth noting that veterans are offered to us – by elite and popular variations of British political culture alike – as the noble and 'non-political' face of British militarism,[6] giving militarism a homely and domesticated feel and permitting all kinds of excuses to be found for its harms. Without seeking to portray my argument as 'anti-veteran' (it is, in fact, quite the contrary), this book aims to uproot the *'militarist terms of reference'* (see Chapters 2 and 3) that present veterans to us as uniquely moral and courageous characters, snatching away any possibility of critical engagement with veterans' stories and their social consequences.

'Veterans' are defined differently by various national governments, the UK's definition being a former service person who has served more than one day in uniform. Veterans themselves often understand the term differently, with some reserving it for 'combat' or 'World War Two veterans', and some preferring alternatives such as 'ex-forces' or 'ex-services'.[7] I will use the term 'veteran' throughout this book, partly because it is the term in common usage, but also because it more succinctly conveys the militarised collection of ideas and symbols that cohere around their stories and public representations. Put simply, 'veteranness' can be powerful. It can be used in numerous and varied ways to legitimise ideas and policies, to express dissent and to foster emotional attachments among communities. Emotive ideas like respect, honour and duty 'stick'[8] to veterans and thereby invest veteran identity with privilege and credibility. Theirs is a subjectivity onto which others project patriotic sentiment, a repository for the expression of patriotic feeling. Veteran identity can thus be used to *do* things, to make certain arguments and ideas more powerful than they might otherwise be. And yet there are other, less normatively 'positive', though equally emotive ideas that also stick. Ideas about veterans as 'damaged' and 'damage-doing' that conjure up feelings of pity, sympathy, apprehension, even contempt. As such, while veteran subjectivity can be privileged – held up as a bastion of (typically male) strength and respectability – it can also be marginalised, and veterans can endure social isolation or disadvantage in the labour market on account of their service and the assumptions others make of them. 'Veteran', therefore, is a complex identity and subjectivity, one that gets bound up in public narratives that are not always of veterans' own making, and that can be deployed in service of radically different political projects.

I focus on British veterans' stories because I believe there is much to be gained from a detailed critical analysis of what these stories are doing politically in British life. Britain has justifiably been described as a 'Warrior Nation',[9] or 'Warfare State',[10] with the willingness and capacity to wage 'humanitarian' war seen by many as a defining feature of our national identity. Britain casts itself, Victoria Basham describes, as 'chivalrous, self-sacrificing and responsibly masculine in valiantly facing the dangers of the world'.[11] In Britain, military history and tradition are fused (albeit selectively) with our national story, with memories of both world wars endlessly revived and reformulated to suit political projects ranging from Brexit to domesticating public opinion in the wake of Coronavirus. Veterans' stories interject in this national story in complex and often contradictory ways: challenging militarism while also depending on it for legitimacy,[12] claiming victimhood whilst being in receipt of unprecedented public and charitable support, and calling for their voices to be heard while, sometimes, sidelining the voices of others. As I set out above, these stories are a key piece of the puzzle in understanding British militarism – something that has significant international ramifications. I therefore argue that we need a critically informed politics of veterans' narratives to untangle the relationships between stories and power (political and military), and to explore the consequences of British veterans' stories for our understanding of war and its manifold legacies.

Given my focus on British veterans' stories, I am aware of the need to expand and diversify the cultural politics of veterans' narratives, even as the idea itself is being introduced. 'Global Britain', by virtue of its long history both of empire and foreign military 'intervention', has created countless war stories in the countries from which veterans return to tell their tales. While these 'Others' – including civilians and enemy 'combatants' – sometimes feature in veterans' narratives, their own stories are given short shrift in Britain as war stories worth telling and hearing. As part of the wider narrative of conflicts like the war in Afghanistan, some stories thus feature prominently while others are excluded. To 'write in' these missing stories, and in doing so to create more equitable and diverse representations of war's impact, other voices need to be heard. I have attempted to include a broader range of voices and stories in this book – beyond those of veterans – but will readily admit that the project of diversifying and democratising veterans' narratives is nowhere near completed by my efforts here. That will require a much more sustained focus, of the kind Ware gives to the stories of Commonwealth-born soldiers fighting in the British Army, for example.[13] And, further, it demands that we listen carefully to the stories of people harmed by our nation's violence. My hope is that by emphasising the violent omissions of veterans' narratives, and by striving to broaden the stories in circulation, this book can be useful to wider demilitarising, anti-racist and anti-colonial projects while fulfilling its main goal of explicating the cultural politics of veterans' narratives in Britain.

Narrative and Cultural Politics

> We have long known that we need to be careful about the stories we tell: for they most surely have consequences. They are the tools for changing hearts and minds. And politics is partially about the management of these stories.[14]

Two core premises underpin the argument of this book: that narrative is a crucial concept for interpreting and giving meaning to experience, and that cultural politics 'happen' – are contested – largely through narrative. Stories are powerful. Not only are they tools for changing hearts and minds, as Ken Plummer suggests, but they are tools for framing events as we want them to be understood and excluding alternative or competing frames of meaning.[15] When Prince Harry speaks of veterans 'fighting to find purpose, fighting to reconnect with family. Fighting to get fit again, fighting to leave the house, and in some cases fighting to stay alive', he wants us to think of the transcendent resilience of these people, and, arguably, not of the *actual* fighting they engaged in during combat. This narrative framing has consequences, for it contributes to a cultural backdrop in which military strength features prominently in the national consciousness. Meanwhile, other narratives – stories about climate breakdown, racial justice or human rights, for example – are pushed into an alternate sphere marked out as zealous, extreme and unpatriotic. Creating space for marginalised narratives to break through is part of what contesting cultural politics is all about. Indeed, political argument generally is partly about who can make their story of the world – how it is and how it ought to be – stick.

Narratives carry out political work: reporting, convincing, inciting and indoctrinating, recruiting, predicting, amusing, inspiring, generating sympathy or antipathy, defining actors and attributing motives, and suggesting appropriate courses of action. They do this work powerfully, but unequally. *Powerfully*, because they shape our ability to understand the world around us in profoundly significant ways. As Annick Wibben says, narratives 'arrest meaning'[16]; they invent an order for events in the world and make this order seem natural, logical, and compelling. But not all narratives do this completely, extensively and successfully, hence: *unequally*. Some narratives are privileged, others are not. Some appear stable, others fragmented and inconsistent. Some are 'accepted' and come to dominate public understanding, others are unruly, disruptive and subversive. The power of a narrative to take hold in public discourse – to arrest meaning in our lives – depends on many factors. Such include the politics embedded in the narrative, and whether this politics seeks to uphold or challenge the status quo. Likewise, they include the version of history a narrative creates, and whether that history is conventional or whether, for example, it is anti-colonial, feminist or populist in its recounting of events. Others include the levels of institutional power and cultural capital invested in those who convey and defend particular narratives. Further still, the contextual dynamics of narrative – such as the audiences to whom they are addressed and the platforms through which they are disseminated – matter greatly in shaping how politics are enacted through stories.

The cultural politics of narrative is about what narratives and stories *do* both personally and politically to those who tell them, listen to them and get caught up in them. Narratives do not only 'contain' and reproduce politics and ideology, they *act* in politically significant ways. The choice of one narrative over another is itself political, as it leads to particular understandings of events while foreclosing other meanings.[17] Narratives 'bound the possible'[18] in thought and action, making certain choices thinkable and others, literally, un-*think*-able. My argument throughout this book is that the stories veterans tell about war and military life are caught up in this political web of storytelling, that these stories matter for our understanding of war and its societal legacy, and also that they matter personally for veterans because they shape the lives they go on to lead as 'civilians'. These stories are playing out around us in culture and society: in the press, on social media, in government and policy discourse, in film and documentary, in cultural products like art, music, theatre and literature, in the memoirs where veterans formally record their war experiences, and in the stories they more casually tell to others. The task of a cultural politics of veterans' narratives, as I see it, is therefore to identify, question and challenge what veterans' stories and stories about veterans[19] are doing both personally and politically.

The framework I shall propose for studying veterans' narratives (see Chapter 1) requires an explanation of 'cultural politics' and its importance in struggles over the meaning of veterans' experiences. Cultural politics, for scholars of cultural studies, is about understanding culture's relationship to power and about the symbolic and institutional function of culture as an educational, political and economic force.[20] It is about the social struggle over meaning, identity and power, and about how relations of inequality are maintained symbolically through cultural practices.[21] In order to ground my study of veterans' narratives in concrete terms, I adopt Nina Schiller's definition of cultural politics as 'the processes through which relations of power are asserted, accepted, contested, or subverted by means of ideas, values, symbols, and daily practices. Power is the ability to make somebody do something, and relations of power include domination, oppression, discipline, struggle, resistance, rebellion, co-option, subversion, and sedition.'[22] This definition captures the essence of struggle over power, meaning and identity which cultural politics entails. The notion of a 'cultural politics of narrative' that I develop in this book reflects the belief that narrative is a vital conduit for the ideas, values, symbols and practices to which Schiller refers, and thus narrative constitutes a crucial process by which cultural politics are enacted. Cultural politics are being contested when, to take but one example, veterans act to defend the idea of 'Remembrance' against others' attempts to 'water down' its meaning by widening its referents. By critiquing the cultural politics enacted through veterans' stories, my aim is to reveal the socio-political consequences of these stories, and in so doing to complicate our engagement with war's legacy.

The terms 'narrative' and 'story' similarly require introduction since their usage – both casual and defined – varies considerably in popular and academic texts. As I shall refer to them, *narratives* are the shared templates that provide tropes and plotlines for organising and understanding events in our lives. As Arthur Frank puts it, narrative 'sets parameters within which predictable kinds of things happen for similar reasons'.[23] They are shared cultural resources that help us interpret the genesis or causality of events and social circumstances. While they cannot technically exist without people to convey them, in a sense narratives do exist externally to, and independently of, any particular individual. They are the *general* templates from which people tell *specific* stories. Stories, then, are the tales people tell about their lives and experiences. As Frank elaborates the narrative/story distinction, 'Narratives make no mention of individual persons; stories depend on characters. *Stories* are about particular people living lives animated by some principle of causality: class conflict, or the tension between fathers and sons, or the human need for true love.'[24] Frank, whose work on narrative influences my own, deliberately provides no formal definition of stories, preferring to recognise them by the work they perform; that is, their 'capacities' for action (see Chapter 1). Nevertheless, there are certain elements that seem to be required. At a minimum, these would include characters along with an event or action that sets in motion a plot. Since most actual stories are not 'fully formed narratives',[25] to insist on definitional criteria would be to impose a rigidity that stories themselves defy. To complicate the distinction slightly, we cannot tell stories without drawing upon shared narrative resources. No matter how individual or unique we might profess our own stories to be, we depend on commonly available narratives to scaffold our stories. And to add one more caveat, the words 'narrative' and 'story', 'overlap so frequently that sustaining this distinction in consistent usage proves impossible'.[26] Nevertheless, I have endeavoured throughout to maintain the distinction where possible.

Outline of the Book

This book draws on more than ten years' experience, observations and insights into veteran storytelling. During this time, I have read, watched, listened to, consumed, and studied many different kinds of stories told by veterans and about veterans across a range of settings. My decisions over which topics and genres to include within this book have been influenced by this prolonged engagement with veterans' stories, and by patiently considering which stories seem to 'move' cultural politics by the messages they communicate about war and military life. The sources I examine are a mixture of systematically and intuitively generated, incorporating my own primary research, existing archives and 'data' sources (e.g., podcast material, memoirs), government policy documents, research by military charities, online veteran communities, and my own experiences as an academic researcher. The result, I hope, is an eclectic view of veteran storytelling and culture that reflects a broad range of possibilities that exist for encountering veterans' stories in everyday life. Within the confines of a single volume, I have done my best to encompass as many of the core narratives – and thorny issues – surrounding veterans and militarism as I could. However, the scope of a cultural politics of veterans' narratives is far from exhausted by my efforts which constitute, perhaps, an introduction to this idea and an orientation to its guiding concerns.

One final clarification, before I introduce the book's contents, regards the manner in which I use the term 'cultural politics of veterans' narratives', which carries a twofold meaning. First, is the empirical situation to which it refers; that is, the politics unfolding in the world through veterans' narratives. I will mostly refer to this as *'the* cultural politics of veterans' narratives'. Second, is the academic practice of critique which aims to develop a better relationship with veterans' stories, as I call for throughout the book. This I will refer to as *'a* cultural politics of veterans' narratives', in recognition of the plurality of critical projects which might be developed in this regard.

The book makes conceptual and empirical contributions to the study of veterans' narratives. Chapter 1 foregrounds the conceptual element by advancing a novel approach to analysing war and military experience. I argue that we face a moral and political dilemma about how to work with and respond to veterans' stories of war and military life. Without reducing the effects of stories to a simplistic binary, I suggest that veterans' stories can act in both 'good' and 'bad' ways in terms of the possibilities they create for lessening the social ills of war and militarism and for promoting the social values of peace and justice. How their stories act depends on many factors, like the justifications they offer for going to war, their treatment of the enemy and civilian 'Other', and the attitudes they foster towards military violence. It also depends on how they weigh the costs – both personal and social – against the perceived successes of war, along with the 'civilian' futures they imagine. My approach opposes the crass rhetoric of patriotism which claims the only proper response to veterans' stories is one of automatic and unthinking 'respect'. It demands instead that we think critically and consider how we *ought* to respond to veterans' stories in ways that promote justice at home and abroad? To facilitate critical inquiry, Chapter 1 sketches five core principles a cultural politics of veterans' narratives might employ, illustrated through stories and examples drawn from a range of different sources and contexts. I show how cultural politics manifests in the tensions between dominant narratives of war and the counter-narratives that claim different versions of events, and how broad political constraints on storytelling inevitably influence the manner in which veterans' stories act.

Chapter 1 therefore serves as the conceptual backbone of the book. The five core principles offer a framework for understanding what stories *are* and what they *do*, building on previous articulations of narrative in critical military studies and related fields.[27] The central argument is that narratives not only 'contain' and reproduce politics and ideology, but they also *act* in politically significant ways. Narratives are a crucial vehicle by which cultural politics 'happens' in social life. For each of the five core principles, a detailed conceptual argument is presented highlighting the individual, cultural and political significance of the stories veterans tell about war and military life. Key theoretical inspirations are drawn from Frank's socio-narratology, which advocates a central concern with stories as 'actors' in people's lives,[28] and Plummer's politics of storytelling which foregrounds questions of power and inequality.[29] The purpose of the chapter is to weave together complex ideas about narrative into a comprehensible framework for interpreting, analysing and critiquing stories about war and military experience.

The book's empirical contribution emerges through a series of chapters addressing different genres of veteran storytelling. Chapter 2 provides a contextual backdrop to veterans' stories. In July 2019, Conservative Member of Parliament and Afghanistan war veteran Johnny Mercer assumed a post at the heart of the UK government in the new 'Office for Veterans Affairs', stating that his purpose was to 'reset this country's relationship with her veterans'. The chapter aims to tell and critique the story of this relationship, and – by way of a 'scene-setter' – to contextualise the stories explored in subsequent chapters. The chapter's argument develops over three sections. In the first, I construct a broad-brush history of British veterans and the interwoven narratives that have shaped their relationship with the nation, arguing that the veteran has always been a disputed or contested figure within British society. The second section considers *who* 'Britain's veterans' are generally assumed to be. I argue that while the veteran is a historically ambivalent figure, there are clear gendered and racialised hierarchies shaping whose stories get to be told *as* British veterans. In the third, I argue that the relationship between 'Britain and her veterans' needs to be understood in terms of the gendered harms that remain permissible in the military. High rates of sexual violence combined with inadequate institutional responses and public 'gaslighting' indicate that Britain is failing to support women veterans when it matters. I conclude the chapter by arguing that the relationship *does* require resetting, but in more fundamental and critical ways than those imagined as part of mainstream political attempts to frame societal understandings of British veterans.

Chapter 3 examines veteran identities and the cultures which shape them. The chapter focuses on *character* as a core feature of storytelling and a key capacity by which narratives influence us.

I argue that veterans' narratives work to construct veteran character as that of 'super-citizen' and that veteran cultures reinforce this character through vivid portrayals of the values veterans live by and the virtues they embody. As such, I argue that cultures of veteran storytelling place veteran character on a morally superior plane – the most deserving among us – and that this construction sometimes has damaging effects on those designated inferior by comparison. To make this case, I draw on two prominent sites of veteran storytelling and identity construction: the podcast series 'Declassified' and social media, both of which are engaged in the construction and defence of veteran character. Through the characters they depict, veterans' stories set in place what I describe as *militarist terms of reference* that enable us to comprehend these stories only from a position of virtue. These terms include an aura of mandatory 'respect' which creates strong emotional attachments to veterans and their stories as well as emotional incentives to support veterans over other potentially vulnerable groups. I argue that to reject militarist terms of reference, and to comprehend war's impact from a more radically egalitarian perspective, we ought to reject the automatic framing of veterans' stories in these exalted moral tones. We ought, that is, to consider veterans as more complex characters and break the conditioned habit of sacralising their stories.

Chapter 4 depicts a narrative power struggle I argue is taking place within the cultural politics of veterans' narratives over representations of 'transition'. Being 'neither civilian nor military',[30] veterans occupy a space in between these two worlds, making the project of transition a narratively difficult accomplishment for veterans. I first argue that a 'state transition narrative' has emerged through policy and political rhetoric regarding veterans' transition, and that powerful actors have attempted to establish this narrative as authoritative. According to the state transition narrative, the vast majority of veterans make the transition to civilian life 'successfully', and representations of the damaged and disillusioned veteran indicate nothing more than a problematic minority responsible for tarnishing the image of veterans as a group. In contrast, narratives of veteran disenfranchisement highlight the anger many veterans feel about how their government and society has treated them since their return to civilian life. Stories of the disenfranchised veteran portray the veteran figure as downtrodden, outcast and alienated, and in doing so risk cornering veterans into a disparaged and deprecated identity. I argue that neither of these archetypal transition narratives are sufficient, in that they obscure and deny the complexity of veterans' lives. Instead, these archetypal narratives essentialise, or 'veteranise', the veteran: attributing success or failure directly to a sense of 'veteranness', whether entrepreneurial or pathological in nature.

Chapter 5 turns towards my own enmeshment in the cultural politics of veterans' narratives by examining my academic journey over the past decade's research. I argue that academics, too, are storytellers: we tell stories about the people whose lives we research, and these stories are tangled up in the broader cultural narratives about veterans. Academics work within narrative confines. There are certain stories that we are pressured to tell and *paid* to tell because of how they underpin political imperatives like 'policy improvement' and 'service delivery'. I identify a 'liberal progress narrative' that shapes how academic research on veterans is conducted and reported so that academics can make over-emphasised claims to 'impact' beyond academia. Within government policy, the liberal progress narrative suggests that great changes are being made to support veterans, whereas, I argue that such changes in reality amount to barely detectable 'tweaks' in the neoliberal system of government to make it slightly more hospitable towards veterans and their families. Within military charities, the demands of liberal progress divert attention from relations of care, leaving vulnerable people feeling 'processed' and unsupported. I argue that research funders such as the Forces in Mind Trust have played a substantial role in shaping academic research in line with the liberal progress narrative, and that the requirement of gaining access to veterans' groups through military charities creates incentives for academics to position their work as supporting the military and the Armed Forces community. The pressures of funding, access and impact contribute to the 'militarisation' of academia and the stories it is possible to tell about veterans through research.

Chapter 6 makes a new contribution to the burgeoning subfield of research on military memoirs through an intertextual reading of four memoirs of the war in Afghanistan. These stories range from the elite to the anti-militarist veteran, and then to the local/Afghan perspective. With the war now widely acknowledged to have failed on its own terms, it is possible to read back over veterans' narratives of the war to understand the various reasons attributed to failure. These memoirs, written while the war itself was still ongoing, diagnosed or predicted failure from an early stage. Reasons for failure are important because they presuppose different political responses to the war. Was the war a political, strategic or ideological failure?

Or was war the result of evil men empowered to enact their evil designs upon Afghanistan's people? While failure itself may be complex and multi-faceted, veterans' stories make compelling arguments that certain actors or circumstances are to blame, and they suggest different responses. Viewing each of their stories as part of a wider 'library' of Afghanistan war memoirs, this chapter reads three veteran's memoirs in dialogue with each other and with one memoir by an Afghan civilian turned refugee. I consider what *kind* of failure emerges through each of these narratives, and how each imagines Afghanistan, the Afghan people and British responsibility in the war's aftermath. The chapter reveals how differently positioned actors construct different narratives of failure and demonstrates the importance of stories in guiding us towards different political responses.

After mapping the broader narrative terrain of veterans and cultural politics in the preceding chapters, Chapter 7 narrows the analytical lens to consider how a specific group of veterans attempted to rebuild their lives in the aftermath of trauma. Reading 'post-traumatic stress disorder' (PTSD) as a direct (personal, embodied) consequence of British militarism, Chapter 7 explores the pursuit of healing through the practice of surfing. Stories of PTSD are 'governed' by an institutional trauma narrative elaborated by the Armed Forces and the medical establishment working in tandem. In this chapter, I first describe the institutional trauma narrative and its approach to diagnosing, domesticating, and treating PTSD. I then introduce three veterans and their stories of surfing as a means of dealing with PTSD on their own terms, outside the strictures imposed by the institutional narrative. I interviewed these veterans as part of my earlier PhD research on the impact of surfing for veterans wrestling with the psychological aftermath of trauma. Their stories show how going surfing and spending time in the ocean environment, together with other veterans, precipitated an 'unlearning' of war's impact on the body, together with a 're-learning' of fundamental components of self that were lost along the journey through military life and PTSD survivor. I describe how an ethos of care and compassion forged strong communal bonds among these veterans, but that also produced moments where compassion seemed to fail. The chapter examines the possibilities and the limits of surfing and nature as a form of healing and makes the case for surfing as an intervention in the cultural politics of veterans' narratives.

The shorter concluding chapter draws together key insights about veterans' narratives and their cultural and political impact in relation to British militarism. It summarises the book's contribution to advances in critical military studies by reflecting on what the cultural politics of narrative has revealed about war, veterans and the complexities of military power as it operates through narrative. Ultimately, I call for a healthier societal relationship with veterans' stories, sketching an imagination of what this might consist of and how we might work to achieve it.

Notes

1. Stories are also time-bound and contextual: this narrative episode occurred prior to Harry's resignation as a senior member of the British Royal family, though he has retained his close involvement with the Invictus Games.
2. Howell, 'Forget "militarization"'.
3. See, for example, Caddick et al., 'Evaluation of the Ministry of Defence Spouse Employment Support Trial'; Godier et al., 'Transition support for vulnerable Service leavers in the U.K.'; Godier-McBard, Caddick and Fossey, 'Confident, valued and supported'; Caddick and Fossey, 'Should we give military families a break?'
4. See, for example, Caddick, 'Life, embodiment and (post)war stories'; Caddick, 'Poetic encounters with war's "others"'; Caddick et al., 'Hierarchies of wounding'.
5. Millar, *Support the Troops*.
6. Rossdale, *Resisting Militarism*.
7. Burdett et al., 'Are you a veteran?'
8. Ahmed, *The Cultural Politics of Emotions*.
9. Dixon, *Warrior Nation*.
10. Edgerton, *Warfare State*.
11. Basham, 'Liberal militarism as insecurity, desire and ambivalence', p. 36.
12. Tidy, 'The gender politics of "ground truth" in the military dissent movement'.
13. Ware, *Military Migrants*.
14. Plummer, 'Narrative power, sexual stories and the politics of storytelling', p. 289.
15. Wibben, *Feminist Security Studies*.
16. Ibid., p. 64.
17. Ibid.
18. Roselle, Miskimmon and O'Loughlin, 'Strategic narrative', p. 76.
19. Of course, an analytical distinction must be drawn between the stories veterans themselves tell and those that others tell about them, or are told on their behalf. There is a politics of authorship and of representation in veterans' narratives (see, for example, Bulmer and Jackson '"You do not live in my skin"'), which is further identified and critiqued in this book.
20. See, for example, Giroux, 'Public pedagogy as cultural politics'; Hall, 'The neoliberal revolution'.
21. Ahmed, *The Cultural Politics of Emotions*.
22. Schiller, 'Cultural politics and the politics of culture', p. 2.
23. Frank, *Letting Stories Breathe*, p. 200.
24. Ibid., p. 200 (emphasis original).

25. Ibid., p. 26. While acknowledging wider definitional debates in narratology, Frank maintains that 'the boundaries of what stories are should remain fuzzy', p. 27.
26. Ibid., p. 200.
27. See, for example, Wibben, *Feminist Security Studies*; Holyfield et al., 'Masculinity under attack'; Barthwal-Datta, Krystalli and Shepherd, 'Narrative in politics and the politics of narrative'; Harel-Shalev and Daphna-Tekoah, 'Bringing women's voices back in'.
28. Frank, *Letting Stories Breathe*.
29. Plummer, *Telling Sexual Stories*; Plummer, *Narrative Power*.
30. Bulmer and Eichler, 'Unmaking militarized masculinity', p. 168.

CHAPTER 1

The Cultural Politics of Veterans' Narratives

GABRIEL TAKES A PAINTING AND PUTS IT UNDER THE CAMERA.

RUBÉN (pointing at the image): That's a painting of the Cruiser General Belgrano that I had on my wall at home. On 16th April [1982] we left Puerto Belgrano under the orders of Captain Bonzo. Our mission was to attack the English fleet south of the Malvinas. On the morning of the 2nd of May the mission was aborted and we were ordered to head for the mainland. I was on guard from 4pm to 8pm. At 3.50pm I leave the mess to start my shift. I touch my face, notice I have some stubble, and decide to shave. So I change direction and go to my bunk to fetch my razor. 4.01pm. I hear a crash like the cruiser has hit a mountain. The power goes off.

LOU: We were relieved to hear that the Belgrano had been hit, because she was a well-armed threat. We didn't care if it was turning away, because she could have turned back and attacked us.

GABRIEL: The veterans have many ways of remembering the war: we get together, and year after year we tell each other the same stories, hoping someone will tell us the missing piece. We travel to the Malvinas to look for the positions where we fought. We take thousands of photos, we put them all together and swap them, as if they were stickers for an album.

These extracts from the theatre production *Minefield/Campo Minado* by Lola Arias show war stories in dialogue, interwoven, stirring and grappling with the minefield of memory.[1] The play features six veterans of the 1982 Falklands/Malvinas war – three of them British, three Argentine – together on stage sharing their memories of the conflict. Watching from the audience, I marvel at how the men's stories make this war vividly present, not past, and how war stories have lived inside them ever since, and now live between them. Having witnessed these stories – which hit a starker emotional note through the interplay of dramatisation, costume, masks, photography, music, models and voiceover – the stories now live with me, too. To me, these feel like 'good' war stories – partly because they are not 'feel-good' stories. They open up the moral complexity of the Falklands/Malvinas war, refusing to privilege one side's recollections over the other's. As the alternating title *Minefield/Campo Minado* asserts, the stories refuse a singular meaning, insisting instead upon multiple coexisting meanings.[2] These stories are 'good' because they enact what Nguyen called an 'ethics of recognition':[3] recalling both the humanity *and* the inhumanity of the self *and* of the other.

For me, the veterans' stories in *Minefield/Campo Minado* exemplify some of the most urgent and critical tensions that a cultural politics of veterans' narratives aims to unpick: how there are a multiplicity of stories and perspectives on any conflict; how stories seek to open up (or alternatively, to foreclose) dialogue with others; how stories *act* in the imaginations of their tellers and listeners; how they make things present; how they reframe, distort and play with memory, and; how they shape our understanding of wars and their international legacies. In several ways, *Minefield/Campo Minado* mirrors the aspirations of a narrative approach; putting stories in dialogue with one another, expanding the range of stories in circulation, and acknowledging the differences amongst stories and storytellers.[4] The approach I take towards a cultural politics of narrative shares these aspirations and adds to them a critical objective designed to interrogate what stories are *doing* as a form of political action. Veterans' stories vary widely in how they relate to war and militarism, and it is only by expanding our sense of what these stories *are* and the *effects* they have that we can explore how cultural politics unfolds as a result. The goal of this chapter is to provide a framework for generating such understanding.

By telling stories we affirm our values and situate ourselves in political communities. For instance, one veteran's war story might position him or her as defender of king and country, secure in the identity of patriotic servant to the nation. Another may imagine patriotism quite differently, as restoring national values deemed to have been violated in the waging of an unjust war, thus marking themselves out as war resisters.[5] When stories affirm values overtly and confidently, they usually polarise responses: either one 'supports the troops' or one doesn't. Yet while cultural politics certainly does operate in this virulent and divisive way, its processes are often more nuanced and contingent. Stories are contextual and can be told in different ways to different audiences on different occasions to make different points. Stories can be fractured, incomplete, hybrid, allowing multiple points of view, exposing the pain and joy of war while deferring judgement on its meaning and purpose. War stories can 'flex': this makes them productive, open to dialogue with other stories. But it also makes them dangerous: stories are 'out of control',[6] and might be used in ways unintended by their authors.[7] Rather than smoothing over stories' inconsistencies, a cultural politics of veterans' narratives, such as I sketch out in this chapter, is about the intricacies of multiple overlapping stories and narratives, and understanding the moral and political work they perform.

This chapter introduces five core principles for a cultural politics of narrative, designed to facilitate a critically engaged analysis of veterans' narratives. These principles are drawn together from a vast body of study on narrative,[8] with two theoretical perspectives providing particular inspiration. Prior to discussing the core principles, I will briefly introduce the theoretical innovations which have helped to shape the ideas put forth in this chapter. First, Arthur Frank's socio-narratology provides a comprehensive understanding of what stories *do* – that is, their capacity to shape meaning, personal experience, embodiment and social life. As Frank describes it, 'Socio-narratology expands the study of literary narratives – narratology – to consider the fullest range of storytelling, from folklore to everyday conversation.'[9] For Frank, stories must be understood as 'actors' in people's lives. Socio-narratology studies *how* and with what *effects* stories act, including the various capacities which enable their action (more on this later in the chapter). It is an ethical project of inquiry into stories, with normative ambitions to reveal the virtue of stories in light of the effects they bring about. In an ethical sense, then, stories are unequal. Whereas some stories seek to narrow the range of human thought and possibility (as might stories told to uphold authoritarian regimes or oppressive social norms), others seek to expand the range of possibilities for expression (as stories told to liberate, to emancipate or to transform societies might do). Importantly, Frank understands stories – and narrative analysis – as dialogical, recognising that 'any individual voice is actually a dialogue between voices'.[10] The significance of this insight for a cultural politics of veterans' narratives lies in understanding how veterans' voices merge with and depart from others', and where these voices carry the broader social conversation on war and militarism.

Second, the framework I present draws upon a 'politics of storytelling' following the work of Ken Plummer.[11] Plummer deals chiefly with questions of narrative power and narrative empathy. On power, he asks *'how does power – domination, subordination, authority and legitimacy, flourishing and autonomy – work its way through stories'*.[12] Storytelling situations are marked by power: by who embodies power in a given situation and by whose interests are being served by particular stories told in particular times and places. There is, therefore, a *'profound inequality of storytelling'*,[13] with stories bound up in wider structures of inequality and division. Linked to this is the politics of narrative empathy, which involves listening to and engaging in dialogue with others' stories, especially the stories of people with whom we might disagree. Plummer sees narrative empathy both as a crucial indicator of our humanity and as a key strategy in politics. In this sense, a politics of storytelling shares the normative ambitions of socio-narratology, in that it is 'ultimately charged with producing better stories told in better ways for a better world for all',[14] and thus there is a useful synergy between these two narrative theories. But whereas socio-narratology provides the more comprehensive insight into stories' social role as actors, Plummer's politics of storytelling provides an overt emphasis on power and politics that I find lacking in socio-narratology. Blending these theories, the approach I take aims to tread a line between critically exposing narrative power, on the one hand, and enhancing narrative empathy through dialogue, on the other.

Five Core Principles[15]

1. *Storytelling and Bodily Experience are Intimately Interconnected Dimensions of Life and World-making*

As feminist scholarship has long advocated, bodies are a fundamental component of war and war experience.[16] Stories about war proceed from the body. This is true both of the storytelling body that retells the experience of war, and of the bodily experiences that are recounted in the telling – such as Rubén's minute-by-minute account of what happened to him during the sinking of the *General Belgrano*. Stories about war are stories about bodies: about what bodies *do* in war, what they are *made* to do, and what is done *to* them. For Parashar, bodies themselves are powerful war narratives, able to speak intimately of war's violence in ways that traditional, 'disembodied' war scholarship overlooks in favour of state-level discourse and explanations.[17] 'Bodies', Parashar writes, 'convey meaning, identity and symbolism in war. War bodies are not all lifeless and mutilated; some are warriors, injured, crippled, raped, held hostage, spying and spied upon, grieving and even celebrating.'[18] I argue that paying attention to stories' embodiment crucially helps us to zoom in on how cultural politics are *lived* and *felt* in real people's everyday lives.

Understanding the embodiment of war stories calls for an appreciation of how these stories are written onto – inscribed on – the body itself. This is strikingly evident in the case of wounded or amputee veterans, where missing limbs and disfigurement convey vivid, visual narratives about war's destruction. The story *Man Down* told by Royal Marine Mark Ormrod in his memoir of Britain's war in Afghanistan, serves to illustrate. In 2007, Ormrod became Britain's first surviving triple-amputee casualty after accidently triggering a Taliban landmine. In this passage from his memoir, he recalls his feelings during the moments after the blast:

> My first feeling wasn't fear or pain, it was anger at myself. I just felt stupid and embarrassed. 'You're a Marine,' I thought. 'You're supposed to be one of the most professionally trained soldiers on the planet. What a prick! What a fucking idiot! How could you do something so stupid?'[19]

Especially revealing here is the extent to which Ormrod's first emotional response to horrific bodily injury is shaped by his identity as a Royal Marine. Despite being 'obviously in a massive state of shock', that Ormrod's first thoughts about injury revolve around the fracturing of his elite warrior identity suggests how deeply military culture infuses his body and bodily sensations. The calamitous moment of injury and subsequent battle for survival marks Ormrod's body with an 'awesome'[20] war story. This story then continues through the agonising struggle of rehabilitation, and later culminates in glory and sporting triumph at the Invictus Games. The latter part of the narrative is told in Ormrod's YouTube documentary 'No Limits', which retells and extends his story from the book.[21] The opening of the documentary shows Ormrod walking onto the Invictus stage on his prosthetic legs, flag-draped, receiving an award for exceptional performance at the games. As inspirational music plays, the film then cuts to an image of Ormrod's grizzled face, focused, positioned against a black background. Then, with eyes focused intently on the camera, his voice emerges, overdubbing the motionless image, and speaking with clarity and authority:

> Here's the thing about life: Life is hard. And throughout this journey that we're all on, we are gonna come across challenges. We're gonna find ourselves facing adversity, and many times we're gonna find ourselves in very difficult situations. But its not those difficult situations that we find ourselves in that define us, its how we overcome them that defines us. Most people's default setting is to face something difficult and to quit, and to give up, and to say 'I can't do this' or 'I'm not good enough, its too hard'. And it is hard; its very, very hard – constantly hard. But it can be done. Just look at the situation that you're facing and think 'Okay, here's what I got, how am I gonna deal with it?' Choosing how you react to the situation you find yourself in – that's what makes the difference between winning and losing. I think a lot of people hugely underestimate what they're capable of. People don't believe in themselves enough anymore. You know, they find something difficult and they get scared, and they give in to fear, and they listen to the people around them that say 'You're not good enough, you can't do it, its too hard'.

This story bristles with meaning, values and beliefs about war, packaged into it both implicitly and explicitly, setting the cultural politics of narrative in motion. Implicitly, Ormrod's story highlights how narratives, like bodies, are marked by gendered expectation and struggle.[22] At the beginning, for instance, Ormrod's response to traumatic injury displays anger – a comfortably 'masculine' emotion, as opposed to fear or pain – as he distances himself from the pain of injury by invoking the elite warrior ideal.[23] If the act of wounding is as much a challenge to Ormrod's sense of elite warriorhood as it is an assault on his physical body, the way he subsequently tells his story serves to repair and rebuild this identity. Explicitly, the story exemplifies the inspirational recovery narrative that has become familiar to audiences through the Invictus Games.[24] As one of the most grievously injured soldiers ever to survive these kinds of war injuries, Ormrod's story of recovery and 'limitless' possibility carries enormous cultural gravitas. Having survived war's harshest violence and 'come back fighting', Ormrod is described by various commentators as 'a living legend', 'a role model', and by Prince Harry as 'Britain's answer to superman'.[25] Within the cultural politics of veterans' narratives, stories like this function as a touchstone of masculine authority on war and its brutality. It reaffirms what Millar and Tidy refer to as the 'myth of the heroic solider' in the public imagination,[26] and, as the most privileged kind of war story, it serves as the backdrop against which other veterans' stories are known and evaluated.

One further observation about storytelling and the body concerns the manner in which these two facets of experience are interconnected. Ormrod's story shows the body in war – devastated by violence, rising from the ashes – as the key subject matter of narrative. Yet how did his experience become 'narrative'? Or, flipping the question, how did narrative become his embodied experience? Narrative theory can shed light on the connections. For Schiff, narrative is an attempt to 'speak life':[27] to articulate the meanings it has for us and to navigate our way through ambiguous life experiences. As he puts it:

> Life and narrative entangle each other in the most intimate sense. The connection between narrative and life is direct but complex, mediated through cultural and social circumstances and the person's ability to creatively imagine alternative possibilities.[28]

Schiff identifies the connection between experience and narrative as one of complex mediation between events that happen in and to our physical bodies, the social and cultural conditions our bodies are situated within, and our imagination. Going beyond Schiff's position, Frank argues that we need to reverse the conventional understanding that narrative simply reflects or reports experiences which have already happened.[29] This is what Frank refers to as the 'mimetic' understanding of narrative, whereby 'stories imitate life that has already happened and is now being represented in the story'.[30] Frank troubles mimetic logic by arguing that it misses the significant extent to which narrative shapes experience. People know stories – most often the ones borrowed from the groups and cultures they live and interact within – and then have experiences. Narrative *then* experience; not experience *then* narrative. In other words, Ormrod is able to experience his recovery from catastrophic injury as an inspirational journey *because* the narrative template for this script was already available and showed him how. However, in reversing the conventional ordering of narrative and experience, Frank is careful to avoid the suggestion that people are 'determined' by narratives. Rejecting determinism means respecting the agency of veterans, and of people generally, as authors of their own experiences and their own stories (but always within limits). Avoiding both determinism and naive mimetic logic, Frank therefore argues that 'mimesis happens, but as a reciprocal process. Life and story imitate each other, ceaselessly and seamlessly, but neither enjoys either temporal or causal precedence.'[31] Narrative therefore shapes experience, and experience also shapes narrative, continuously and recursively.[32]

2. Veterans' Stories are Borrowed From, and Situated In, the Societies and Cultures they Inhabit

To tell stories, veterans depend on the genres, tropes, themes and metaphors embedded in the 'public' or 'cultural' narratives circulating in their societies. By expanding the cultural component of narrative, this second principle develops and advances the idea (expressed above) that culture infuses embodied experience with meaning. Molly Andrews' description of political narratives provides a useful summary of the simultaneously personal and social nature of stories:

> Discussion of political narratives always turns to an examination of the relationship between macro and micro narratives, in other words the relationship between the stories of individuals and the stories of the communities in which they live. Political narratives which individuals tell may or may not be explicitly about politics; often the most telling of them are not. But in the stories which they weave, individuals reveal how they position themselves within the communities in which they live, to whom or what they see themselves as belonging to/alienated from, how they construct notions of power, and the processes by which such power is negotiated. For individuals, political narratives are the ligaments of identity, revealing how one constructs the boundaries of, and the connections between, the self and the other.[33]

For Andrews, then, 'political stories, even when they relate to individual experience, are never just the property of isolated selves'.[34] The notion that individuals borrow their stories from the cultures they inhabit affirms the belief that people possess *narrative agency*; that is, the capacity to select which stories to tell about their lives and which cultural narratives they seek to be part of. If no story is ever completely original – the 'property of isolated selves', in Andrews' terms – individuals at least have the ability to influence their narrative destiny. The degree of narrative agency people can exert is always contingent, for example, upon the strength of free speech and democratic institutions within a given society, and the extent to which dominant narratives (e.g., around military service or the legitimacy of any given war) become hegemonic in ways that limit the freedoms of counter-narratives or render them too risky or subversive to embrace publicly. Tied to this second principle, therefore, is the understanding that stories are not only *borrowed from*, but also *situated within* cultural, societal and political contexts. If the notion of 'borrowing' implies too much in the way of freedom to spin culture into personal stories as we please, that of stories as 'situated' reminds us that circumstances weigh heavily on the kind of stories we can tell. As Ashplant and colleagues argue, 'individual subjects come to identify their experiences through the pre-existing narratives fashioned by the agencies of the nation-state and civil society'.[35] If the range of pre-existing narratives is limited, or if certain narratives dominate to the exclusion of others, the possibilities for representing experience become narrowed. Because most individuals do not have control over the public narratives which frame their stories and give them meaning within a wider context, they must find ways of accommodating their personal stories within this narrative context, even (or perhaps especially) if that means challenging the dominant narratives.

How veterans' stories interact with social narratives about war influences the cultural politics which unfold through these stories. For example, veterans' stories offer varied perspectives on the justification of the wars they fight, with these perspectives set in dialogue with the official justifications that governments provide. One method by which historians and scholars of war have grappled with the logic of conflict, as refracted through narrative, has been to examine the genre of military memoir.[36] These are the autobiographical narratives published by veterans who participated in war, providing a means of public education and enlightenment. Some examples can be used to illustrate commonalities and divergences in veterans' accounts of war's logic:

> The officers were clear enough as to why we were in Afghanistan. Helmand Province was the Taliban's backyard and cradle of the 9/11 attacks. Our job was to deny a safe haven to terrorists who posed a threat to the people of the United Kingdom. Personally, I was there to do a job and test myself to the limit. If I did any fighting it would be for myself and the lads who stood next to me and to stop any bastard having a crack at us. Taking on the terrorists was fine by me and if my being there meant some group of girls went to school for a bit, then I was happy with that. (Mark Ormrod, *Man Down*[37])

The safety of our streets (and Underground) is the reason soldiers board RAF planes bound for Kandahar, it is the reason soldiers return in coffins draped with the Union Jack flag, it is the reason they are fighting in Helmand in the first place, but it is not the reason they fight. War today is not about defending and invading territory. There isn't the obvious patriotism of protecting British soil like the Falklands or defending allied borders as in the World Wars, because the wars in Iraq and Afghanistan are more obtuse. It isn't the threat of Al Qaeda bombs in London that drives a soldier to arms, because today's PlayStation generation are not motivated by religious zeal or political ideals. They don't go to war so Fat Cat bankers can sit more comfortably on the Tube, and they don't patrol around the villages of Helmand Province concerned with spreading democratic values (not to say this doesn't occupy more senior commanders). They do it because of their friends, their mates and their Army family. (Héloïse Goodley, *An Officer and a Gentlewoman*[38])

Every day in Iraq I felt like a hypocrite, and it tore me apart inside to fight in a war I didn't believe in. I wanted to throw down my weapon and refuse to promote the injustices I executed. My integrity to fulfil my oath and the compassion for my comrades kept me at my post. The battle within raged, but the light at the end of the tunnel was near. I swore to myself that I would one day make a difference in this world. On May 31, 2005, I was honorably discharged from the United States Army, though in my heart and mind I felt I had been part of a dishonorable action. I would spend the next nine years going to school, learning to understand my experience, and the reasons I feel the way I do. I would also spend that time as an activist, fighting to make the world a better place, as well as seeking penance for the things I felt I had done wrong. (Ben Schrader, *Fight to Live, Live to Fight*[39])

Leaving aside the relative merits of their arguments, evident in each of these examples is that individual stories are framed within wider conflict narratives, such as the 'liberal militarist' narrative of foreign war as domestic security. As a collective genre, military memoirs have been described as 'vectors of militarism', in that they constitute 'mechanisms by which the logic of military intervention and the use of military power comes to be justified and rationalised'.[40] The similarities of their stories notwithstanding (such as the near-universal trope of 'fighting for one's comrades'), there is variety in how veterans respond to the logic of intervention and the use of military power. These stories are all situated within dominant war narratives, but they manoeuvre differently within them. Exploring the 'situated' telling of veterans' stories opens up fascinating questions for a cultural politics of narrative: do their stories share or oppose the logic of the dominant war narratives? How do counter-narratives emerge to contest the dominant narratives? Do counter-narratives actually undermine the dominant narratives or, paradoxically, do they maintain them by keeping the parameters of narration intact? How do veterans share similar narrative forms in telling their stories, and how do they differ? Where are the fissures and fractures in veterans' stories, and how might the inconsistencies be used to undermine military power? Keeping such questions in mind helps us to explore the connections between stories and wider cultural narratives as a key site where militarism unfolds and politics occurs.

3. Stories are 'Actors' in the Sense that They Take On the Capacity to Shape the Thoughts, Beliefs and Actions of Those Who Are Caught Up in Them

The capacity for 'action' raises the stakes of narrative by showing that stories have consequences which render them transformative and (potentially) dangerous.[41] The notion of stories as 'actors' develops the previous two principles by advancing a bolder definition of the role of stories in social life. The capacity of stories to act is not deterministic, and to argue as such would cede too much power to stories while underplaying the agency of the storytellers themselves. Rather, to claim that stories are actors is to acknowledge the very significant extent to which they form our interpretations of the world and make particular courses of action seem worthwhile, compelling or necessary. Frank explains the manner of stories' action:

> People do not simply listen to stories, they become *caught up*, a phrase that can be explained only by another metaphor: stories get under people's skin. Once stories are under people's skin, they affect the terms in which people think, know, and perceive. Stories teach people what to look for and what can be ignored; they teach what to value and what to hold in contempt.[42]

Stories, therefore, are performative; they make things happen, at both the micro and macro levels of narration. At the micro (personal) level, stories act to shape the course of a life by teaching, in Frank's terms, 'what to value and what to hold in contempt'. Tracing a line between narratives and their effects on individuals can be relatively straightforward. For example, gendered narratives about war trauma act on veterans by reinforcing the masculine imperative to 'man-up and get on with it' rather than seek help for post-traumatic stress disorder.[43] That such narratives may result in veterans avoiding or delaying help-seeking can be demonstrated empirically by analysing veterans' stories of masculinity and PTSD. At the macro (structural) level, narratives act by framing social, economic and political events or agendas, and by establishing the templates through which different groups understand their place in society. Identifying the action in macro-level narratives can be more convoluted. Narratives at this level of social organisation are channelled through many sources (e.g., news, film, radio and television, books, social media, research, everyday conversation). They are not the product of an individual storyteller, but rather they involve many 'tellers' and many 'listeners'. Such narratives are diffused throughout culture and society, may or may not have a clearly identified origin, and are sometimes articulated only loosely or through 'fragments' which gradually accrue into narratives.[44] Given the complexity of narratives at this structural level, attributing causality to narrative is slippery and imprecise. When examining the impact of narrative on cultural politics, therefore, it is often most useful to consider how narratives *create the conditions* under which certain events, actions, values and prejudices are more likely to occur.

Frank lists thirteen capacities by which stories perform their social role as actors. Without rehearsing the whole list, some of the most influential capacities for a cultural politics of veterans' narratives include the following:

- *Truth-telling*: Stories have the capacity not only to report, but to *enact* truth. That is, stories bring new truths into being by depicting events in a particular light. Things happened *this* way not *that*, and *these* are the consequences. The truth of stories is often contested by those who tell other stories about events or circumstances; counter-narratives which seek to enact different truths in order to claim a different version of social reality. Stories' truth telling capacity is therefore complex, bound up with the constant and uncertain social process of establishing 'the truth' of complex matters like war. Power is integral to this process, and the capacity of stories to enact truths that take hold depends upon the social and political power flowing through their tellers.

- *Interpretive openness*: Linked to truth-telling, stories possess interpretive openness, which is the capacity to 'narrate events in ways that leave open the interpretation of what exactly happened and how to respond to it'.[45] The same story might make different points – communicate different truths – to different readers or listeners. The point a story makes will often depend upon the predispositions, perspectives and values with which a reader or listener approaches and interprets the story.
- *Point of view*: Contra interpretive openness, stories also possess the capacity to make a particular point of view appear both plausible and compelling. Being too caught up in a story can feel like being compelled to share the viewpoint of a particular character. This is the character whose 'side' we come to take – the hero or heroine of the story with whom we associate. The more deeply we come to identify with one character's point of view, the less we are able to appreciate the perspective of others.
- *Inherent morality*: Stories possess an inherent morality in that they 'inform people's sense of what counts as good and bad, of how to act and how not to act'.[46] This moral quality suggests what we *ought* to do to resolve a conflict or a disruption to the status quo.

As influential as these capacities may be, the most potent capacity of stories, according to Frank, is their capacity to arouse imagination.[47] Stories, 'create imaginations of how the past might have gone differently and the future is open to any possibility'.[48] In stories about war, imagining what might have been – alongside future possibilities – takes on great significance. How might war have been fought differently, or avoided altogether? How can we tell stories that lead to peaceful futures? For Andrews, the generative potential of our narrative imagination is about this opening up of human possibilities, rather than relying on settled certainties: what she refers to as the 'subjunctive' quality of narrative.[49] It is also, she argues, integral to our ability to form ethical relationships with others through imagining that which is different from ourselves. The imaginative capacity of narrative to open up possibility is most productive and expansive, therefore, when it happens as part of open dialogue with others. Returning to this chapter's opening, this dialogic means of imagining difference is well exemplified by *Minefield/Camp Minado*. The Argentine and British veterans invite the play's audience to reflect on the human commonalities existing between former enemies, and to imagine the Falklands/Malvinas war differently as a result. As part of this audience, I feel my moral imagination of the war broadened, rather than constricted to a singular point of view. The possibilities of stories are best realised when they inspire hope, lead us towards healing, or help us to find solutions to intractable problems. Good stories are those that reveal multiple points of view, permit different interpretations, acknowledge complex truths, unpick moral complexity and expand rather than constrict the imagination.

Yet veterans' stories *do* sometimes constrain and restrict the imagination, often by enacting silences regarding others and their stories. Stories enact silences when they become privileged interpretations of war, when they 'orientalise' the other,[50] and when they render others' voices mute or irrelevant. To understand how, we must put veterans' stories in dialogue with others', particularly those whose lives are disrupted by the wars veterans fought in. Such stories are easily missed against the torrent of veteran war stories, but they do exist. One example is Qais Akbar Omar's memoir *A Fort of Nine Towers*, which tells his story of growing up in Afghanistan during a period of brutal conflict. His story begins 'In the time before', as time itself has been carved up by the convulsions of war in Afghanistan:

> In the time before the fighting, before the rockets, before the warlords and their false promises, before the sudden disappearance of so many people we knew to graves or foreign lands, before the Taliban and their madness, before the smell of death hung daily in the air and the ground was soaked in blood, we lived well.[51]

Omar writes fondly of his family, his school, his uncles and their businesses, and about 'the heart of our world'[52]; his grandfather's house where they all lived. 'Living well', for Omar, meant holding onto all that was worth preserving about Afghanistan throughout the subsequent destruction: his family's nomadic heritage, his love of world literature, the natural beauty of the land, and the warmth and generosity of Afghanistan's people who, even during the brutality of war, never 'failed in their hospitality even for a moment'.[53] Reading stories like Omar's in dialogue with veterans' stories, it is possible to create different, perhaps deeper and more nuanced 'imaginations' of Afghanistan.[54] Veterans' stories often depict Afghans as backward villagers, ancient tribesmen, hapless military partners or as fanatical yet formidable opponents. Assumptions and generalisations are constantly being made about Afghans, and veterans' stories often act by reinforcing an imagination of Afghanistan as somewhere that requires intervention, protection and democracy. Omar's story, on the other hand, claims a rich history and culture for Afghanistan and its people, one that he and other Afghans now wish to rebuild. Omar's story acts by humanising those whom veterans' stories sometimes render 'Other'. Rather than a place of violence – a 'Desert of Death'[55] – Afghanistan becomes a place where stories exist to be told. By listening to these stories, we develop a broader view of cultural politics, widening the circle of people imagined as citizens with a stake in the struggle over meaning and value. Indeed, the cultural politics of narrative is about what happens when stories like Omar's come into contact with veterans' stories: which meanings and interpretations gain the status of truth and are allowed to shape our understanding of war, and how might other stories upset these moral certainties?

4. Narratives are Relational and Historical: They Forge Communities Around Shared Understandings of History

In November 2019, I was invited onto my local radio station to discuss a move by the Royal British Legion (RBL) to broaden the meaning of its iconic red poppy – the traditional symbol of Remembrance for British soldiers killed in war. That year, for the first time in nearly 100 years of commemoration events, the poppy was to incorporate recognition of civilian victims of war and terrorism alongside soldiers. Recent years had witnessed an annual furore over the poppy's symbolism, and so the move by the RBL could be read as an attempt to subsume diverse viewpoints within its system of meaning while maintaining its authority to speak on behalf of the nation. As an RBL spokesperson claimed: 'remembrance is inclusive of all modern Britain and its important communities know their views and values are reflected in our activity'.[56] I went on record supporting the decision, arguing that dead civilians are no less dead than the soldiers who lose their lives in war, and reflecting on the vastly greater number of civilians than soldiers killed during the Second World War. In hindsight, I can better appreciate the hierarchical manner in which the RBL were attempting to incorporate civilians into their symbolism, though I still view the attempt to acknowledge different viewpoints as a step forward in practices of commemoration. However, rather than defusing controversy surrounding the red poppy – and its alternative, the pacifist white poppy symbol – the RBL's attempt to modify its messaging stimulated further argument. Callers to the radio programme worried that the meaning of the red poppy was being 'watered down', while veteran communities online continued to angrily reject the white poppy. Further striving to distance the poppy from political debates, the RBL began to state on their website that 'Everyone is free to remember in their own way, or to choose not to remember at all.'[57]

Acts of commemoration and the debates that encircle them exemplify the notion that narratives gather people into communities based on shared understandings of history. Narrative should be understood as a form of social practice – as constituting social relations and historical representations that become organised *by* and *as* narrative.[58] By articulating what it is that people share in common with each other, such as shared struggles, histories and traditions, narratives give people a means of relating to one another. Behind the red poppy lies a national story about the wars Britain fought to maintain its 'way of life', anchored by quintessential Second World War memories of Winston Churchill, the 'Blitz spirit', and the Battle of Britain.[59] There is a 'nation-defining' quality to the narrative of Britain's resilient defence of freedom and decency against Nazi tyranny. Wearing the poppy marks one out as belonging to a national community which shares this core historical narrative. Narrative is thus a *means of belonging*: those who share the same story about being from this or that place, or membership of a particular social group, share a key focus for communal identification and bonding. The communities that narratives help forge can be 'real', as in groups of people with reciprocal patterns of relationship situated geographically or virtually, or 'imagined', as in a wider collective assumed to cohere on the basis of shared identities such as racial, national, and/or political identities.[60]

Narratives are historical both in the sense that they develop over time, possessing a genealogy that can be traced to the past, and in the sense that they 'create' history by constructing particular versions of past events. As Andrews argues:

> Political narratives play a critical role in creating and recreating history – at the level of the individual, community, and the nation. In as much as identity is inextricably linked to story, and is forever a project in the making, political narratives are, by extension, a mechanism through which the past is reformulated in light of a desired future.[61]

Just as the creation of identity through narrative is forever in the making, it is also *contested*, as the fractious poppy debates serve to illustrate. As Ashplant and colleagues argued, 'The politics of war memory and commemoration is precisely the struggle of different groups to give public articulation to, and hence recognition for, certain memories and the narratives within which they are structured.'[62] While many communities within Britain may locate themselves comfortably within the dominant story, displaying the red poppy on their lapel as a symbol of their belonging, others struggle to do so, and may oppose the dominant narrative. Basham, for example, argues that British practices of Remembrance create a gendered and racialised image of a 'white, muscular, masculinist British state, threatened by irrational enemy others'.[63] Wearers of the white poppy therefore challenge what they see as the association of war with militarist pride and glory, choosing instead to commemorate a pacifist history of opposition to war.

The relational component of narrative is often, therefore, just as much about who is left out of the story as it is about who is included within it. Official practices of commemoration not only help to preserve dominant narratives, but function also to police the boundaries of who belongs within those narratives. When the Peace Pledge Union (creators of the white poppy symbol) pledge remembrance for 'all victims of war', including 'people of all nationalities',[64] their actions are seen as inflammatory by those for whom remembrance ought to be restricted to British soldiers. They are accused of 'playing politics' with Remembrance. The ethical move to remember 'others', argues Nguyen, is seen as 'explicitly political in that it goes against the grain of the natural and by doing so becomes visible'.[65] Remembering one's own, by contrast, has 'the luxury of appearing to be natural and hence invisible'.[66] A cultural politics of veterans' narratives, as I set out in this chapter, aims to practice Nguyen's 'ethics of recalling others', in addition to one's own, by bringing multiple voices into the social conversation on war and its legacy. The central questions here are which histories are promoted by which narratives, and in whose interests? And, relatedly, which relationships – for example, of dominance and subordination, privilege and marginalisation – do these narratives enable and reinforce?

One reason why contest over narrative often feels divisive is because people feel there is much *at stake* in their narratives,[67] such as defending identities which resonate with the core of who people feel themselves to be. Narratives teach us to attach value to certain norms and ideologies (e.g., the proud, triumphant nation) and this valuing has a strongly emotive character. We feel invested in these norms, we are drawn to them and they become *ours*. Likewise, we are repelled by other norms and ideologies that stories make suspect, such as a pacifist 'disrespect' for fallen soldiers. We feel disgusted by them, and we are *opposed*. Stories contain emotional scripts,[68] the effects of which are profoundly political because they unconsciously generate support for social norms in ways that depoliticise war and its societal legacy.[69] The emotional logic of narrative is extraordinarily powerful; tightening social bonds within communities while hardening opposition to others, legitimising the wars of the present based on the glories of the past, and justifying nationalist myth-making. Effective storytelling does much of this work beyond the level of conscious reflection – locking us into emotional responses without us realising it is having this effect.

5. *Power is Everywhere in Stories, and Politics is about Influencing, Controlling, Regulating, and Challenging Different Narratives*

I want to speak on behalf of the generation of women who experienced the rampant misogyny of the 80s as well as those who are living through the more covert biases and bigotry of today. It wasn't all bad – as pioneering military women, we had a lot of fun and brilliant experiences along the way. And we dated, even married, quite a few of those male officers as well, because serving British women and men are exactly the sort of characters you would want to marry; reliable, resilient, faithful and kind. But there are still too many holding minorities back within the British Army – a small, but toxic cohort of senior, misogynistic white middle-class males. These are the enemy of Good. Of a high-class British Army. They are not the ones you want to marry . . . So even though I am leaving I will continue to fight. I will remain a Woman at War.[70]

Diane Allen's memoir, *Forewarned: Cockups, Conspiracy and Misogyny in the British Army (1983–2020)*, tells of an embattled personal encounter with power and privilege built into the institutional structures of the British Army. It is a story that many within the institution would likely deny, particularly those who devise recruitment ads claiming the army to be a welcoming and egalitarian employer. As Allen's subtitle makes clear, hers is a story long in the making, but one kept silent for many years because of the devastating impact speaking out would have had on her career. Now that her career is over – Allen says, 'Its way too late to fix my career now; the Patriarchy has beaten me and that is a source of great sadness to me'[71] – Allen tells her story in the hope of influencing change. Her complaint identifies no shortage of necessary changes: sexism and privilege built into an unaccountable promotions system, a culture that remains hostile for whistleblowers, and assumptions of female incompetence that cut deeper than the casual groping she also experienced.

Allen's story is an intervention in the cultural politics of narrative, for it challenges deeply cherished norms, such as 'pride in service', which underpin veteran storytelling. She writes, 'In my view, we don't currently have an Army that we can be proud to serve in'.[72] By questioning the foundations of military pride – something culturally integral to the military's authority – her story aims to expose the failings of the powerful within the army. Her story illustrates the last core principle of a cultural politics of narrative I wish to introduce: that stories are everywhere subjected to, reproductive of, and imbricated in relations of power. Power is the complex social force that shapes the telling of all stories in the arena of war and politics. Following Plummer, power is best understood as an interaction between different social actors and the conditions within which they exist.[73] That is, power is not a property of individual people, and it is not zero-sum – either lacked or possessed. Plummer provides a description of what he terms 'narrative power':

> Narrative power is a relational and dialogic process oscillating and undulating throughout the social world and working to pattern the degree of control people experience and have over their own lives and the lives of others. We can speak of narrative power relations as domination and regulation. Produced ubiquitously in everyday living, narrative power sensitizes us to the ways lives are asymmetrical and can be dominated, shaped and influenced (sometimes damaged and exploited) by stories; how, in turn, people resist and sometimes empower themselves through new stories.[74]

Power creates the conditions for some stories to be told and heard, and others silenced or made untellable. Power, diffused throughout networks and associations, replicated in 'traditions', and manifested in interpersonal relationships, prevents people from telling stories they know would further marginalise them. Following Plummer, I suggest that we can understand narrative power as a dynamic interaction between three key components; the storyteller, the story, and the context/audience. First, storytellers vary in the amount of institutional power or 'cultural capital'[75] that they can leverage behind their stories. Simply put, stories are more likely to be heard, and more likely to be granted legitimacy, when those who tell them occupy positions of social or political power and privilege. This is the key problematic in Allen's narrative – on account of multiples statuses as female, Reservist and non-privately educated, she lacks power and privilege, and her stories are easily silenced as a result. Privileged storytellers – in Allen's narrative, as in so many others – are often those who are White, male, heterosexual and privately educated, and by virtue of such characteristics possess greater access to the public platforms needed to get their stories amplified. When it comes to narrating wartime experience, some storytellers *count* while others do not. One key task of a critically informed cultural politics of veterans' narratives is thus to constantly question *why*?

As with storytellers, stories themselves can be imbued with power. Some stories conform to and confirm the existing social order because they occupy a cosy space within its confines.[76] Such stories flow easily through social conversations, in the media, and through the halls of power. At the scale of macro-narratives (i.e., those that define wider political, social and economic systems), one example is the liberal militarist narrative of Britain as a tolerant and peaceful nation that will reluctantly use military force only when called upon to defend its citizens.[77] The cultural dominance of this narrative means that it can be voiced 'safely', as it repeats the ideals upon which economic and political power is maintained. By contrast, counter-narratives – such as Dixon's characterisation of Britain as a 'warrior nation'[78] – may be heard and even legitimised, but, lacking the 'common-sense' authority of the dominant narrative, they can struggle to enact change or to upset the wider narrative consensus.

Finally, audiences – whether implied or actual – also shape how stories unfold within relations of power. Thinking about the role of audiences encourages us to consider how contextual factors are implicated in storytelling. As Plummer suggests, 'Different stories will be told in different times and places to differing audiences with different motivations and impacts.'[79] For instance, Allen's story of sexism and misogyny within the British Army might be read differently when the audience is the UK Parliament's Defence Select Committee compared with the elites and generals who held her back from promotion. How this story *acts* in each scenario might be quite different, depending on whether the response is characterised by defensiveness and dismissiveness, or, for instance, moral outrage. How people respond to stories can sometimes be unpredictable, and how cultural politics unfold through narratives depends on the management of these unpredictable responses. Examining contextual factors such as how and to whom stories are told highlights the centrality of storytelling *situations*, and guards against a decontextualised analysis of veterans' stories. It is in the balance between stories' expressions of normative ideals, the power and cultural capital invested in the storytellers, and the context and dynamics of audiences that narrative power is enacted.

Conclusion

Using the principles sketched out in this chapter as orienting premises, this book proceeds by critically analysing the cultural politics of veterans' narratives across a range of different storytelling situations and genres, from trauma to transition, veteran cultures to academia, and from Britain to Afghanistan. In order to cultivate a critical attention to veterans' stories, I have used the method described by Frank as 'dialogical narrative analysis', though it is less a 'method' than a heuristic guide for paying attention to stories and their effects.[80] Insofar as it *can* be described as a method, in the traditional social scientific sense of the term, then it is best understood as a 'method of questioning', recognising that, in Frank's terms 'some methods are more useful for the questions they offer than for any procedures they prescribe'.[81] Frank identifies various questions that may guide an analysis of stories, while stressing that the particular questions posed within any individual project will reflect the analytical interests at hand. Questions of relevance to a dialogical narrative analysis invariably call attention to the *work* that stories do in dialogue with others. Throughout this chapter, I have indicated the kind of questions of interest to a cultural politics of veterans' narratives; from understanding how stories shape the conditions of possibility for individual lives, to exploring the ethical relationships that stories and narratives sustain between groups of people. Ultimately, the questions I pose aim to examine the possibilities that emerge from diverse veterans' stories for understanding British militarism and its national and international consequences.

In order to explore these questions as widely as possible, I have drawn upon a variety of source material throughout the book, including newspapers, podcasts, broadcast media, social media, theatre, government policy documents, research interviews, memoirs and existing academic research. How stories and narratives emerge varies according to the source, as *context* – both the local context of an individual instance of storytelling as well as the wider social and political context at the time of telling – is considered crucial to understanding narrative production. The conventions of form and genre (contrast, for example, how stories are told in memoirs versus newspapers) influence both the content and structure of the narrative – *what* gets told and *how*. Understanding how context shapes narrative is therefore important to exploring the work these narratives perform, as the motivations for telling a story, as well as the intended audience, often determine the choice of one storytelling 'platform' over another. By incorporating a variety of sources into my analysis, I have therefore attempted to consider how the context of stories' production influences how the cultural politics of veterans' narratives plays out as a result.

Drawing upon a rich tradition of narrative scholarship, this chapter laid out the conceptual tools necessary for undertaking a critical study of veterans' narratives. In doing so, I hope to have provided a clear sense of narrative's social role in shaping beliefs and values about war, in moulding the ideological character of cultural and political life, and in sustaining – and questioning – inequalities and relations of power. Guided by the above five principles as key analytic concepts, the subsequent chapters of this book present original arguments about different types and topics of veterans' narratives and the cultural politics at stake in them. Whereas each chapter deals with a distinct topic, there are multiple connections and themes running throughout them, foremost among these being how certain ideological and political agendas are promoted and others undermined or attacked through the cultural politics at play in veterans' stories. As I seek to make the case throughout, it is only by calling attention to this politics that we may garner the means to engage with and contest it. This book provides a narrative vocabulary for doing so.

Notes

1. The text of the play appears in Arias, *Minefield/Campo Minado*
2. Wibben, *Feminist Security Studies*.
3. Nguyen, *Nothing Ever Dies*.
4. On a narrative approach to dialogue and difference, see Plummer, 'Narrative power, sexual stories and the politics of storytelling'; Wibben, *Feminist Security Studies*; Frank, *Letting Stories Breathe*; Frank, 'Practicing dialogical narrative analysis'.
5. See, for example, Schrader, *Fight to Live, Live to Fight*.

6. Frank, 'Health stories as connectors and subjectifiers'.
7. The danger extends to analysis, of course, and I am aware that I may be using veterans' stories in ways other than those in which the author intended. On the ethics of talking about other people's stories, see Alcoff, 'The problem of speaking for others'; Frank, 'Practicing dialogical narrative analysis'.
8. The study of narrative has grown substantially over the last few decades, with many notable conceptual and methodological advancements taking place over this time. See, for example, Andrews, *Narrative imagination and everyday life*; Andrews, Squire and Tamboukou, *Doing Narrative Research*; Bruner, *Acts of Meaning*; Frank, *Letting Stories Breathe*; Freeman, *Hindsight*; Nelson, *Damaged Identities, Narrative Repair*; Plummer, *Telling Sexual Stories*; Plummer, *Narrative Power*; Polkinghorne, *Narrative Knowing and the Human Sciences*; Riessman, *Narrative Methods for the Human Sciences*; and, *A New Narrative for Psychology*; Smith and Sparkes, 'Contrasting perspectives on narrating selves and identities'; Somers, 'The narrative constitution of identity'; Wibben, *Feminist Security Studies*; Harel-Shalev and Daphna-Tekoah, 'Bringing women's voices back in'. Given the vastness of this narrative literature, then, the framework I develop is necessarily selective, and is grounded in a strand of narrative theorising with its roots in social constructionist theory; see Sparkes and Smith, 'Narrative constructionist research'.
9. Frank, *Letting Stories Breathe*, p. 12.
10. Frank, 'Practicing dialogical narrative analysis'. The method Frank proposes for studying narrative, dialogical narrative analysis, has as its central concern an understanding of what stories are doing as part of a dialogue with other stories and storytellers.
11. See Plummer, *Telling Sexual Stories*; Plummer, 'Narrative power, sexual stories and the politics of storytelling'; Plummer, *Narrative Power*.
12. Plummer, 'Narrative power, sexual stories and the politics of storytelling', p. 281 (original emphasis).
13. Ibid., p. 289 (original emphasis).
14. Ibid., p. 290.
15. These include but expand upon, the three principles I introduced in my 2021 paper on studying narrative in critical military studies (see Caddick, 'Life, embodiment and (post)war stories'). Throughout the book, these five principles are the core threads that unite the arguments put forth in subsequent chapters. Not all of them feature in every chapter of the book, as different chapters are animated by different concerns. Rather, throughout the book as a whole I will use all of these principles as the basis for my analysis and critique of the cultural politics of veterans' narratives.
16. See, for example, Sylvester, *Experiencing War*; Sylvester, *War as Experience*; Parashar, 'What wars and "war bodies" know about international relations'; Bulmer and Eichler, 'Unmaking militarized masculinity'; Tidy, 'War craft'; Dyvik, '"Valhalla rising"'; Dyvik, 'Of bats and bodies'; Jude, 'Breaking the silence'; Baker, *Making War on Bodies*; Harel-Shalev, '"A room of one's own(?)" in battlespace'.
17. Parashar, 'What wars and "war bodies" know about international relations'.
18. Ibid., p. 621.
19. Ormrod, *Man Down*, p. 3.

20. As fellow veteran Andy McNab's dedication on the book's front cover attests.
21. Elliott and Ormrod, 'No Limits'.
22. See, for example, Bourke, *Dismembering the Male*; Sylvester, *War as Experience*.
23. Joanne Bourke describes this distancing of the self from pain as a typical feature of post-2001 military memoirs. See Bourke, 'Bodily pain, combat and the politics of memoirs'.
24. See Cree and Caddick, 'Unconquerable heroes'.
25. Elliott and Ormrod, 'No Limits'.
26. Millar and Tidy, 'Combat as a moving target', p. 143.
27. Schiff, *A New Narrative for Psychology*, p. 67.
28. Ibid., p. 68.
29. Frank, *Letting Stories Breathe*.
30. Ibid., p. 21.
31. Ibid.
32. This point distils (perhaps simplistically) wide-ranging social theory on the relationship between language and the body: see, for example, Burkitt, *Emotions and Social Relations*; Cromby, *Feeling Bodies*; Shilling, *The Body and Social Theory*; Soloman, 'Embodiment, emotions, and materialism in international relations'. Essentially, human experience is at once both corporeal and social, physical and discursive. It is *enabled* by the body but not *reducible* to it, and therefore we cannot make sense of embodied experience (e.g., sensation, emotion, affect) outside of social relations, language and historical and political contexts. The point echoes Soloman's suggestion that bodies and matter are 'ambiguously interwoven with "ideas", discourse, the social field, etc' (p. 63), and that nuanced ways of integrating social constructionist thinking (exemplified in narrative theory) together with materiality are needed within research on war and politics.
33. Andrews, *Narrative Imagination and Everyday Life*, pp. 86–7.
34. Ibid., p. 87.
35. Ashplant, Dawson and Roper, *Commemorating War*, p. 33.
36. See, for example, Woodward and Jenkings, *Bringing War to Book*; Harari, *The Ultimate Experience*; Dyvik, '"Valhalla rising"'; Dyvik, 'Of bats and bodies'; Klein-reesink and Soeters, 'Truth and (self)censorship in military memoirs'; Klein-reesink, 'On military memoirs'; Dwyer, 'Making sense of the muddle'.
37. Ormrod, *Man Down*, p. 36.
38. Goodley, *An Officer and a Gentlewoman*, pp. 169–70.
39. Schrader, *Fight to Live, Live to Fight*, p. 1.
40. Woodward and Jenkings, '"This place isn't worth the left boot of one of our boys"', p. 505.
41. Frank, *Letting Stories Breathe*. The notion of stories as 'actors' is developed most completely within Frank's socio-narratology, but is also resonant in much recent social scientific writing and narrative theory. See Andrews, *Narrative Imagination and Everyday Life*; Mattingly, *The Paradox of Hope*; Mattingly, *Moral Laboratories*; Plummer, *Narrative Power*; Riessman, *Narrative Methods for the Human Science*; Wibben, *Feminist Security Studies*.
42. Frank, *Letting Stories Breathe*, p. 48 (original emphasis).
43. Caddick, Smith and Pheonix, 'Male combat veterans' narratives of PTSD, masculinity, and health', p. 101.

44. Bruner, *Acts of Meaning*.
45. Frank, *Letting Stories Breathe*, p. 34.
46. Ibid., p. 36.
47. For an extended discussion of narrative's role in stimulating the imagination, see Andrews, *Narrative Imagination and Everyday Life*.
48. Ibid. p. 40.
49. Andrews, *Narrative Imagination and Everyday Life*.
50. Said, *Orientalism*.
51. Omar, *A Fort of Nine Towers*, p. 9. I revisit Omar's stories in depth in Chapter 6.
52. Ibid., p. 10.
53. Ibid., p. 167.
54. Manchanda, *Imagining Afghanistan*. Manchanda discusses the imperial 'imagination' of Afghanistan as acts of representation and knowledge production that allow Afghanistan to be 'defined, delineated and spoken for' (p. 22). 'Through the power of representation Afghanistan is introduced to the world, alternately and often concurrently, as potential ally, as dangerous enemy, as gendered space, as an exotic or mysterious locale and as the nemesis of modernity' (p. 13). Such representational practices are frequently found in the stories veterans tell about their experience of war in Afghanistan.
55. Docherty, *Desert of Death*.
56. Robert Lee, speaking to *The Guardian* newspaper.
57. Royal British Legion, 'What is Remembrance?'
58. See, for example, Bruner, 'The narrative construction of reality'; Crossley, *Towards Relational Sociology*; Gergen, *Relational Being*; Gubrium and Holstein, *Analyzing Narrative Reality*; Smith and Sparkes, 'Contrasting perspectives on narrating selves and identities'; Somers, 'The narrative constitution of identity'
59. Dawson, 'The theory of popular memory and the contested memories of the Second World War in Britain'.
60. Anderson, *Imagined Communities*.
61. Andrews, *Narrative Imagination and Everyday Life*, p. 88.
62. Ashplant, Dawson and Roper, *Commemorating War*, p. 16. Much scholarship on war memory and commemoration reinforces this notion that narratives operate to forge shared historical understandings, contested between different communities. See, for example, Baines, *South Africa's 'Border War'*; Bourke, *The Second World War*; Bourke, 'Remembering war'; Dawson, 'The theory of popular memory and the contested memories of the Second World War in Britain'.
63. Basham, 'Gender, race, militarism and remembrance', p. 885.
64. Peace Pledge Union, 'Remembrance and white poppies'.
65. Nguyen, *Nothing Ever Dies*, p. 60.
66. Ibid.
67. Frank, 'Practicing dialogical narrative analysis'.
68. Cree and Caddick, 'Unconquerable heroes'.
69. Åhäll, 'Feeling everyday IR'.
70. Allen, *Forewarned*, p. 6.
71. Ibid., p. 254.
72. Ibid. p. 4.
73. Plummer, *Telling Sexual Stories*.
74. Plummer, *Narrative Power*, p. 30.

75. Bourdieu, *The Logic of Practice*.
76. Wibben, *Feminist Security Studies*.
77. Basham, 'Liberal militarism as insecurity, desire and ambivalence'.
78. Dixon, *Warrior Nation*.
79. Plummer, 'Narrative power, sexual stories and the politics of storytelling', p. 281.
80. Frank, *Letting Stories Breathe*.
81. Ibid., p. 72.

CHAPTER 2

Britain and 'Her Veterans': Narrating the Veteran Figure

I come here, unapologetically, to improve the plight of veterans and their families. The last government under this Prime Minister did more than any before it in this cause, but there is still some way to go. It is a deep privilege to come to this House with the hopes of tens of thousands of Plymouthians, and I do not underestimate the duty that is incumbent upon me in the years ahead. I cannot promise anything but noble endeavour, relentless positivity and an abounding sense of duty to look after those who, through no fault of their own, find themselves on the fringes of society, and who find life an interminable struggle. I look forward to the challenge.[1]

On 1 June 2015, the newly elected Conservative MP for Plymouth, Johnny Mercer, took his seat in Parliament. As a recent veteran of the war in Afghanistan, he used his maiden speech, an excerpt from which is quoted above, to shine a light on 'the plight of veterans and their families'. Four years later, he would go on to lead the newly established Office for Veterans' Affairs (OVA), situated at the heart of the UK government in the Cabinet Office at 10 Downing Street. Announcing the creation of the new Office just days after becoming the (now former) prime minister, Boris Johnson stated, 'We are rightly admired throughout the world for our Armed Forces, and it is a stain on our national conscience that any veteran who has served should be abandoned by the country they have fought so courageously to protect.'[2] The mandate for the OVA was broad, covering, in Johnson's words, 'the full gamut of veterans' civilian lives', including further professionalisation of veterans' care and treatment, support in transition, and preventing veteran suicide and homelessness. In particular, the OVA was tasked with ending what had been deemed 'vexatious prosecutions' against veterans accused of historical human rights abuses in Iraq, Afghanistan and Northern Ireland; something the newspapers had branded a 'witch hunt'. Grasping the opportunity to fulfil the parliamentary purpose he set out in his maiden speech, Mercer said of his appointment to the OVA, 'I am delighted with this role, and am resolutely determined to reset this country's relationship with her veterans.'[3] But what was, and is, Britain's relationship with 'her veterans'? And why does it need resetting?

By telling a story of Britain and her veterans – past and present – this chapter establishes the social, historical and political context in which the cultural politics of veterans' narratives are contested and sets the scene for the rest of the book. This story oscillates between two dominant narrative threads about the figure of the British veteran: the marginalised outcast and the patriotic servant/hero. Clear in Mercer and Johnson's comments is a sense that veterans are getting a raw deal from their country: they face a 'plight', they are 'abandoned', left at the 'fringes of society'. This is the *tragic* veteran, abandoned, betrayed, ousted from the society he serves. By juxtaposing this narrative with another – the heroic veteran, courageous protector of the nation – Johnson highlights an intolerable injustice, a 'stain' that must be removed. Often these two narrative threads are combined: veterans are *tragic heroes*,[4] and this combined image works to create all kinds of emotional and political attachments to the figure of the British veteran. In casting his government as the new veterans' champions, Johnson pledged a fresh start for Britain's relationship with 'her veterans'. In this chapter, I consider how the core narratives about British veterans developed historically, how they weave together to shape impressions of veteran character, and how they influence British culture, politics and society. The chapter begins with a brief history of British veterans and the narratives that have shaped their encounters with civilian society and British militarism. I then address questions about the diversity of British veterans in the twenty-first century and *whose* stories are assumed to be representative of veteran experience. In the final section, I explore how sexual violence and the politics of storytelling surrounding this violence fundamentally undermines the relationship between 'Britain and her veterans', casting a long shadow of doubt over claims that Britain is in the midst of transforming this relationship for the better. My main argument is that the relationship between 'Britain and her veterans' *does* need resetting, though not in the narrow sense of further professionalising veterans' care implied by Mercer and Johnson. Instead, I will argue for a more fundamental reorganisation of our understanding of *who* Britain's veterans *are*, and how their stories intersect with the national story.

Before embarking on this argument, it is first worth reflecting on the character of British militarism and the role of veterans' narratives within it. In contrast to its pre-Second World War status as a predominantly imperial power, Britain's military operates today under the guiding ethos of 'liberal militarism', which has been described as 'the commitment by liberal democratic states and societies to maintain and use military force'.[5] As Chris Rossdale points out, British militarism 'is not a static entity', and is composed of 'a complex of social, political and economic processes'.[6] Manifestations of British militarism are hugely varied and include (for example): wars disguised as humanitarian intervention in the Middle East; oversized defence budgets and mandatory commitments on military spending; a nuclear arsenal capable of destroying the planet several times over; and a neoliberal war economy hospitable to the profiteering of arms companies. Importantly, each of these elements depends on a broader cultural militarism, whereby military virtues, history and personnel are celebrated components of the British national 'story'. As I stated in the Introduction, veterans and their stories can be understood as the noble face of British militarism. While individual veterans may themselves be critical of militarism (or indifferent to it, or perhaps even its cheerleaders), advocates of British militarism have always found the generalised figure of the veteran to be a dependable resource for legitimising their objectives, relying on the notions of duty, nation and service these figures represent. Despite considerable historical ambiguity and contestation over representations of the veteran in society (see below), veterans' narratives reliably reproduce a sense of pride in the military and the nation which provides British militarism with enduringly powerful ideological resources. As I will show later in this chapter, the morally courageous character that British militarism takes on by virtue of the reputation it plunders from veterans enables it to withstand all manner of scandals and criticisms.

The principal means by which veterans and their stories construct a noble and virtuous version of British militarism is by reinforcing what I will further describe in Chapter 3 as *'militarist terms of reference'*. Terms of reference set the tacitly agreed social context for discussion of veterans' narratives, forming the boundaries of acceptable discourse. To transgress the terms of reference for a given subject is to utter a 'taboo'; one feels the energy in a room change when it happens. Conversations shut down, defences go up, hackles rise. Breaking terms of reference renders one suspicious and inappropriately 'political'. The militarist terms of reference which accompany veterans' narratives are what maintain the veteran figure as apolitical, having transcended the realm of political debate. These terms strongly suggest that 'politicising' veterans' narratives is disrespectful and inappropriate, thereby undermining the possibilities for critique, or even engaged discussion.[7] Militarist terms of reference are also a 'travelling' feature of veterans' narratives, detectable across multiple genres of veteran storytelling. Whatever the narrative framing – positive or negative, triumph or outrage – militarist terms of reference position our responses in line with military ideals of service and sacrifice. As I will argue in Chapter 3, these militarist terms of reference are the dominant position for understanding veterans' stories in the contemporary social realm. Yet even where veterans appear in the social imagination as undesirable outcasts, as they have been throughout much of British history, there is always an undercurrent of injustice pointing towards veterans' service and/or character as an indicator of moral deservingness, and a reflection of military virtue.[8]

A Brief History of British Veterans

Veterans' history is a field of research in its own right and it is far beyond the scope of this chapter to offer more than a short introduction to the rich and complex history of veterans even within Britain.[9] Any such history must, however, in the words of Angel Alcade, approach 'the "veteran" as a culturally constructed symbol, rather than a strictly delimited actor, allow[ing] us to understand phenomena such as the emergence of stereotypes about veterans and their utilization by other historical actors'.[10] My focus is therefore a kind of 'narrative history' – or history of narratives – identifying narrative threads that have worked to construct and re-construct notions of 'veteranhood'[11] throughout British history, in recognition that the historical trajectory of such narratives is important for contextualising the role veterans play in the public life of the nation.

Writing and research about veterans throughout history shows that there are longstanding narrative associations with the figure of the veteran in British society. Kate McLoughlin's study of veterans in British literature from 1790 to 2015, for example, shows how literature has both reflected and constructed societal perspectives on veterans.[12] Alongside other studies of the 'literary veteran',[13] McLoughlin argues that veterans historically were presented as figures of considerable social uncertainty, subjected to a 'spectrum of constructions - from delinquent to superhuman'.[14] For McLoughlin, veterans pose the unsettling question of whether the person who comes home from war is the same as the one who went away, which is a question wrought with difficulty for both the individual and his or her community. In response, veterans are held nervously in abeyance by the communities to which they return, constructed as 'Xenos' (Other). McLoughlin explains that literary treatment of the veteran often paints him (and in the period and works of interest, almost exclusively *him*) as alien, marred by the violence of war, and mistrusted by society over fears that he brings back home with him violence, non-conformity, dissent, even revolution. And yet poised alongside these anxieties are other, more normatively positive qualities and constructions such as wisdom, insight and worldliness. McLoughlin collects these 'veteran virtues' under the concept of *Erfahrung* (from the German verb *fahren*; to travel), signifying cumulative experiences earned through journeying, suffering and learning. As such, while the veteran figure has often been feared and reviled, he may also be associated with a kind of mystique, imbuing him with the qualities of a 'natural pedagogue' with the capacity to edify and to instruct or warn society.[15] Historically, then, veterans might have been assumed to possess certain noble qualities, but these tend to be offset by marginalisation, outcasting and ambiguity.

Historically rooted stereotypes inform the capacities that veterans' stories have to act in public life. Invoking the nobler qualities associated with military service may be a strategy for veterans to establish their 'truths' in a context where suspicion and indifference have dominated social responses to their stories. Indeed, it is only comparatively recently that veterans have begun to occupy their extraordinarily prestigious position in the national imaginary, and yet this prestige is still held in contrast to the popular image of veterans as damaged by their service.[16] As Ingham suggests, 'Until the latter half of the nineteenth century, civilian society regarded regular soldiers as "other", a potentially dangerous underclass'.[17] Even after this period, elite and public understanding of and support for veterans has ebbed and flowed over the course of Britain's martial history. Contemporary revisionist claims that Britain enjoys a unique historical bond of unity with its military and its veterans – claims intended to buttress patriotic sentiment in a time of frequent humanitarian-justified interventionism – have therefore been described as unfounded.[18] The veteran is, and always has been, a much-contested figure in British national life.

Scholarship on soldiers and veterans of the First World War has likewise demonstrated that veterans experienced mixed post-war fortunes and were subjected to capricious responses in Britain both from the public and the state.[19] Joanna Bourke, for instance, has written about the extraordinary impact of industrialised mass warfare on veterans' bodies, and argued that the war in general failed to produce significant changes either in British society or in the treatment of veterans.[20] Indeed, Prime Minister Lloyd George's famous promise of a 'Land fit for heroes' failed to materialise, with veterans quickly forgotten about along with society's desire to forget the war. Relations between veterans and the state were defined largely in terms of the war pensions system, whose ministers and administrators quickly developed excuses for limiting payments to veterans disabled by their service.[21] Such treatment caused anger and resentment among veterans who felt they were being cheated, but as David Swift argues, these feelings were not strong enough or widespread enough to mount a significant challenge to the state.[22] Swift thus writes of the 'relative quiescence of British veterans' compared with their post-war European counterparts and suggests that the ex-soldier organisations formed by veterans advocating for better treatment rapidly lost any significance they had achieved in the immediate post-war period.[23]

The First World War experience – or, at least, the writing it generated – did much to reinvest the social narrative of veterans as marginalised and disillusioned. In his much-cited work *The Great War and Modern Memory*, Paul Fussell promoted the idea of veteran disillusionment by suggesting 'irony' as the dominant mode of interpreting the First World War experience, based on canonised writing from the conflict.[24] Others dispute this notion. Bourke, for instance, rejects the claim that the war produced widespread feelings of betrayal and alienation among veterans, arguing instead that, 'bitterness was only *one* response to wartime experiences: and it was a response that few could afford to maintain for long periods, or were willing to maintain in the face of renewed hope for happiness'.[25] Indeed, 'disassociation', or the rejection of veteran identities in preference for the civilian, seems to have been a more typical response to the First World War in Britain.[26] Whether or not veterans throughout British history *have* in fact been disenfranchised by their treatment, the notion provides powerful narrative resources that continue to influence how veterans narrate their post-war experiences and that continue to furnish claims of injustice towards veterans with a sense of historical provenance.

This is not to suggest that there were no legitimate reasons for a sense of disenfranchisement, particularly among certain groups of veterans. Alison Fell's study of women as veterans after the First World War, for example, shows that women who served in various capacities often struggled to gain the recognition they deserved for their service.[27] This was especially so if their service could not be interpreted as an appropriately gendered contribution to the war effort, such as caring and devoted nurses to front-line soldiers. Women's claims to veteran identity were therefore contested, and the status and benefits that veteran identity conferred were jealously guarded by those who felt the sole rights to a 'veteran story' belonged to male soldiers who had fought at the front. Others whose stories were overlooked include the forgotten soldiers of empire whom David Olusoga writes about in *The World's War*.[28] Despite the indisputable significance of empire in securing victory in both world wars, veterans from Britain's colonies have been racialised, marginalised and forgotten *as* veterans, at least until very recently.[29] As Olusoga argues, 'More words have been written over the past century about the few-dozen middle-class officers who wrote their war memoirs and penned their war poetry than about the 4 million non-White, non-Europeans who fought for Britain, France and their allies.'[30] The history of veterans in Britain is thus marked by gendered and racialised struggle over who gets to claim veteran identity, and what this identity represents in the image of the nation.

Yet it was arguably not until the post-1945 period that veterans in Britain became clearly recognisable as the ultimate embodiment of national patriotism. As numerous scholars have suggested,[31] the Second World War has provided Britons with seemingly inexhaustible narrative resources for constructing a sense of national belonging, virtuous militarism and a mythic sense of homogeneous national community. The national story of the Second World War, of Britain's resilient defence against the incontrovertible evil of the Nazis, has acquired the status of an 'ethnic myth' in Paul Gilroy's terms, though one which necessarily subsumes the content of veterans' *actual* stories of the conflict and its aftermath.[32] Many Second World War veterans returned to Britain embittered by their treatment in the forces, encountering a civilian society that had itself been deeply scarred by war and offered little sympathy for the plight of veterans.[33] They were told by their officers not to burden their families with their memories – to forget their war experiences – and many suffered lifelong psychological harm as a result.[34] When they did speak, their stories testified to the brutality and horror of war, and some also warned against being seduced by belligerent nationalist ideologies scaffolded around their stories.[35]

Commemorative culture in Britain – a key battleground of cultural politics – has long relied on the stories of Second World War veterans. Narrative reproduction of the Second World War takes place in numerous spaces (e.g., online, broadcast and podcast media, newspapers, etc.), not only around Armistice Day in November, but also around celebrated anniversaries such as Victory in Europe (VE) and Victory in Japan (JD) days. One example (out of many that I regularly encounter), is the story of Jim Wren, whose story appeared on the SSAFA[36] Facebook page in the days leading up to the 75th Anniversary of VJ Day in August 2020. Wren was one of around 50,000 British troops taken prisoner by the Japanese Imperial Army in 1942. Presented by SSAFA as an exemplary representation of Second World War memory, the story recounts the brutal conditions Wren suffered in captivity; 'Jim was a Prisoner of War for three and a half years and spent time in four different camps. He was subjected to slave labour and brutality every day. He witnessed many atrocities in that time, which he finds it difficult to discuss, even 75 years on.' Quotes from Wren then offer reflections on the war and its impact on his life:

> It's had an effect on me mentally over the years. I find it rather difficult to communicate or converse with people. That whole experience is in the back of my mind all the time because some things never go away . . . I'm glad the war ended, but it's important to remember the world has changed too. The Japanese today are different people to the way they were then. And what happened at the end of the war shouldn't be forgotten either. The atom bomb saved my life, and the lives of thousands of men, but it took lives as well. It's a thing I never want to see again. Never.

Wren's story is but one example of popular memory being performed in the public sphere, with SSAFA's contribution framed as honouring the historic legacy of Second World War veterans. The manner of these stories' presentation, however, results not in an invitation to inhabit and discuss veterans' stories, but rather in a *foreclosure of dialogue*. Britain's Second World War 'industry of memory', to use Nguyen's phrase,[37] demands not that we *discuss* these stories, merely that we *respect* them. This aura of mandatory respect and the accompanying taboo against questioning serves the ideology of British militarism well. Wren's story, for instance, might have provoked discussion on the ethics of the atomic bomb, or civility in international relations, both themes poignantly evoked by his reflections. Instead, comments on the post showed an outpouring of respect, gratitude and Union Jack emojis. Notwithstanding the limits of social media as a site for nuanced debate on world affairs, it was striking how uniform the responses were to Wren's story. I argue that such uniformity is a pattern we can routinely observe in response to veterans' stories, akin to how the phrase 'thank you for your service' typifies America's engagement with its veterans.[38] In terms of the 'national story', the history of the Second World War is closed, not open to discussion or revision. Yet we ought to question whether it is the stories themselves that foreclose dialogue, or, in Nguyen's words, 'the material and ideological forces that determine how and why memories are produced and circulated'.[39]

Post-1945, the history of British veterans can be broadly characterised as a history of forgetting, at least until the resurgence of public support occasioned by Iraq and Afghanistan. Conflicts such as the Korean War, which had rather more complicated moral and geopolitical rationalities, which were 'messy', could not be easily assimilated into Britain's sense of a 'usable past'.[40] Likewise, the bloody retreat from empire saw small colonial wars in Suez, Kenya, Cyprus, Borneo and Aden quickly forgotten – and in some cases, deliberately expunged – from popular memory and culture. As Paul Gilroy suggests, 'the mysterious evacuation of Britain's postcolonial conflicts from national consciousness has become a significant cultural and historical event in its own right'.[41] The later humanitarian-justified interventions in Sierra Leone, Kosovo and Bosnia have similarly failed to register in the national psyche. Even the longest military campaign in modern British history – nearly four decades in Northern Ireland – has been marginalised from the dominant narratives of commemorative culture. It has been argued that the Falklands/Malvinas War, during which Margaret Thatcher overtly channelled Churchillian Second World War rhetoric to generate popular support, stands outside this pattern of ambiguity as a much-vaunted defence of British sovereignty and identity.[42] Yet in subsequent decades, this too has arguably moved to the periphery of memorial culture, particularly after the 'War on Terror' began to dominate media headlines.

The Second World War's enduring, perhaps definitive, influence on the British 'national story' has thus eclipsed subsequent wars and their memory in popular culture.[43] For the veterans of latter conflicts, apathy and indifference towards their stories often left a bitter taste. Grace Huxford, for instance, writes of the resentment Korean War veterans felt at the lack of recognition they received within British culture.[44] Such resentment could often darken or damage veteran identity, particularly for veterans who fell on hard times after leaving the military. With national commemorative culture focused on the two world wars – and to some extent, the wars 'of the moment' – telling stories about Britain's later twentieth-century conflicts seems to be the more private affair of those who fought in them. The cultural politics of *forgetting* veterans' narratives thus plays a constitutive role in maintaining the idea of veterans generally as the custodians of an idealised national patriotism. Indeed, it may be argued that the increasingly celebratory, some might say *vulgar*, tone of commemoration in Britain is linked to deep-seated anxieties surrounding the imminent passing of the Second World War generation and to a growing willingness to question Britain's imperial military past in mainstream debate; both occurrences which threaten to undermine patriotic ideals as a distinguishing feature of British national identity.

Who Are British Veterans?

British veterans today are more diverse than ever before, though White male veterans still comprise the majority. Despite the absence of accurate demographic data on veterans, a survey carried out by the Ministry of Defence in 2017 estimated that there were around 2.4 million veterans in the UK, with 99 per cent of those believed to be White, 89 per cent male, and 60 per cent over the age of 65.[45] The demographic homogeneity of Britain's veteran population, combined with the popular imagination of veterans as masculine defenders of a racially defined homeland,[46] has undoubtedly made it easier for British society to ignore non-White, non-male, non-heterosexual and foreign-born veterans. Throughout history, gendered, sexual and ethnic minorities have been marginalised and discriminated against in the British Armed Forces. The figure of the veteran is assumed White and male by default. As female veteran-scholars West and Antrobus argue, 'The term "veteran", to a British audience, conjures up the image of an elderly white man – a veteran of the First or Second World Wars or a more contemporary image of an injured serviceman from Iraq or Afghanistan, perhaps an Invictus Games competitor.'[47] Underpinning this image is the ideological fusion of masculinity with the practice of soldiering, and with the ideal, mythologised figure of the heroic combat soldier in particular[48]. Veterans are assumed male largely because the authority to enact violence on behalf of the nation is considered an inherently male privilege. Military institutions are replete with gender-based norms and interactions as a result, and a great deal of critical feminist scholarship has examined the consequences of this ideological arrangement.[49]

Still today, women veterans' stories are rarely heard or acknowledged *as* veterans' stories. One report on British women veterans' experiences describes them as a 'hidden population', 'a marginalised and disenfranchised subgroup of civilian society',[50] and suggesting that 'Women who served aren't seen as veterans'.[51] As a result, support services designed to meet veterans' healthcare or employment needs did not recognise women's experiences.[52] Echoing these sentiments, West and Antrobus described the 'deeply odd' experience of having their gender consistently identified and problematised by the military and by society. In their words:

> Women veterans are problematic. We are problematic both as military insiders and as academic outsiders. As military women we were in a minority and had to find ways to fit in, ways that did not challenge the male warrior stereotype. And only now can we see that we never achieved the acceptance we thought we had at the time. But our identity is not just a challenge to the military: society is not sure what to make of us, these women who have seemingly left their families to live and work in this male environment, the goal of which is life-taking when women are supposed to give life. And then as women veterans, as we reclaim our civilian female identity we are largely invisible both to the military which surrounds itself with and sees one type of conventional veteran, and in scholarship where women veterans voices are rare.[53]

West and Antrobus highlight how transgressing *civilian* notions of women as carers and nurturers led to their being excluded from dominant conceptions of veteran identity, and from academic circles where veterans' voices predominate.[54] Despite the British military's ban on women serving in combat roles being lifted in 2016, women in the military are not expected to have engaged in the 'definitive' act of soldiering – the enactment of violence – which gives veteranhood its privileged status in the popular imagination. The *assumed insignificance* of women veterans' stories therefore plays a key role in keeping them at the margins of civilian ideas about *who* veterans *are* as well as *what* they do. A clear sense of whose stories matter thus ensures that the power to influence cultural politics is concentrated in male veterans' stories, which tend to assume representative status *as* 'veteran stories'.

Non-White and foreign-born veterans have similarly struggled to find acceptance as 'British veterans'. As well as being gendered, veteran identity is racialised such that whiteness is the norm and non-whiteness aberrant.[55] Issues of race and nationality are crystallised in the figure of the 'military migrant', recruited from Britain's former colonies in order to assuage a perpetual recruitment shortfall. Vron Ware suggests that whereas White British soldiers are automatically recognised as having served their country, migrant soldiers are caught in the curious position of being 'alternately lauded as heroes but stigmatised as immigrants'.[56] Ware's study of Commonwealth-born soldiers in the British Army revealed that they frequently experienced racial prejudice, sometimes in the form of outright abuse, but often by being funnelled into certain roles or regiments on the basis of their assumed 'martial' characteristics. On leaving the military, non-British veterans have often been forced to negotiate complex legal scenarios and have been charged exorbitant visa fees to allow them to remain in the country. Their right to belong as British citizens is not granted automatically in exchange for their military service, but, rather, as Ware puts it, citizenship is 'a privilege yet to be earned', or, indeed, paid for.[57] The story of Taitusi Ratucaucau exemplifies such issues. Ratucaucau is a Fijian-born veteran who served for ten years in the British Army. In April 2020, *The Guardian* newspaper reported that Ratucaucau had been ordered to pay £27,000 in NHS hospital bills to finance the cost of brain surgery to remove a tumour. Categorised as an illegal immigrant, unable to access free NHS treatment, Ratucaucau feared deportation while recovering from surgery in hospital. In a witness statement recorded by his lawyer, Ratucaucau said:

> As I had served for 10 years, I expected that I would be able to remain in the UK after being discharged . . . I feel that the position I have had to endure since being discharged from the army is very unfair. The army let me down badly by not giving me enough notice about steps that needed to be taken in order for me and my family to remain in the UK, and also about the cost of the Home Office applications. I feel that the fees that the Home Office charge foreign

national veterans for the right to remain is extremely unfair, considering the committed service we have given to this country.[58]

While it constitutes a more striking example of non-British veterans' marginalisation, Ratucaucau's story highlights the barriers that many face to inclusion and acceptance.[59] It also underscores the reality that, as women veterans have found, the ability to claim a veteran identity, and to have that identity validated by society, is not equally distributed on the basis of one's service. As Ware argues, drawing a connection between notions of 'service' and 'citizenship' in Britain, 'Asking who serves, under what conditions and for what rewards are crucial questions for a post-imperial democracy that cannot agree about its role in the world, and cannot afford to maintain the status to which it aspires.'[60] Whether veterans can claim the status and entitlements associated with being a veteran is an important way in which their 'relationship' with the nation can be considered.

Understanding who British veterans are also requires attention to the kind of labour they have undertaken on the nation's behalf. The dominant image of a veteran is one who has 'fought' for the country. Indeed, much of the reverence shown towards veterans is based on the popular belief that they have 'fought so courageously to protect' the country.[61] Yet it is not always accurate to say that veterans have 'fought' anyone at all. As Paul Higate asks in his autobiographical examination of veteran pride, 'What if the realities of many – if not the majority of those who are/have served were antithetical to the mythologised understandings that continue to dominate? Should we hold these actors in such high esteem if their experiences were closer to the lives of the stereotypical civilian employee, for example?'[62] Much of the critical scholarship on veterans' lives (my own previous work included) focuses on those who served in 'combat' roles. Given that many (though by no means all) of the potentially devastating consequences of military service – such as traumatic injury, post-traumatic stress disorder, killing and death – are concentrated among those who serve in front-line combat or infantry roles, this focus is perhaps understandable. However, this focus on violence and its aftermath risks exceptionalising veterans' stories and reifying the dominant image of veterans as masculine patriotic warriors. It also obscures the more prosaic ways in which lives become 'militarised', for example, by performing 'civilian'-type roles such as clerks, cooks, drivers and logisticians while wearing a uniform. Such diversity in veterans' stories and experiences of military life, while often overlooked, is important for a critical account of the cultural politics these stories perform, and for undermining the automatic associations between veterans, violence, and moral authority on armed conflict.

Sexual Violence

> I used to be full of shame. Now I know the shame is not mine, it's his. I hope that I can help other people come forward and get help. I am a survivor not a victim. I survived it. It was not until I flipped things on their head, stopped being a victim and started being a survivor that things began to change. The more I speak about it, the less frightened and more empowered I feel. I hope that by speaking I can help other people who have gone through military sexual trauma to go and get the help they need. The MoD needs to acknowledge military sexual trauma amongst its serving personnel and veterans and stop sweeping it under the carpet. Military sexual trauma is going to be the next scandal to hit our armed forces and the powers that be should get in front of this and do something about it. Survivors matter so acknowledge our pain and help us. We are not a dirty secret to be hidden away.[63]

Many years after experiencing violent abuse by a colleague, Royal Air Force veteran Helen Bolland told her story of military sexual trauma to a newspaper reporter as a way of speaking out against the Ministry of Defence, and of reclaiming voice in the wake of trauma.[64] Helen described being raped while posted to Iraq in 2005, of being 'blackballed' by her colleagues who assumed her encounter had been consensual, and of being unable to report the abuse she had suffered. After returning from Iraq, Helen described how she began experiencing symptoms of post-traumatic stress disorder (PTSD), which were dismissed by a psychiatrist because they had not resulted from a 'combat' incident. She then faced a lengthy battle for justice and support. As Helen tells it, 'It has taken years of fighting to get my service medical pension, to get the right diagnosis, treatments, housing, some compensation, state benefits, and to see light at the end of a very long tunnel.' Highlighting the dilemma and embarrassment in first telling a story of sexual violence, it took seventeen years for Helen to get to a point where she felt able to report the rape to the civilian police, who passed the case to the Service Justice System (SJS) to deal with. While 'refusing to comment on individual cases', the Ministry of Defence stated in response to the *Sunday Post* article, 'We continue to improve reporting mechanisms so personnel feel safe in raising issues and confident allegations will be acted on.' Helen's story and the military's response to it – and to all stories of sexual violence in the military – reveal a key point of struggle in the politics of veterans' narratives.

I argue in this section that Britain's relationship with 'her veterans' ought to be considered in terms of the gendered harms that can occur during service, and how these harms are dealt with at an individual as well as a systemic level. Internationally, evidence suggests that sexual violence within military organisations remains at 'epidemic proportions' despite decades of publicity on the issue along with more recent policy and culture-change initiatives.[65] Britain's military is no exception to this trend. Depending on the survey, and the variation on terms like 'sexual assault', 'sexual harassment', 'sexual violence', and the more euphemistic 'inappropriate behaviours', data indicate that anywhere between 21 per cent and 52 per cent of female personnel have experienced some form of serious, traumatic and unwanted sexual contact during their service.[66] Men are affected by sexual violence in the military too, though proportionally less so than women, as the hyper-masculine, sexualised culture of military life more readily targets women. Given the often devastating consequences of sexual violence to the veteran her- or himself – as attested to in Helen's story – any honest assessment of Britain's relationship with 'her veterans' therefore needs to consider institutional responses to the national scandal of sexual violence which remains permissible in the military.

Sexual violence takes place against the backdrop of an enabling institutional culture which routinely tolerates sexualised comments, jokes and behaviour at the expense of women. The extent of the gendered harm produced by this culture has until recently been unrecognised at the official level. The Wigston review, published in 2019 by Air Chief Marshal Mike Wigston into 'inappropriate behaviours' across UK Defence acknowledged for the first time the scale of the issues at hand. The review clearly identified inappropriate behaviours (taken to include bullying, harassment and discrimination as well as sexual offending) persisting at unacceptable levels within the British military. Coming from a senior military official, the report was widely received as an urgent call for change, including with regard to how complaints are handled within the SJS. However, Wigston's presentation of the report also took great care in emphasising the 'aberrant' character of inappropriate behaviour within the British military, stating upfront that:

> There are nearly 250,000 people in Defence, military and civil service, and the overwhelming majority serve with great pride collectively protecting the UK 24/7. The UK Armed Forces are a formidable fighting force and the commitment of all military and the civilians that support them is rightly celebrated. In bleak contrast, however, inappropriate behaviour persists which harms people, the teams they serve in and, ultimately, operational output.[67]

While identifying clear internal problems within military culture, the report thereby still manages to partition inappropriate behaviour – including sexual violence – at the fringes of 'majority' behaviour, with a problematic minority of individuals responsible as the perpetrators. As such, the problem of military sexual violence, along with culpability for its prevalence in the military, remains firmly attached to *individuals*, rather than the institution itself.

The Wigston review, together with subsequent high-profile reviews such as the Atherton review, led by Sarah Atherton MP in 2021 into women's experiences in the Armed Forces,[68] offers insights into the politics of storytelling around military sexual violence. This is a complicated politics that envelops the official narratives about Britain's institutional response to sexual violence together with the stories of veterans as victims/survivors. The politics of sexual violence storytelling is framed by risk and precarity on all sides: for the institution with regard to its public image and potential to recruit female trainees, but especially so for victims/survivors with regard to the sharing of highly personal and traumatic stories of abuse – stories which risk calling forth all manner of gendered responses, thereby emphasising vulnerability. Research by Megan MacKenzie into the stories we tell about military sexual violence in public culture reveals that dominant narratives act to uphold the image of the 'good soldier' and the honourable military institution in the face of sexual violence reporting.[69] MacKenzie argues that public narratives about military sexual violence amount to 'institutional gaslighting' in that they 'create a series of excuses and rationales to help make sense of the violence in ways that tend to variously remove institutional accountability, evade the acknowledgement of a systemic and persistent institutional problem, and diffuse or weaken efforts to address the problem'.[70] As a result of institutional gaslighting – that is, political strategies that resist critiques of the institution – inaction on sexual violence becomes justified, and the 'vast majority' of 'good' soldiers are absolved of 'any responsibility for the regular, predictable, and high rates of MSV'.[71]

While MacKenzie's focus is on media reporting of sexual violence in the US, Canadian and Australian contexts, I argue that the same patterns can be observed in Britain's institutional response to sexual violence, with some of this 'institutional gaslighting' replicated in the reports and reviews purportedly holding the system to account. This is evident in the Wigston review's framing of the problem as one belonging to a tiny minority of servicemen, thus insulating the military culture at large. Similar framing issues have enabled the British military to respond to other reports with little more than platitude. The Atherton review, published two years after Wigston in 2021, has perhaps done more than any other previous report in drawing attention to institutional inaction on sexual violence. Atherton constituted a watershed moment in Britain's relationship with its female service personnel and veterans, in that an institutional ban on serving military members speaking to the UK Parliament was lifted to enable women to come forward and tell their stories. Yet the report still offers the military a generous overall framing which enables its rhetorical defence. On the one hand, Atherton offers the following unequivocal statement of the problem:

> There is too much bullying, harassment and discrimination – including criminal behaviours like sexual assault and rape – affecting Service personnel (both male and female), and the MOD's own statistics leave no room for doubt that female Service personnel suffer disproportionately. We were alarmed and appalled that the Army's Sexual Harassment survey of 2018 found that 21% of servicewomen had either experienced or witnessed sexual harassment at work in the previous 12 months. Such a figure should have raised major concerns in the Army but appears not to have done so. The stories that we heard are truly shocking and they gravely concern us.[72]

However, the report's opening lines also make clear that 'nearly 90%' of over 4000 women who responded to the review's survey stated they would recommend a career in the Forces to other women.[73] As MacKenzie suggests, such statements of support for the military institution from women themselves are a familiar strategy that enables the institution to deflect or deny criticism of its handling of sexual violence. Whether or not Atherton intended to grant the military this positive framing, the effect remains. For example, the UK Defence Secretary in responding to the review directly quoted this 90 per cent figure (with no mention of other figures from the report), and rather than *apologising* to women for the military's failures, instead *thanked* them for their contribution to the review, stating that 'I am grateful to all the women who contributed to the Defence Committee's report' and further that 'I look forward to continuing to work with them to hold all three services to account, and ensure we see meaningful progress.'[74] Following MacKenzie's observations, I suggest that such responses typify the British institutional response to military sexual violence. The overall character of responses is about highlighting the 'ongoing efforts' to address the problem, while emphasising the narrative, as MacKenzie puts it, 'Everything is OK because we're committed to change.'[75] This narrative, designed to placate criticism, is further evident in the MoD's 'Tackling sexual offending strategy', released in July 2022, which stated that Defence will '*continue to create* an environment where everyone, but especially women, can feel safe and confident to report offending', with the strategy itself exemplifying 'Defence's commitment to crack down on unacceptable sexual behaviour and sexual offences.'[76]

While the institutional response sets the tone and backdrop for sexual violence narratives, the politics of sexual violence storytelling arguably take on higher stakes at the personal level. Decisions over whether, and how, to tell one's story are riddled with complexity and fear. Women fear not being believed, being blamed for the abuses they suffered, and being stigmatised as weak, feminine or a 'victim'. To tell a story of abuse feels like an 'admission'; once made, it alters perceptions of the teller. Narration itself can be a powerful act of reclaiming voice in the wake of violence, and is integral to the pursuit of justice. As Wieskamp argues, 'storytelling has been central within the movement against military sexual violence'.[77] This is evident in Atherton (quoted above) whereby women's stories of abuse formed a key component of the evidence mounted against the Ministry of Defence, accentuating the report's policy recommendations. There are always pitfalls, however. If stories rely on feminised notions of victimhood in order to be heard, or if responses succeed in positioning the veteran in this way, they will be disempowering. If, on the other hand, stories of sexual violence can represent strength and healing alongside calls for justice – and, importantly, the *systemic* rather than individual nature of the problem – the result may be empowering not only for the teller but for others living with 'silent' stories of abuse.[78] Of utmost importance to a cultural politics of veterans' narratives is thus to support the conditions which make such stories 'shareable' while also respecting silences which confer protection on the storyteller.[79]

Ultimately, I argue that Britain's relationship with its female veterans ought to be assessed by the provision of justice to veterans who experienced sexual violence, and by the military's ability to prevent future abuses. Continued high rates of sexual violence in the British military indicate that efforts to prevent abuses are still failing at the systemic level, with sexual violence therefore still effectively tolerated within the institution. For example, an official progress review carried out a year after publication of the Wigston report indicated that progress in implementing Wigston's many recommendations was 'slower than desired'.[80] Likewise, both Wigston and Atherton's reviews present stark evidence that the SJS is failing to provide justice for those who complain about the sexual violence they encountered in the military. Those who do report abuses are in the minority, with most service personnel and veterans lacking faith in the system to handle their cases appropriately. Indeed, of rape cases that proceed to Court Martial (trial in the SJS), conviction rates remain appallingly low at around 16 per cent, which is lower even than the (similarly poor) conviction rates in the civilian criminal justice system.[81] Accordingly, research by Herriott and colleagues into the SJS reported that case handling is 'characterised by substantial failings during the investigation and prosecution of sexual offences, victims being pressured into dropping charges, and victims being subjected to investigations of their own conduct'.[82]

Evidence therefore indicates that female veterans and servicewomen are not being supported by the British military when it really matters. The larger paradox here, identified by MacKenzie in her work on US, Canadian and Australian militaries, is that institutional failure to provide a safe working environment for women, or to enact justice on their behalf, does not damage overall public trust in the military. Despite the evidence of systemic ingrained misogyny and violence, British militarism still trades on the outstanding reputation of the British soldier/veteran. Militarism as a cultural ideal easily weathers the storm of sexual violence scandals through its continual promotion of the proud, committed service of 'the majority', and through the wider cultural resonance of British veterans' narratives.

Conclusion

Efforts to improve state support for veterans led to the development of a 'Veterans Strategy' in 2018, jointly published by the UK government and devolved administrations. With clear moral certainty, the foreword to the strategy stated: 'It is right that we as a nation – government, charities, business and the wider public – support and empower those who have served us in our Armed Forces. We have a long history of doing this in the UK, and it remains our duty to support those who step up to serve this country.'[83] As this chapter has shown, however, the claim to a 'long history' of supporting veterans is exaggerated at best. The strategy sets out the vision that by 2028, 'Those who have served in the UK Armed Forces, and their families, transition smoothly back into civilian life and contribute fully to a society that understands and values what they have done and what they have to offer.'[84] This vision is the result of ideological processes that have, over many decades, come to constitute dominant ideas of 'the veteran'. Most significantly, the concern with ensuring veterans are 'understood and valued' reflects a deep-seated anxiety that veterans are widely perceived as *damaged* heroes, and that this image is harmful to the military's popularity and legitimacy; that British militarism may yet weaken.[85] As Ross McGarry argued, 'it is the construction, representation, and illustration of British soldiers as vulnerable subjects that is said to hold the greatest threat, rather than augmentation, to civil–military policy and the military institution'.[86] The convergence of two public narratives discussed in this chapter – veterans as marginalised outcasts and as patriotic servants – reveals how this dominant image crystallised in the popular imagination. Politicians and military elites have simultaneously *fuelled* this image by decrying the 'plight' of veterans and *railed against it* by striving to promote 'a more nuanced public understanding of Veterans' experience' and by 'dispelling popular myths'.[87]

British veterans have a complex, ambiguous, often ambivalent relationship with the nation. It is not correct to state that Britain has a long history of supporting its veterans, but neither is it true to suggest (as many veterans have done) that veterans are unsupported and unappreciated in the current political context. Veterans are supported by a large and well-funded charitable sector, along with modifications to statutory services (e.g., an increase in 'veteran friendly' GP surgeries and specialist care such as a new NHS-run 'high impact' mental health service) designed to help alleviate problems and promote 'successful transition' to civilian life.[88] Yet many veterans still report feeling alienated from and marginalised by British society. Bulmer and Jackson, for example, describe veterans' experiences of living in an 'alien world' due to the archetypal narratives that define and colonise their experiences of civilian life.[89] Despite effusive public 'support' for veterans, it is clear therefore that many veterans do not experience understanding or empathy within British society.

Like a steamroller flattening out differences in character and plot, the public narratives that act to define various 'veteranhoods' (e.g., Invictus Games warrior, honest and dutiful servant, dignified commemorator, tragic victim) easily eclipse the nuances and contradictions of veterans' actual lives and stories. As long as they can be inserted into these recognisable genres, veterans' stories reliably maintain the terms of reference for any dialogue as a mandatory respect for military ideals and a reverential view of 'service'. Breaking down these norms – which involves a more fundamental 'resetting' of our relationship with veterans – is an important first step both in shifting the ideological terrain of cultural politics and emancipating veterans from society's dominant imagination of them. It requires us to rethink and to question *who* British veterans *are*. Are they a social underclass of marginalised figures exploited by the nation for a sense of glory during Remembrance? Are they privileged 'super-citizens', honoured by the nation as heroes and rewarded with benefits and services? Are they, even, a potentially subversive group with the ability to disrupt common-sense beliefs about the nation, the military and the violence perpetrated 'on our behalf'? Most of the time, most veterans are just people living ordinary lives like the rest of us. Yet these lives are constantly being valued and valorised in ways that reinforce military ideals and, occasionally, in ways that denigrate other social groups, such as migrants, protestors and welfare claimants.[90]

Given these ideological entanglements, it is impossible to ignore the role that veterans' narratives have played in tightening the grasp of militarism on Britain's politics, policies and values.[91] Each of the various 'veteranhoods' outlined above derive from a common ideological formation: that is, a reverence for, and fascination with, the military and its contribution to the nation. Popular versions of this ideology frequently manifest in anger at the victimised condition veterans have been made to endure in civilian life. Meanwhile, elite manifestations increasingly advocate a 'single view of the veteran'[92] as a positively contributing, non-disruptive subject, capable of maintaining the warm glow of patriotism as the backdrop to British national culture. This book argues for a rejection of patriotism as uncritical allegiance to, and solidarity with, the nation and its representative institutions. Love for one's country involves holding it to high and difficult standards of morality. It involves wanting it to *do* and to *be* better, casting a critical eye over the past while working to repair a damaged present. Further, it involves changing the established grammar of responding to veterans' stories as simple, automatic 'respect'; a convention which reliably diverts attention from the acts veterans carried out 'in our name' and guarantees our continued ignorance of their lives and experiences.

This book calls for a breaking down of the discursive walls that prevent a better social conversation about veterans' stories from emerging. Unthinking patriotism as the response to veterans' stories degrades our commemorative culture, harms a 'just memory' of war,[93] and forecloses the possibility of a future-enhancing dialogue. In line with the narrative approach I set out in Chapter 1, such dialogue is morally necessary, both for grappling with the aftermath of military violence, and for developing more empathic relations with others. For the narrative theorist Arthur Frank, empathy begins with knowing others' stories. 'Knowing someone's stories precipitates perceiving them differently. Their claims may not be more likable or more honorable, but they make more sense and thus require a different response. Empathy thus depends less on some intra-psychic will – a moral resolution to be empathic –and more on habitual ways of interacting with others.'[94] Dialogue relies not only on conversation (though engaged conversation with veterans is certainly a key element of the approach I am advocating), but also on paying detailed attention to veterans' stories wherever we find them. We need to *know* veterans' stories better, while appreciating that there will sometimes be aspects of these stories that are hard to know.

Notes

1. The text of this Parliamentary speech appears as the epilogue to Mercer's memoir, *We Were Warriors*, p. 326.
2. HM Government, 'PM creates new Office for Veterans Affairs to provide lifelong support to military personnel'.
3. Ibid.
4. See, for example, Woodward, Winter and Jenkins, 'Heroic anxieties'; McCartney, 'Hero, victim or villain?'; MacLeish, *Making War at Fort Hood*.
5. Basham, 'Liberal militarism as insecurity, desire and ambivalence'. p. 33.
6. Rossdale, *Resisting Militarism*, p. 4.
7. Cree and Caddick, 'Unconquerable heroes'; Cree, 'Sovereign wives'.
8. As Rudyard Kipling's famous poem 'Tommy' eloquently captures.
9. Within this unavoidably brief and selective history, I have chosen to focus mainly on the period beginning with the First World War, given the undeniable centrality of the two world wars to the modern imagination of the veteran figure in British culture. It is impossible within the scope of this chapter to cover

numerous important components of history, such as the Empire before 1914 (e.g., Dawson, *Soldier Heroes*), or the rich history of veterans *resisting* the military establishment (see Glenton, *Veteranhood*). Nor have I been able to pay more than the briefest attention to the history of women veterans (see Fell, *Women as Veterans in Britain and France after the First World War*; Noakes, *Women in the British Army*), or racialised veterans (Olusoga, *The World's War*). Other more detailed historical accounts are available on each of these topics, and I direct the reader to these sources for a more complete historical analysis.

10. Huxford et al., 'Writing veterans' history', p. 125.
11. See, for example Glenton, *Veteranhood*.
12. McLoughlin, *Veteran Poetics*.
13. See, for example, Pividori, 'Of heroes, ghosts, and witnesses'; Lyon, 'Continuities and discontinuities'; Corley, 'Epistemological interference and the trope of the veteran'.
14. McLoughlin, *Veteran Poetics*, p. 68.
15. Ibid., p. 110.
16. McCartney, 'Hero, victim or villain?'
17. Ingham, *The Military Covenant*, p. 21.
18. Ibid.
19. Swift and Wilkinson, *Veterans of the First World War*.
20. Bourke, *Dismembering the Male*.
21. Cohen, *The War Come Home*; Purdy, 'Paternalism and prosthesis'.
22. Swift, *For Class and Country*.
23. Ibid., p. 92.
24. Fussell, *The Great War and Modern Memory*.
25. Bourke, *Dismembering the Male*, p. 20 (original emphasis).
26. Swift and Wilkinson, *Veterans of the First World War*; Wilkinson, 'Ex-prisoners of war, 1914–18'.
27. Fell, *Women as Veterans in Britain and France after the First World War*.
28. Olusoga, *The World's War*.
29. Against a backdrop of mounting criticism of 'Remembrance' in Britain as a racialised and gendered practice of commemoration (see, e.g., Basham, 'Gender, race, militarism and remembrance'), the Royal British Legion has begun to increase efforts to incorporate the service of non-white, non-British soldiers into its commemorative rhetoric and activities. For example, in 2020 Tweets about Black and Asian service in the world wars were being marked by the hashtag #RememberTogether, while the RBL's website specifically mentions Remembrance 'from Britain and the Commonwealth'.
30. Olusoga, *The World's War*, p. 40.
31. See Gilroy, *After Empire*; Dawson, *Soldier Heroes*; Dawson, 'The theory of popular memory and the contested memories of the Second World War in Britain'; O'Toole, *Heroic Failure*; Dorling and Tomlinson, *Rule Britannia*.
32. Gilroy, *After Empire*, p. 97.
33. Allport, *Demobbed*.
34. Hunt and Robbins, 'Telling stories of the war'.
35. Bourke, *The Second World War*. See also, Smith, *Don't Let My Past Be Your Future*.
36. Soldiers, Sailors, Airmen, and Families Association; one of Britain's oldest military charities.
37. Nguyen, *Nothing Ever Dies*, p. 106.

38. Wool, *After War*.
39. Nguyen, *Nothing Ever Dies*, p. 107.
40. Huxford, 'The Korean War never happened'.
41. Gilroy; *After Empire*, p. 96.
42. Dawson, *Soldier Heroes*.
43. Huxford, 'The Korean War never happened'.
44. Ibid.
45. Ministry of Defence, 'Annual population survey'.
46. See, for example, Basham, 'Gender, race, militarism and remembrance'.
47. West and Antrobus, 'Deeply odd', p. 25.
48. Millar and Tidy, 'Combat as a moving target'.
49. See, for example, Enloe, *Maneuvers*; Enloe, *Globalization and Militarism*; Enloe, *Nimo's War, Emma's War*; Sylvester, *War as Experience*; Parashar, 'What wars and "war bodies" know about international relations'; Eichler, *Militarizing Men*; Basham, *War, Identity and the Liberal State*; Kronsell and Svedberg, *Making Gender, Making War*; Gray, 'Domestic abuse and the public/private divide in the British military'; Hyde, 'The present tense of Afghanistan'; Tidy, 'Fatherhood, gender, and interventions in the geopolitical'.
50. Edwards and Wright, 'No man's land', p. 6. See also Dodds and Kiernan, 'Hidden veterans'.
51. Edwards and Wright, 'No man's land', p. 19.
52. Godier-McBard, Gillin and Fossey, 'Treat everyone like they're a man'; Godier-McBard et al., 'Barriers and facilitators to mental healthcare for women veterans'.
53. West and Antrobus, 'Deeply odd', p. 36.
54. See also Bulmer and Eichler, 'Unmaking militarized masculinity'.
55. Darda, 'Military whiteness'.
56. Ware, *Military Migrants*, p. xvii.
57. Ware, 'Whiteness in the glare of war', p. 316. See also, Pearson and Caddick, 'Meeting the needs of Commonwealth personnel and families'.
58. Gentleman, 'British army veteran faces £27,000 NHS hospital bill'.
59. Pearson and Caddick, 'Meeting the needs of Commonwealth personnel and families'.
60. Ware, 'Whiteness in the glare of war', p. 178.
61. Boris Johnson's words, quoted at the beginning of this chapter.
62. Higate, 'Proud to "fly a desk" and wear a medal?'
63. Stewart, 'I'm not a victim. I'm a survivor'.
64. Despite her story already being in the public domain, I approached Helen for permission to reproduce her story in this chapter and she kindly agreed. Helen names her experience as 'military sexual trauma', which is a term used in an official capacity by most Western militaries (at the time of writing, this does not include the British military) to identify the particular trauma experienced as a result of being raped or assaulted by a fellow service person. In this chapter, I have chosen to use the term 'sexual violence' because it clearly identifies both the *violence* inherent to unwanted sexual activity perpetrated within militaries and the problematic nature of the sexual behaviours which remain prevalent. Both terms – 'military sexual trauma' and 'sexual violence' – remain important in a larger sense for grasping the serious nature of the *effect* and the *criminality* of the violent behaviour itself.
65. Wieskamp, 'I'm going out there and I'm telling this story', p. 134.

66. British Army, 'Sexual harassment report'; Edwards and Wright, 'No man's land'.
67. Wigston, 'Report on inappropriate behaviours', p. 4.
68. Atherton, 'Protecting those who protect us'.
69. MacKenzie, *Good Soldiers Don't Rape*.
70. Ibid., p. 9.
71. Ibid., p. 151.
72. Atherton, 'Protecting those who protect us', p. 25.
73. Ibid., p. 3.
74. HM Government, 'Defence response to the "Women in the Armed Forces" report'.
75. MacKenzie, *Good Soldiers Don't Rape*, p. 14.
76. HM Government, 'Tackling sexual offending in Defence', p. 2 (my emphasis).
77. Wieskamp, 'I'm going out there and I'm telling my story'.
78. Ibid.
79. On the conditions which make stories shareable, MacKenzie offers useful guidance for media reporting on sexual violence, including not centring the reputation of the military or perpetrator, and not seeking to offer 'balance' by including the perspectives of women who defend the military on account of never having personally experienced sexual violence. See MacKenzie, *Good Soldiers Don't Rape*. Widespread adoption of such guidelines would do much to shift the politics of sexual violence storytelling in favour of veterans who have experienced abuse while serving.
80. Ministry of Defence, 'Unacceptable behaviours progress review 2020', p. 4.
81. The 16 per cent conviction rate figure is reported in the Atherton review (p. 63) and is taken from MOD official statistics on sexual offences.
82. Herriott et al., 'Sexual offences committed by members of the armed forces'.
83. HM Government, 'The strategy for our veterans', p. 3.
84. Ibid., p. 4.
85. For example, the *Veterans Transition Review*, carried out by Lord Ashcroft in 2014 on behalf of the British government, demonstrates an overriding concern with correcting the common view of veterans as damaged by their service. Likewise, a survey conducted in the same year by the Royal British Legion commented: 'There is a pervading myth that serving and ex-Service personnel are "mad, bad and sad" i.e. that most suffer mental health problems, that many veterans end up in prison or sleeping rough on the streets, and that many are suicidal.' See Royal British Legion, 'A UK household survey of the ex-service community', p. iv.
86. McGarry, 'Demystifying the "victimised state"', pp. 69–70.
87. HM Government, 'The strategy for our veterans', p. 14.
88. On the politics of 'successful transition', see Bulmer and Eichler, 'Unmaking militarized masculinity'.
89. Bulmer and Jackson, '"You do not live in my skin"', p. 28.
90. For an insightful discussion of the equation of pro-veteran with anti-migrant politics in the US context, see Darda, 'Like a refugee'.
91. Dixon, *Warrior Nation*.
92. Office for Veterans Affairs, 'Veterans' Office marks one year since establishment'.
93. Nguyen, *Nothing Ever Dies*.
94. Frank, 'Knowing other people's stories', p. 154.

CHAPTER 3

The 'Super-Citizen' Character: Veteran Cultures and Identities

> I would recommend it to any youngster, you know people say to me would you let your daughter join the military? I say of course I would if that's what she wanted to do. I think it gives you the best grounding in life that money can't buy. And ten years after I've left, they're still installed in me: the courage, respect, integrity, selfless commitment, you know these things are ingrained in every aspect of my life and I try and pass them on to people I meet when I talk in schools, assemblies. Those core values take you so far in life if you believe in them and you live by them.
>
> Jordan Wylie, on the 'Declassified' podcast

One of the most compelling aspects of veterans' narratives is the characters their stories present to us. In narrative terms, characters are a crucial component of how storytelling compels the imagination. They invite reflection on who that character is, what their motives and their choices are, and they invite us to imagine life in their shoes. Good stories give us richly drawn characters who provide wisdom and/or warning. Characters instruct, teach and guide us. Building on the 'capacities' of stories introduced in Chapter 1, another is the capacity to 'display and test people's character'.[1] As Frank writes, 'Socio-narratology is interested in how stories work to make characters available as generalizable resources that listeners use to engage in work on their own character. Stories form character by evaluating different expressions of it as possibilities for action and as possible identities.'[2] In this chapter, I argue that cultures of veteran storytelling give us a well-formed image of veteran character: that of 'super-citizen'. The super-citizen is one who has surpassed the moral expectations and requirements of ordinary citizens, who through enacting their inherent noble qualities and committing to exemplary values has earned the admiration and respect of others.

This characterisation is a *generic* feature of veterans' narratives, one which travels across multiple genres of veteran storytelling, infusing our background understanding of who veterans *are*. It is a characterisation that *precedes* the actual veteran, prefiguring the possibilities we have for engaging with their stories.

Characterisation does political work. It is ideologically laden, reinforcing the militarist terms of reference that veterans' narratives impart to us, often in the most 'common-sense' or seemingly innocuous of ways. My argument here develops the idea, introduced in the previous chapter, that veterans' stories reliably maintain the terms of any dialogue as mandatory respect for military ideals and a reverential view of 'service' (i.e., militarist terms of reference). This argument is key to understanding how the veteran figure manages to transcend politics, and how their stories thereby influence our politics all the more powerfully. I suggest that any effort to reshape the ideological terrain of cultural politics must contend with the notion of 'supporting' veterans (as per the familiar refrain 'support the troops') as an unquestionable moral good. The call to 'support veterans' often entails first agreeing with things that veterans say – investing veteran speech with superior moral value – and secondly casting others' suffering or need for support as subordinate.[3] In refusing militarist terms of reference, I argue that we ought to question the certainty and centrality of these ideals and ask how other moral goods might come to contest them. In particular, I advocate refashioning the ideological demand to 'support veterans' away from notions of patriotic duty and towards a perspective grounded in notions of radical equality, of the kind proposed by Judith Butler in her work on non-violence and grievability, for example.[4] This is to suggest that if we reject the ideology that constructs the veteran character as 'super-citizen', possibilities might emerge for a more equal social distribution of compassion and solidarity which could better encompass other groups who continue to be rejected as worthy of our support.

Stories about veterans petition us with the demand to support them *because* of their military service and presumed heroism, rather than because they are human beings affected by war. Notions of a moral debt of gratitude constitute the backdrop to such demands.[5] No matter the content and context of the argument – 'veterans are unjustly portrayed as damaged goods', 'veterans are suffering higher rates of joblessness or homelessness', 'women veterans are systematically discriminated against', etc. – the premise is nearly always that the situation is undesirable because veterans are exemplary characters and any disadvantage they encounter is therefore either tragic or the result of intolerable neglect. In Chapter 1, for example, I cited the example of Diane Allen's story of misogyny in the British Army. Nestled within her legitimate complaint about sexism is a robust belief in the fundamental value and virtue of military culture. As Allen states, 'The culture is still strong. It produces those who are resilient, pragmatic, humorous and level-headed in crises, problem solvers who are capable of game changing energy or incredible patience.'[6] Further, in defence of the many 'good' officers she encountered, she asserts that 'serving British women and men are exactly the sort of characters you would want to marry; reliable, resilient, faithful and kind'.[7] The argument that women are badly treated is couched within familiar exhortations about the exceptionality and valour of British service personnel. Such qualities and exhortations are typical of stories about veterans told in the public sphere.

Refusing the automatic framing of veterans' stories in these terms is, I argue, vital to understanding war from a more radically egalitarian perspective. If we state, for instance, that suffering experienced by veterans is unacceptable because war itself is bad and inherently harmful, rather than because veterans are uniquely special characters, we may open up the possibility of addressing other groups such as refugees who also suffer as a result of war. This argument is not antiveteran; on the contrary, it considers how 'veteranness' gets transformed in ways that many veterans themselves – especially 'critical' veterans – do not recognise.[8] To advance this position as a means of contesting the cultural politics of narrative, in this chapter I will examine storytelling cultures that work to construct the character of the British veteran as 'super-citizen', alongside the ways in which this characterisation designates other potentially vulnerable groups as suspect or unworthy. In a general sense, this argument is informed by my embeddedness within veteran cultures over the past decade of research and study. As specific sites for analysis, I focus on two domains of storytelling that stand out to me as culturally significant examples of characterisation and identity construction: podcasting and social media. Given the growing popularity of podcasts as a form of 'infotainment', the creation of veteran-themed podcasts provides intriguing new opportunities for engaging with veteran stories. Likewise, the ubiquitous infiltration of social media into our everyday lives has enabled new forms of digital narratives and cultures to emerge in ways that harness and transform existing veteran cultures. While I cannot lay claim to a systematic method of gathering social media content for analysis, my extended, habitual exposure to veterans' online activity has provided me with a wealth of analytical reflections worth utilising. I argue that paying attention to these 'everyday' iterations of veteran culture and identity reveals much about how cultural constructions of veteran character are working to shape our values and politics in contemporary Britain.

Inside Veteran Cultures

When analysing veteran culture it is important to acknowledge that this culture is not one 'thing', but multiple overlapping and fragmented cultural forms. Furthermore, within veteran cultures there exist many complex, shifting and sometimes contradictory veteran identities which resist straightforward categorisation.[9] Veteran identities are constructed (and deconstructed) in dynamic ways and over extended time periods as veterans find themselves immersed in different cultural forms. This complexity is further compounded by the artificial and tenuous separation of 'military' versus 'civilian' worlds, and the ambiguous position of the veteran figure within this binary construction.

Notwithstanding the inevitable fractures and fault lines inherent within any cultural grouping, there are, nevertheless, distinguishable forms of veteran culture. One distinction can be drawn between what we might describe as 'elite' and 'popular' veteran cultures. The notion of an elite veteran culture can be understood as comprising (predominantly) the former officer class who go on to adopt leading civilian roles as politicians, military charity bosses, defence journalists, policy and security analysts, military historians, and corporate executives in the defence industry and beyond. The primary function of this elite culture is arguably to act as a 'civilian' branch of the military establishment, extending military values and power into civil society in ways that help to maintain the military's privileged role as a key constitutive element of 'the nation'. Cultural veteran elites might not necessarily operate in this way by conspiratorial or intentional means, but rather through the reliable selection of those who can reproduce tradition as part of the dominant cultural formation.[10] Elite veteran culture thereby empowers certain influential voices as its privileged representatives, while aiming to manage or contain other voices in subordinated positions.

It is also possible to identify a broader 'popular' veteran culture based around the more 'ordinary' or everyday veteran experience.

Popular veteran culture is patterned by common 'structures of feeling',[11] which typically include an embrace of the ideals of service and patriotism, pride in military service and in the monarchy, a feeling of being separate from civilian society, and an alternately respectful and antagonistic relationship with military and political authority. Veterans who position themselves within – and who are positioned by – this cultural form are often strong advocates for veterans' 'issues', are active in debating these issues online, and are more likely to vocalise dissatisfaction or disillusionment with the way veterans are treated by the government or the nation. In some ways, this culture works in tandem with 'elite' veteran culture by reproducing patriotic sentiment and military ideals as the pervasive backdrop to British cultural and political life. Yet it can also work antagonistically by marshalling resentment towards the government and military establishment for its neglect of veterans. This latter dynamic highlights a key element of struggle within iterations of veteran culture, which can at times also manifest as a variation of class struggle.[12]

Third, there is a small but increasingly vocal 'critical' veteran culture (or *counter*-culture) comprising dissenting veterans who seek to undo the military's influence upon their own lives and to counteract the effects of military power in society. This culture hails veterans who become part of organisations such as Veterans for Peace and Forces Watch who aim to critically analyse military power and hold it to account, campaigners, journalists and activists such as Joe Glenton and David Gee, as well as veterans turned critical scholars such as Paul Higate, Ben Schrader and others. Critical veteran cultures contest the ideological representations of militarism which characterise other iterations of veteran culture, though often they do so by drawing upon a shared repertoire of meanings and concepts such as service, moral courage and bravery.[13] Critical veterans thereby seek to imbue veteran identity with transformed meanings and representations, posing a challenge to militarism both from within and from outside of its own ideological terrain.

Finally, there are veterans who mostly avoid any association with veteran culture and identity, who do not identify as 'veterans', preferring at most to think of themselves as 'ex-service', who do not view their military service as consequential in their broader life story, and who slip quietly back into civilian society. They might not choose to keep their military past 'hidden' per se, but neither is it front and centre in their lives. While they might be quietly proud of their military service, or view it as a professional or developmental experience, they do not advertise or discuss their military background, do not wear medals or attend Remembrance services, and prefer to drift quietly along in civilian life without adopting a 'veteran' posture or presence for themselves. In this regard, they might not really be considered as a constituency within 'veteran culture' at all, since they are unlikely to associate with it in the first place.

All forms of veteran culture, it must be noted, are marked by gendered norms and expectations. From the hierarchical privileging of front-line combat and special forces infantry roles, to sexualised 'banter' and other masculine conventions of storytelling, to the near absence of women within the dominant cultural forms, to the privileging of masculinity even within critical veteran cultures, the hyper-masculinity for which the military itself is renowned is reflected in different ways in all forms of veteran culture.[14] Veteran cultures therefore produce a gendered 'veteranhood' which delineates the boundaries of inclusion and exclusion according to one's ability or willingness to conform. Within the broad portrait of veteran cultures I have sketched out above, there is clearly room for actual veterans to manoeuvre between and within different cultural forms, to adopt certain practices of veteranhood while rejecting others, and to shift the positions they reflexively choose to occupy. This portrait therefore serves as nothing more than an analytical touchstone for identifying key trends or features of veteran cultures; that is, it is not intended as a tool for categorising individuals. The examples I select to form the basis of my critique in this chapter predominantly conform to the 'elite' and 'popular' forms of veteran culture, since these are the formations which arguably exert the strongest influence on our national culture and politics, and which are most consistently reproduced as portrayals of 'the veteran' in British society. These are the dominant cultural forms, buttressed by their association with 'the nation' and the symbolic power of the monarchy, which are most capable of influencing social representations of veteranhood.

Veteran cultures are, furthermore, coextensive with the wider cultural context of contemporary Britain. As I began gathering ideas and material for this chapter, in the febrile atmosphere of the summer of 2020, numerous developments within and beyond Britain began to frame my understanding of how veterans' stories dovetail with the broader culture. Some of these developments felt like a crystallisation of long-established trends, while others emerged in the more proximal disruption of the COVID-19 pandemic. They included the continued cultural–political argument over Brexit and trade deals, the robust defeat of Jeremy Corbyn's Labour at the 2019 general election, the rapid transfer of economic and social activity into online spaces as a result of COVID-19 (as well as controversy surrounding the government's response to the virus), an ongoing refugee crisis unfolding on Europe's shores and across its borders, and the rise of mass protests against racism sparked by the international Black Lives Matter movement. Associated with the latter was a noticeable rise in public debate about historic legacies of slavery and empire, which found climactic expression in the toppling of the Edward Colston statue in Bristol. Such events triggered a further conservative backlash, spurred on, for example, by then Prime Minister Boris Johnson's call to end 'our cringing embarrassment about our history, our traditions and about our culture, and that we stop this general bout of self-recrimination and wetness',[15] and by the UK equalities minister Kemi Badenoch's pronouncement that 'this government stands unequivocally against critical race theory'.[16] Moreover, each of these developments can be read as episodes in a longer-running 'culture war' characterised by ideological contestation about 'Britishness' and 'British values'.[17] This is the background against which veterans' narratives play out, which they feed into, contest and transform. Furthermore, it is in this context that we can observe the resurgence of the veteran figure as 'super-citizen'.

Constructing the Super-Citizen

> With great British values and standards, we can achieve the unachievable
> Brian Wood, interview on 'Declassified' podcast

> I don't think there's any finer example of a role model in the military community, but just in our society mate, people would do a great service to themselves by looking at you and how you operate. And from everyone here, I thank you; I thank you for today, I thank you for your future support and everything you're doing for our guys, girls, dependants and all the rest of it – thank you!
> Michael Coates, host of 'Declassified' podcast, to David Wiseman

> One thing that's shining through is your passion for it and your dedication for this . . . Why do you care so much, why do you go way over and above, why are you doing this, why have you taken the day off to come here for a one-hour podcast with me: why do you care so much?

I'm not really sure, it's a sort of instinct – its instinctive. I think it's because of what you do and what you have done, and how you have borne those injuries. I'm very impressed, I'm grateful.
>> Exchange between Michael Coates and Alexandra Crick on 'Declassified' podcast

Constructing the veteran character as 'super-citizen' is an ongoing habitual process that takes place across different spheres of society and cultural activity. In this section, I focus on how character is constructed in one example of cultural production, the podcast series 'Declassified: Documenting Military Stories'. The podcast launched in 2018 as a vehicle for telling stories of military life and sharing honest, hard-hitting conversations about mental health. Guests reflect the diversity of constituents within what the podcast frequently affirms as 'the military community', and have included veterans, charity executives, politicians, business leaders, healthcare professionals, spouses and, in one harrowing episode, the parents of a soldier who died by suicide. Notable public figures including Johnny Mercer MP, the adventurist and TV personality Levison Wood, and numerous stars of the Invictus Games along with Prince Harry have also featured as guests. The podcast styles itself as a platform for breaking taboos about mental health and generating inspirational stories of courage and bravery in overcoming trauma. The host, Michael Coates, himself a former soldier, gently coaxes stories from his guests, often nudging the conversations towards recurring themes like values, community, and post-traumatic growth.

'Declassified' quickly resonated with the podcast-listening public, achieving recognition as 'best interview podcast' at the 2020 British Podcast Awards, along with a bronze award for 'best wellbeing podcast' that same year. As at early 2021, the podcast had published ninety-three episodes, including a sub-series featuring conversations designed to offer support and guidance during the COVID-19 pandemic. The podcast medium allows for a sense of intimacy between the speakers, giving the impression of an 'overheard social conversation',[18] and thereby contributing to the 'community' ethos of the podcast. Regular listeners are invited to become part of this community through their identification with the characters and contributors featured. Skilful and attentive community-building through the podcast medium thus lends itself well to the ability to influence that community politically. The success of the podcast suggests that the public has a strong appetite for stories of gritty combat, heroic feats and inspirational journeys. As a site for veteran storytelling, then, the podcast provides a rich and influential narrative resource that aims to represent veteran experience to both a military and a wider civilian audience, and which seeks to promote the value and virtue of veterans' stories for teaching wisdom, inspiration, and overcoming adversity.

Each of the above extracts illustrates what I argue to be the core effect (or moral purpose) of the stories told on 'Declassified': that is, the co-construction of character. Frank argues that 'Many stories, if not most and possibly *all*, involve some test of character: a decisive moment at which a character's response declares what sort of person she or he is.'[19] In veterans' stories, the test of character is assumed to have been passed already by virtue of military service. It is a background assumption that informs our expectations of veteran character. Veterans are virtuous characters simply by virtue of being veterans. On 'Declassified', the test of character – the 'decisive moment' in which character is both formed and displayed – is made explicit through vivid illustrations of the storytellers' responses to adversity, through 'bombs and bullets' combat stories, and through continuous attention to the values that military communities hold dear. Combat itself is notoriously considered a test of character, or a 'proving ground' for heroic masculinity.[20] While 'Declassified' features numerous different kinds of story, combat stories seem especially revered for their capacity to demonstrate strength and resilience of character. Yet whatever kind of story is being told, the host's questions draw out examples of his guest's strength and resilience which depict their character.

In production terms, 'Declassified' episodes stake an early claim for character, with the host's introduction to each guest (voiced over dramatic crescendo music) providing an 'abstract' to the upcoming tale. For example:

> The word 'warrior' accurately describes our next guest. She followed in her father's footsteps and at the age of sixteen joined the British Army. After serving in some of the most hostile environments on the planet, she now faces her hardest battle: her battle with cancer. (Episode 28: Mandy Islam)

This example is interesting for its portrayal of a woman as 'warrior', though as the story unfolds it becomes clear that warrior character is attributed more to her battle with cancer than to her career as a military officer. Indeed, while women feature on the podcast, they are mostly represented in the roles of mother, spouse and sometimes professional, rather than as 'military cross winner', 'special forces soldier' or 'combat veteran', as per other prominent guests. The character under the brightest spotlight is notably that of the male soldier as proud, values-driven servant of the nation. References to the fighting spirit of 'the blokes' are commonly used to emphasise virtuosity. This focus on the valour of the male combat soldier works alongside a habitual emphasis on the 'values' espoused by soldiers – and reflected in the wider military community – to paint a portrait of aspirational character.

The role of 'values talk' is, I argue, integral to constructing the veteran character as super-citizen, to elevating veteran personhood morally above the civilian. As well as the overt references to values, 'Those core values take you so far in life, if you believe in them and you live by them' (Episode 9: Jordan Wylie); '. . . good values, and living with them, really good, mate' (Episode 13: Levison Wood); '. . . that values base was I'm assuming then what took you to Rwanda in 1998' ('Housing special', with Ed Tytherleigh), values are frequently implicit within discussion of soldiers' professionalism, service, self-sacrifice and empathic relations with others. 'Declassified' celebrates 'living by values' as an ideal form of life, a source of pride, and something which defines and separates the military community. Such a strong emphasis on values in veteran storytelling undoubtedly reflects the doctrinal emphasis on 'Values and Standards' within military life, which are codified and listed as 'Courage', 'Discipline', 'Respect for Others', 'Integrity', 'Loyalty' and 'Selfless Commitment'.[21] These abstracted values are brought to life in stories about people being rescued from childhood trauma by the welcoming embrace of the military community (e.g., Episode 18: Paul Watson; Episode 16: Amanda Jones; Episode 10: Alexander Khan); recovery from life-changing injury (e.g., Episode 23: Dave Henson; Episode 12: David Wiseman; Episode 5: Simon Harmer; Episode 34: JJ Chalmers; Episode 36: Cassidy Little); or about heroic individual efforts to raise funds for others through extreme adventure challenge (e.g., Episode 29: Dean Stott; Episode 28: Mandy Islam; Episode 9: Jordan Wylie). In offering these stories to the public, 'Declassified' aims to showcase what is possible when character is based around these essential militarised values. Moreover, in constructing militarised values as special and superior to civilian ones (constituted by implication as selfishness and inefficiency), these stories bind us to militarist terms of reference that allow us to comprehend veterans' lives and experiences only from a position of virtue.

The reason why construction of character is such an important feature of veterans' stories is that it is this which fundamentally underpins their elevation to the status of 'super-citizens'. And, as I will argue in the next section, this super-citizen status has serious implications for how we think about war, nation and belonging. The links between military service and idealised framings of citizenship are well established, and feminist scholarship has long critiqued the equation of the two as a practice guaranteed to reproduce gendered and racial hierarchies internal to citizenship regimes.[22] Less apparent in such scholarship is how superior citizenship is maintained through narrative – through the political *work* undertaken by characterisation – along with the 'othering' effects that veterans' stories can exert through the juxtaposition of character.

Constructing super-citizen character through stories that espouse values-based conduct is a feature of narrative enabled by trends in citizenship practices. Margaret Somers' eloquent treatise on the 'genealogies of citizenship' makes the important point that citizenship is not a 'thing' or an immutable status one holds but is, at heart, 'a matrix of institutional relationships, technologies, political idioms, and rights-claiming practices that are always dynamic and contingent'.[23] Citizenship, therefore, is a *practice*, the effects of which determine 'the right to have rights', or, in other words, the right to inclusion within a social and political community. In this sense, it is also a mechanism for inclusion *and exclusion* based on certain configurations of rights and obligations. In feminist studies of citizenship, the balance between rights and obligations is a key point of political interest.[24] Veterans' stories, like those told on 'Declassified', implicitly draw from citizenship practices which emphasise obligations, rather than rights, as the basis for inclusion. That is, the obligation to subordinate self-interest by serving the common good is held as the definitive criterion of model citizenship.[25] This in contrast to a liberal rights-based discourse which emphasises membership of a polity based on fundamental legal rights.[26] By extolling the values of service and sacrifice, veterans' stories lay claim to this subordinated self-interest which underpins super-citizen character. Another example from the podcast, from a summary episode reflecting on previous editions, illustrates self-sacrifice as a hallmark of veteran character. Commenting on the aspirational qualities of one of his guests, Coates says:

> Another thing that episode taught me was also that leadership is about sacrifice. And that preparing yourself to sacrifice or to sacrifice yourself, not just like getting blown up, but by leading and by putting yourself in a really uncomfortable position, that to me is leadership, the ability to sacrifice yourself. (Episode 22: Summary)

'Declassified' stories are intended to instruct and inspire; to illustrate how ordinary people might cultivate superior virtue and character by modelling their behaviour on these inspirational super-citizen characters. These stories are 'narrative maps' that offer templates for character development, though they also establish an exclusionary measure of worthiness through which emerges the enduring (and, for many, alluring) notion of male military service as the epitome of democratic citizenship.[27]

Beyond the 'obligation' model, which confers superior citizenship on the veteran in return for answering the call to service, citizenship practices grounded in 'contractual exchange' logic also provide opportunities for narrating the veteran figure as super-citizen. Somers' argument is that contemporary citizenship is conferred by a contractual logic of exchange: one must 'exchange commensurable quid pro quos to be treated as a valued member of civil society who is entitled to protection as a right of membership'.[28] Citizenship is therefore a privilege to be earned through the exchange of goods of commensurate value. Here, again, military service emerges as an influential barometer of contribution and contractual fulfilment. For example, it is often argued or implied that by serving the country and sacrificing youth, health and innocence to the brutalising rigours of warfare, veterans have *exceeded* their contractual obligations to the nation and are deserving of special recognition in return.[29] As former SAS soldier Phil Campion comments in Episode 3 of the podcast, 'If you're first in line to help the country out, you should be first in line to get some help.' By the same logic, others who are considered to have nothing to offer in exchange for their citizenship (e.g., migrants, the unemployed, welfare claimants) risk being constructed as inferior, especially when direct comparisons are drawn with the super-citizen. However, the contractual logic also poses risks to veterans as it can undermine their status if veterans are seen to be a drain on the state's resources. If veterans are not perceived to be 'net contributors to society',[30] for instance, through homelessness, unemployment or criminality – all forms of contractual non-fulfilment under a marketised citizenship ethos – their collective reputation is harmed and their status lowered. Character, therefore, is not immutable: it can be undermined and degraded as well as celebrated and revered. As such, character sometimes needs *defending*.

Defending the Super-Citizen

Threatened identities fight back.

Afua Hirsch[31]

I have argued that construction of the 'veteran-as-super-citizen' is a practice that requires ongoing maintenance through narrative. Yet it also seems to require others whose citizenship is constructed as inferior by comparison. Others' claims to *equal* citizenship can come into conflict with veterans' claims to *super*-citizenship, and as such there is a need to defend veterans' social standing against threats to identity and belonging posed by 'outsiders'. Outsiders include all those whose potential inclusion within the body of society is considered to undermine the character and values of the nation, with national character generally epitomised by the institutions of the military and monarchy.[32] Outsiders may take the form of *literal* outsiders (e.g., refugees, migrants, asylum seekers), but can also include those imagined to be outside the national community by virtue of their ethnicity, sexuality or through adherence to 'alternative' value systems (e.g., socialists, activists, feminists). These outsiders become threatening when their struggles for inclusion and equality begin to challenge the dominant narratives of our history and who 'we' are as a people, as has taken place following periods of colonial consciousness-raising in Britain.[33] Following Hirsch, I argue that vigorous re-assertions of the veteran as super-citizen can be understood as 'threatened identities' fighting back against outsiders who would unsettle the norms in which they are deeply invested. This defence of the super-citizen is a process that can be readily observed in online spaces of communication through social media.[34]

Social media is understood as a core site of cultural production and social interaction.[35] Social media platforms – and I focus here on Twitter in particular – are spaces where the cultural politics of everyday life takes place; where people exchange messages and jokes, construct and manage identities, and where they represent emotion and provoke emotional responses in others.[36] As Duncombe explains,

'"Tweets" are powerful mechanisms for the circulation of affect and transmission of emotion, whereby emotionally charged content quickly resonates with others, sparking debate and often anger."[37] Moreover, the power of Twitter as a mode of cultural politics is not limited to the online world, with online exchanges spilling over into offline interpersonal and political relationships as well as shaping debate in the wider mass media. My interest in Twitter (and, to a lesser degree, Facebook) derives from the opportunities it presents for observing and engaging with veteran culture and socialisation. As an academic, I am a habitual Twitter user. As well as keeping in touch with colleagues and finding out about events and articles, I use it as a means of staying up-to-date with news and discussion regarding veterans and their political affairs. I follow, and am followed by, a large number of veterans and veterans' organisations. As a result, every day I am exposed to reams of online content which represents veterans' experiences and opinions in the form of highly interactive and shareable posts. My engagement in this space is not always comfortable, as I am occasionally exposed to content which carries racist and misogynist undertones, or political viewpoints which I find objectionable. Rather than challenge this material, my typical response is to let it wash over me, to privately consider the political work enacted by content which actively reproduces inequalities. I recognise this response is passive and politically ineffective, though it derives from a sense of having never experienced a productive exchange of views over social media, and the emotional costs involved in constant argumentative Twitter 'spats'. As such, I am largely an observer, and occasionally a participant, in online veteran cultures.[38]

Much of the content which represents veteran identities and cultural norms is shared in the form of 'memes'; images superimposed with text designed to capture meaning and share ideas. As Gbadegesin writes, memes are 'important meaning making artefacts created, and spread through the social media',[39] are often intended to convey humour, and in veteran cultures, also function as statements of character and moral authority. Memes are 'vehicles for cultural proliferation',[40] and are a means of encoding ideology as normative cultural practice.[41] Within online veteran cultures, different 'meme genres' exist, performing subtly different roles in cultural politics. Three genres I will consider here include what I describe as 'identity memes', 'betrayed veteran memes' and 'military banter memes'. Identity memes are a prominent genre in veterans' online communications, involving a robust presentation of veteran pride, often combined with nationalist expressions of identity. Examples from the many I have encountered include an image of the Union Jack flag captioned with the words 'I am and will always be a UK veteran', and another showing a UK veterans' lapel pin captioned with the phrase 'WE ARE NOT JUST VETERANS, WE ARE ONE BIG FAMILY. DON'T MESS WITH MY BROTHERS AND SISTERS'. Messages like these play a role in 'collectivising' emotions within veteran communities and, indeed, in recreating communities in online spaces. Memes are potent symbols of veteran identity, and capable therefore of pricking the emotive attachments to identity and belonging which form the communal basis of military life and 'brotherhood'.[42] Through these memes, the 'affective energies'[43] evoked by themes of pride, loyalty and family encoded in the memes' text and images are communicated and shared, just as memes themselves are 'shared' at the click of a button. By networking emotion, then, meaning-saturated memes give veterans a means of experiencing the collective politics of identity despite their geographical dispersion or isolation.

Identity memes might not necessarily contribute to an 'othering' of other groups, but they do work to create a solid representation of *who* British veterans *are* that can be read against a backdrop of antipathy towards 'multiculturalism' and its supposed failings.[44] As Dixon writes, within British culture 'a conservative, assimilationist, British nationalism has been promoted as a means of dealing with an existential security threat',[45] with that threat imagined as multiculturalism's destabilising of the national community, provoking increased militarism and securitisation in response. In this context, the veteran-as-super-citizen becomes the ideal bulwark against such threats: the literal and symbolic defender of the nation.

'Betrayed veteran memes' work more directly than identity memes to foster separation from, and moral authority over, other civilian groups and cultures. Such memes draw upon the narratives of disillusionment and betrayal I discussed in Chapter 2 in order to highlight ill-treatment and misunderstanding by the civilian 'other'. Illustrative examples include an image of a green military tunic pierced by a bullet-hole, with blood stains around the hole forming the shape of a poppy, and the caption 'IF ANYONE EVER QUESTIONS WHY A POPPY SHOULD BE RED, SHOW THEM THIS PICTURE' (see Figure 3.1[46]).

Likewise, the more satirical meme showing a tapestry-style illustration of historic battles captioned with the mock headline 'SOLDIERS INVOLVED IN THE 1066 BATTLE OF HASTINGS TO FACE FRESH INVESTIGATION INTO MURDER CLAIMS!' Each of these memes works

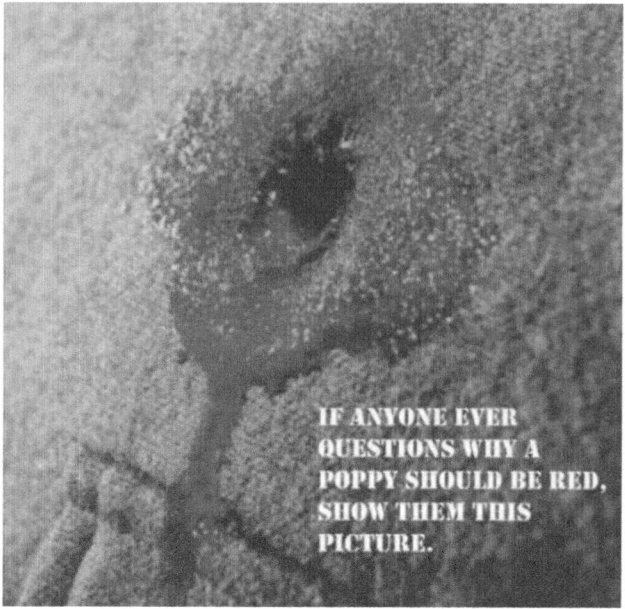

Figure 3.1 Bullet hole poppy. *Source*: Twitter/X

to defend veterans' moral authority against threats both seemingly benign (e.g., the 'white poppy' symbol) and malicious (e.g., the prosecution of veterans for alleged war crimes). As with the identity memes which typify popular veteran culture online, betrayed-veteran memes likewise rely on fiercely emotive imagery and meaning to create 'communities of feeling', whereby veterans enact and experience feelings of 'collective national selfhood'.[47]

Moreover, like the stories on 'Declassified', identity memes and betrayed-veteran memes both construct a vivid portrait of veteran character as uniquely brave, honest and self-sacrificing. What unites the meanings and emotions which circulate via these messages – both on and offline – is the underpinning ideology of 'service', so deeply and uniquely attached to veteran character. It is the rhetorical weight of 'service' that so powerfully establishes the notion of an unpayable debt that society owes to its veterans.[48] The abiding notion that veterans have sacrificed themselves in order to serve their country is, above all, what legitimises their status as super-citizens. The ideology of service is the foundation of the moral contract that demands that society honours its veterans. And, moreover, it is the unpayable debt to 'service' that so readily lends itself to feelings of betrayal and neglect, as highlighted by another meme titled 'Combat Veteran' which presented a list of eleven 'rules' for interaction, including '1: NEVER QUESTION THE LOOK IN HIS EYES: You really don't want to know what he's thinking', '4: NEVER ASK HIM IF HE HAS KILLED ANYONE: He may say your [sic] next', and '6: NEVER DISRESPECT HIS FLAG OR COUNTRY: He has lost friends defending both'. Through such sentiments, the ethos of service and self-sacrifice acquires deep moral resonance and bestows a sense of moral deservingness upon the veteran as super-citizen.

Crucially, it is when the unimpeachable ethos of service conflicts with claims that others might make to belonging and inclusion that the 'othering' effects of the super-citizen character are realised. This is most evident when veterans' virtuosity is contrasted to other less deserving groups, whereby support for veterans is imagined as a zero-sum transaction against support for vulnerable others. Two examples – each of which foreground the tensions around nationalism, patriotism and racialised belonging which cut across the cultural politics of veterans' narratives – occurred during the summer of 2020 with the Black Lives Matter (BLM) protests and the ongoing refugee crisis in Europe.[49] Both events received substantial media attention at the time, and both provoked significant reaction on social media by veterans and others connected to the military community.[50] As well as drawing attention to police brutality and structural inequalities experienced by Black people in the present, the BLM protests sparked heated debate about Britain's imperial past and the legacies of slavery and colonialism. Right-wing commentators and politicians accused the protestors of attempting to 're-write' history and of tarnishing Britain's international reputation for fairness and equality.[51] Concurrent with the government and media backlash against BLM, the protestors aroused anger and suspicion among military communities given the links the former were drawing between the militarised violence of empire and histories of racial prejudice in Britain. The critical approach towards history advocated by the protestors arguably conflicted with conservative trends towards *celebrating* British history,[52] and thereby threatened to destabilise the military's association with freedom and democracy as part of the dominant historical narrative.

A third meme genre, 'military banter memes', aimed to satirise and undermine the BLM movement's attempt to bring race discrimination onto the political agenda, as in Figure 3.2 showing a soldier with a rifle 'taking a knee' (as per the symbolic act of protest) in the 'correct' fashion.

For those taking a 'knee', this is the correct position.

Figure 3.2 Taking a knee. *Source*: Facebook

Through the use of humour (or 'banter', in military terms), this meme works to devalue and emasculate the anti-racist protestors while reinforcing the primacy of military masculinity. The protestors are succinctly othered by the meme's humorous presentation of the 'correct' (read: heteronormative, nationalist) gender ideology. Similarly, 'betrayed-veteran' memes circulating at the time of the protests contrasted BLM's suspect political agenda to the morally unassailable causes advocated by veterans (e.g., defence against malicious prosecutions), as in one meme proclaiming, 'Standing with soldiers A-Z: Veteran's lives matter'.[53] Pitching its message within the familiar 'betrayed-veteran' narrative, this meme casts the White male veteran (rather than the racialised Black protestor) as the *real* voice of minoritised difference.[54] Indeed, as Joseph Darda has argued in an American context, it has become possible for a sense of White grievance to invert the discourse of liberal multiculturalism in order to protest the alleged decentring of the White male veteran in favour of immigrants, feminists and racial minorities.[55] Thus, the betrayed veteran emerges as multiculturalism's true victim, with a strong response of assimilationist nationalism required to restore the order disturbed by the protestors.

Similar racialising processes are set in motion by the next ('banter') meme I wish to highlight, picturing a stern-faced Queen Elizabeth II on the massive electronic billboard at London's Piccadilly, captioned with the mock-attributed quote 'Carry on you little fuckers and I'll set the Gurkhas on you' (Figure 3.3). This example is notable for its construction of the Gurkhas as an ideal form of non-White, non-British racial belonging compared with the contingent, always suspect forms of pseudo-belonging inhabited by other racialised groups. In veteran cultures, as in British society more generally, Gurkhas are 'popular' immigrants, their favour derived from historic ties to the British Army and from their fearsome reputation, as invoked by the Queen's ventriloquised threat.[56] Implied in each of these examples is a sense that the protestors do not belong here, that their accusations of unfair treatment and their demands for inclusion are unwarranted, unwelcome, and fundamentally at odds with the tolerant and decent society we know ourselves to be. Veterans, by contrast, are the embodiment of that society; having offered their service to Queen and country, they become society's most dignified representatives. Indeed, as Somers argues, 'accusations of questionable patriotism and loyalty are always more directed against fellow

Figure 3.3 Ventriloquising the Queen. *Source*: Facebook

citizens than actual foreigners, for it is by "othering" internal dissenters and the socially excluded that the included are able to distinguish themselves as true patriots ready to defend the nation against the threats from without or within.'[57]

As with the BLM protestors, the imagined threats to the national community posed by refugees also provoked an 'othering' response online, particularly when the refugees' need for safety and inclusion was brought into conflict with the needs of the veteran-as-supercitizen. One meme in the 'betrayed-veteran' genre depicted a homeless man (potentially imagined as a veteran in this scenario) lying on the street being told by a police officer 'I'M SORRY SIR BUT YOU NEED TO MOVE ON IMMEDIATELY, THE MIGRANTS IN THE HOTEL ACROSS THE ROAD HAVE COMPLAINED ABOUT YOU' (Figure 3.4). Another 'banter' meme showed a group of male refugees in a small dingy captioned with the phrase 'Its only six to a boat from Monday!'.[58] Elsewhere, a veteran's tweet compared 'miscreants' crossing the English Channel illegally with the case of a Fijian veteran of the British Army being threatened with deportation over an irregular immigration status.[59] Following Butler, I understand such articulations of anti-refugee sentiment as belonging to a 'tacit war logic [that] enters into the biopolitical management of populations',[60] such that veterans' lives are understood

Figure 3.4 The migrants have complained about you'. *Source*: Facebook

as worthy of protection – and their needs for support of being met – whereas refugees' lives are considered a threat to the existence of our society and culture. 'According to that war logic', Butler explains, 'it is a matter of choosing between the lives of refugees and the lives of those who claim the right to be defended against the refugees. In such instances, a racist and paranoid version of self-defence authorizes the destruction of another population.'[61]

Of course, the racist biopolitics which pits veteran lives worth nurturing against refugee lives which may be abandoned cannot be said to originate with veterans themselves, but rather inheres in social relations and logics of nationalism, contractualised citizenship and securitisation more generally. In this sense, veterans who promote anti-refugee narratives cannot be held responsible for the death and destruction which results from political decisions to close down safe routes of passage to vulnerable people. There are, moreover, complex drivers of anti-refugee narratives in veteran communities, as in the population at large, often involving a deep sense of class injury.[62] Where veterans find themselves and their communities impoverished by neoliberal Britain, class injury combined with the moral entitlement of the super-citizen can resolve itself onto the familiar target of those most excluded from society. Popular militarism, like xenophobic nationalism, 'piggybacks' on economic inequalities. Thus, even while hateful content posted by veterans online will frequently be challenged by their peers and by others in the military community, there exists a pernicious form of othering whereby the cultural politics of the veteran-as-super-citizen reinforces the demand to put '*#VeteransBeforeMigrants*', and in so doing contributes to the precariousness of refugee lives. When support for refugees is imagined as antithetical to support for veterans – that is, a zero-sum transaction whereby the availability of support becomes finite and non-transferable – the needs of the most deserving super-citizen will trump the needs of the undeserving non-citizen, even when it is the latter who experiences the greater existential threat.

Conclusion

Prior to this chapter I have focused on the overarching narrative structures which shape the individual stories veterans tell about their military and post-military lives. In this chapter, I focused on the *characters* at the heart of these narratives; the honourable veteran as 'super-citizen' and the 'other' characters constructed in relation. Character is an integral component of narrative, and its capacities are both constructive and destructive. On the one hand, a strong sense of character creates a vivid and highly relatable imagination of the storyteller, promotes empathy, and highlights the 'complexity and the fluidity of people's motives'.[63] Yet, on the other hand, the construction of character can essentialise people, fixing them into a predictable 'type' of person with motives and characteristics which always tend to precede their actual spoken stories. I have demonstrated how situations of veteran storytelling always seem to be framed by the construction of the veteran figure as 'super-citizen'. The super-citizen is a character type who can be cast into all manner of veteran storytelling genres, and who functions as a militarising figure in that his story gives us a world framed by an aura of mandatory respect for the military and gratitude for his service. These *militarist terms of reference*, as I refer to them, obstruct a critical examination of that 'service', including the geopolitical projects and forms of violence it enables.

Like the memes that circulate on social media, the militarising ideology of respect for service produces a deeply affective response. Affect 'sticks'[64] to the notion of service, such that we feel – *instinctively*, as one of the 'Declassified' guests put it – a sense of awe, respect and gratitude when it is invoked. Just as Cynthia Enloe argues that virtually anything can be militarised if it is capable of being coopted and directed towards military logics of power,[65] I argue that 'service' militarises our feelings by compelling our gratitude and respect towards the character of the veteran-as-super-citizen. From this position of mandatory respect, critique is stifled and alternative values are deprived of capacity to take root. My aim in this chapter has not been to single out particular individuals or practices and label them as 'problematic', but rather to highlight enduring features of veteran culture that reproduce a gendered moral hierarchy between veteran and civilian ways of being, premised on ideals of service and respect. These ideals function in an exclusionary manner to elevate veterans and veteran ways of being as inherently worthy, despite certain facets of this culture reproducing harmful social relations of sexism and racism.

Following Butler's call for a radically egalitarian political imaginary – which permits no differentiation between the value or 'grievability' of people's lives[66] – I argue that we ought to reject the militarist terms of reference which elevate veterans to the status of super-citizens and consequently render the needs and demands of other groups inferior. Practically, this might entail refusing to be awed by 'service' – particularly when it is uncritically accepted *apriori* as a moral good – as well as granting equal social status and citizenly protection to people from *all* backgrounds whose lives are impacted by war and structures of inequality. It would also certainly entail, as this book calls for, a more critical appreciation of the stories veterans tell about war and military life and an examination of what these stories are *doing* in the cultural politics of the nation.

Notes

1. Frank, *Letting Stories Breathe*, p. 29.
2. Ibid., p. 30. There is a parallel meaning to character here, in the sense of the agent within a story, and closely linked, the personal qualities or 'characteristics' that characters embody.
3. Caso, 'The political aesthetics of the body of the soldier in pain'.
4. Butler, *The Force of non-Violence*.
5. Wool, *After War*.
6. Allen, *Forewarned*, pp. 312–13.
7. Ibid., p. 6.
8. See, for example, Higate, 'Proud to "fly a desk" and wear a medal?'; Clarke et al., 'The good, the bad and the rebels'; Messner, *Guys Like Me*; Schrader, *Fight to Live, Live to Fight*.
9. Bulmer and Eichler, 'Unmaking militarized masculinity', p. 172.
10. Hall, *Cultural Studies 1983*.
11. Hall's use of Raymond Williams' term 'structures of feeling' explains it as 'the description, even re-creation of how life is actually lived, of what it is like to think and act about a particular problem in a society. It seems to come naturally to people who are inside the society because they share the results of the historical experience which has produced this particular set of ideas about the family, culture, masculinity, the economy, et cetera' (p. 37). Structures of feeling within veteran cultures create common points of reference for articulating ideals, goals, and relationships with other cultural groups (and other forms of veteran culture).
12. How social class and manifestations of class struggle map onto veteran cultures is a much neglected phenomenon in need of its own detailed study. Class-based identities and relationships are often traceable in the stories through which cultural politics are enacted and contested. While classed dimensions of cultural politics are clearly present in the subtext of my analysis, they regrettably do not feature as a key analytic given the overarching concerns with nationhood, citizenship, and processes of 'othering' in this chapter. For a discussion of class relationships and veteran cultures and identities, see Glenton, *Veteranhood*.
13. Jo Tidy, for instance, reveals how veterans in the US military dissent movement oppose wars by drawing upon the sense of legitimacy they gain by virtue of gendered notions of combat experience and heroism. See Tidy, 'The gender politics of "ground truth" in the military dissent movement'.
14. See, for example, Bulmer and Eichler, 'Unmaking militarized masculinity'; Tidy, 'The gender politics of "ground truth" in the military dissent movement';

Holyfield et al., 'Masculinity under attack'; 'Basham, Gender, race, militarism and remembrance'; Gallagher, 'Burdens of proof'.
15. These off-handed comments were made to a reporter as part of a row about whether the BBC would permit the words to 'Land of Hope and Glory' and 'Rule Brittania' to be sung as traditionally they would be at the 'Last Night of the Proms' ceremony. The lyrics had come under renewed public scrutiny due to their association with British colonialism and slavery.
16. Badenoch, 'Black History Month', speech.
17. See, for example, Hirsh, Brit(ish); Gilroy, After Empire.
18. My thanks to Katy Parry for this point.
19. Frank, Letting Stories Breathe, p. 29 (original emphasis).
20. Millar and Tidy, 'Combat as a moving target'.
21. British Army, 'Values and standards of the British Army'. As espoused in Army doctrine, 'Our Values and Standards set us apart from other occupations and, often, from our enemies. Whilst they have been refined over time, they remain constant, non-discretionary principles that define the behaviours expected of all members of the British Army, whatever the circumstances', p. 3.
22. See, for example, Tidy, 'The gender politics of "ground truth" in the military dissent movement'; Ware, 'Whiteness in the glare of war'; Sasson-Levy, 'Constructing identities at the margins'; Enloe, Maneuvers; Lister, 'Citizenship'.
23. Somers, Genealogies of Citizenship, p. 35.
24. See, for example, Lister, 'Citizenship'.
25. Within citizenship scholarship, this is known as the 'republican' tradition of citizenship. See Lister, 'Citizenship'.
26. Ibid.
27. Sasson-Levy, 'Constructing identities at the margins'.
28. Somers, Genealogies of Citizenship, p. 34.
29. Ingham, The Military Covenant.
30. Ashcroft, Veterans Transition Review, p. 8.
31. Hirsh, Brit(ish), p. 268.
32. The deeply intertwined relationship between these two British institutions, built on centuries-old historical ties and emphasised in the royal names attached to various services and regiments, performs a great deal of symbolic work in maintaining cultural imaginations of Britain and British tradition. The deep cultural resonance of this relationship is demonstrated (for example) in the annual Remembrance Day parades at the Cenotaph, during which the Royal Family – and the solemn figure of the monarch in particular – plays the central role. Images of the Royals dressed in black and emblazoned with the symbolic poppy create a highly visual link between nation, military and monarchy at this time. The same can be said of the ceremonial pageantry associated with events such as the monarch's birthday, Trooping the Colour ceremonies, and the Changing of the Guard at Buckingham Palace.
33. Leigh, 'From savages to snowflakes'; de Orellana and Michelsen, 'Reactionary internationalism'. See also, Qureshi, I Refuse to Condemn.
34. Given the enormous volumes of content uploaded onto social media by the minute, my choice of material for analysis is necessarily selective, and represents a distillation of the messages and content to which I am exposed via the online networks I am part of. Whilst the possibility, of course, exists therefore

that I am viewing only a narrow range of content, I make an effort to follow and engage with politically diverse groups and individuals as part of my online immersion in veteran cultures. I do not strive for representativeness here, rather for critical examination of the logics of representation inherent within spheres of online communication.
35. Beneiot-Montagut, 'Ethnography goes online'.
36. Duncombe, 'The politics of Twitter'
37. Ibid.
38. This is certainly not to discount the diversity of views expressed by veterans on social media, often in measured and respectful tones. Rather, that the tendency of debate on Twitter is towards fractious, aggressive and fiercely emotive exchange which serves to enrage rather than to edify.
39. Gbadegesin, 'Gender ideology and identity in humorous social media memes', p. 530.
40. Ibid., p. 531.
41. Memes, of course, are not 'stories' as such, but they are related. Content posted on social media often derives from and feeds into larger cultural narratives; it references or conforms to these narratives. Memes and other posts which reproduce commonly held ideas may constitute 'narrative fragments' which, with repetition, amass or accrue into narratives. Regarding online content as narrative fragments, see Holyfield et al., 'Masculinity under attack'.
42. On the centrality of social emotions in sustaining life in military institutions and cultures, see, for example, Hast, 'Synching the martial body'; McSorely, *War and the Body*.
43. Holland, 'Constructing crises and articulating affect after 9/11'. p. 170.
44. Gilroy, *After Empire*.
45. Dixon, *Warrior Nation*, p. 5.
46. All images are shared under guidelines on the reproduction of online content established by Twitter and Facebook's 'fair use' policies.
47. Berezin, 'Secure states', p. 44. See also Basham, 'Gender, race, militarism and remembrance'.
48. Wool, *After War*.
49. There is a danger when discussing the 'European' refugee crisis of centring Europe itself as the referent subject of the 'crisis', rather than refugees themselves and the *actual* crises of war, famine and economic deprivation which forced them to flee their countries. Without wishing to reify the notion of a 'European' crisis, then, I refer to the refugee crisis in Europe as the dominant media and social media construction of these events.
50. I do not wish to suggest that reaction by veterans was homogeneous or was in any way wholly negative. Indeed, there were nuanced and sympathetic posts made by veterans on these subjects. However, the dominant responses were arguably characterised by a degree of hostility, anger and defensiveness. It is these responses which served to further inflame the racial and national tensions at issue here with regard to the denigration and exclusion of minoritised groups.
51. See, for example, Badenoch, 'Black History Month'.
52. See Hirsh, *Brit(ish)*.
53. 'Soldiers A-Z' is a reference to the media pseudonyms (e.g., 'Marine A', 'Soldier F') given to veterans undergoing prosecution in order to protect their anonymity.

54. Darda, 'Military whiteness'.
55. Ibid.
56. Ware, 'Whiteness in the glare of war'. For a discussion of how the Gurkhas acquired their reputation as a 'martial race', see Chisholm, 'From warriors of empire to martial contractors'.
57. Somers, *Genealogies of Citizenship*, p. 139.
58. The 'six to a boat' quip is a reference to the 'rule of six' introduced by the UK government regarding the number of people allowed to gather in outdoor spaces during COVID-19 restrictions.
59. To be clear, I am not suggesting that such anti-refugee sentiments are in any way representative of veteran communities or the opinions they may hold with regard to asylum in Britain. What I am interested in is the logics of difference and hierarchical separation reproduced by these memes and posts, along with the political effects they have in bolstering anti-immigrant politics and abuse online.
60. Butler, *The Force of non-Violence*, p. 62.
61. Ibid.
62. McGarvey, *Poverty Safari*.
63. Frank, *Letting Stories Breathe*, p. 31. What characters *do* with their character casting – how they might resist or seek to change it – is a question worth pursuing as part of a cultural politics of veterans' narratives. Particularly interesting here would be whether and to what effect 'critical' veterans (i.e., those who have turned towards anti-militarist activism) can escape from or reframe their casting as super-citizens.
64. Ahmed, *The Cultural Politics of Emotions*.
65. Enloe, *Maneuvers*.
66. Butler, *The Force of non-Violence*.

CHAPTER 4

In Failure and Success: The Politics of Transition Narratives

The Army taught me a lot and it was only when I left that I actually realised how many transferable skills that I had to bring away from it. People skills is a huge one; from day one in the Army, team building is drilled into you. You look out for one another, build relationships and work together through everything. When I was an Area Manager, I managed up to 150 employees in my department and the experience of managing teams in the Army, helped me be successful in driving that positive culture of teamwork that resulted in a very efficient team.
Army Veteran Jessica Masterman MBE[1]

I was living on the streets. I slept in a local park for about six months. I'm not alone; five of us ended up homeless. You go from being this soldier everyone respects to being the lowest of the low. People judge you. They think you're a druggie. You just want to be respected like when you were serving . . . You need to learn how to adjust to civilian life. The second you feel worthless everything spirals out of control very quickly. In the space of a year I went from being a healthy young man in a great regiment to someone sitting in a park wondering what the point of my life was.
Army Veteran David Swift[2]

Plural, public and increasingly politicised, stories of 'transition' have become a key site of contestation in the cultural politics of veterans' narratives. The core struggle for meaning is not about what transition 'is' – which is not a settled question – but rather, it is about whether veterans are making the transition to civilian life 'successfully'. The two excerpts above represent two contrasting story archetypes of veteran transition, one 'successful' and the other 'failed'. The former 'success' story is taken from a promotional news item featured on the army.mod official website. Along with many similar stories, it seeks to highlight veterans' achievements after service, and to claim these achievements as having been produced by the army through its training and the unique characteristics it instils. The latter 'failure' story is taken from a report by the Soldiers, Sailors, Airmen and Families Association (SSAFA) designed to highlight the struggles of a 'forgotten' generation of younger, working-age veterans. This story, and countless others like it across the media and military charity sector, seeks to highlight the extent to which veterans are neglected by society and are reliant on the support of charities like SSAFA to pick up the broken pieces of their lives.

Personal testimony is often used to evoke wider truths about the transition experience. We can contrast the different kinds of testimony that are used for different political purposes. Each of the above testimonies are, of course, heavily mediated, curated for public consumption in ways that seek to communicate a different 'truth' about transition. While neither testimony could be considered to be representative, statistically speaking, of veterans' transition experiences, both make representative claims: that a military career is foundational for later success as a civilian, or that civilian life is irrevocably different, devoid of meaning, and that soldiers are prone to struggle. While these archetypal narratives offer contrasting versions of contemporary transition, they each have different origins and temporalities. Stories of struggle and failure have a longer trajectory, built on narratives of disenfranchisement and disillusionment traceable throughout the history of British veterans (see Chapter 2). Stories of success have emerged comparatively recently, as a deliberate response by the British state seeking to counter 'broken-veteran' narratives and to rehabilitate the image of the veteran in the eyes of the British public.

In this chapter, I analyse the political stakes at play in the reproduction of transition narratives and consider the work that each of the archetypes *does* in the cultural politics of veterans' narratives. Here, I build on the idea of 'veteranness' as a collection of traits, qualities and narrative plots that define social imaginations of the veteran figure. Veteranness is that abiding feature of veterans' narratives that makes them recognisable *as* veterans' narratives. It is also what limits and constrains social understandings of the veteran. A sense of veteranness 'veteranises' the veteran, tying veterans' qualities and characteristics solely to their veteran status and identity. That is, veterans are the way they are *because* they're veterans, and that is their nature or their enculturation. Most importantly, however, veteranness is contested, and nowhere more so than in the realm of transition narratives. The central contest is over whether veteranness will come to be associated with the 'successful' or entrepreneurial veteran, reflecting positively on British militarism and its role in shaping veteran character to the benefit of society, or whether veteranness will be dominated by stories of the 'failed' veteran crashing and burning in Civvy Street, provoking anger and sympathy over the betrayal of their sacrifices.

This chapter works in tandem with the next. In this chapter, I identify the emerging 'state narrative' of veterans' transition; that is, the narrative the state is working to construct as the dominant, authoritative story of veterans in transition. In the next chapter, I consider how government, academia and the military charity sector collaborate in producing a 'liberal progress narrative' based on incrementally improving transition for all veterans. As an overarching framework for the production of academic research, I argue that this narrative 'militarises' academia while co-opting researchers like me in a game of narrative politics which legitimises only certain knowledge claims about transition. The preferred state narrative of transition, together with the liberal progress narrative, work to regulate transition; that is, to construct a benign story of veterans in transition which serves the interests of the state, which rewards conformity and which marginalises discord and dissent. As I outline in Chapter 1, *narrative power* – in Plummer's terms[3] – is the dynamic mechanism underlying the interplay of different transition narratives, and its operation can be observed throughout the infrastructure of veterans' transition. Before considering how the interplay of narrative power and politics further militarises the academy, in this chapter I turn first to the construction of the state's preferred transition narrative.

The State's Story to Tell

In 2012, the wealthy businessman, former deputy chairman of the Conservative Party, peer and military history enthusiast Lord Ashcroft was commissioned by then-Prime Minister David Cameron to conduct a review of veterans' transition in the UK. The review was to be a wide-ranging report on how transition was managed at different levels within the UK public, private and third sectors, together with a comprehensive set of recommendations on how transition could be improved for veterans. Published in 2014, the *Veterans Transition Review* would become the key touchstone in political and academic debate about transition for many years to come. The review set the terms of debate by establishing what would be the key concerns in relation to veterans transitioning from the military into civilian life. With separate chapters examining provision for veterans in the areas of education and training, resettlement and employment, housing, health, welfare, finance, advocacy, the provision of information and a further chapter on reservists, much of the report concerns itself with the technical policy detail of transition across these various domains. For example, details of the review include the process of service leavers moving from military accommodation into social housing or the private rental sector, the transfer of healthcare from Defence Medical Services to the National Health Service, and the availability of training courses for reorienting service leavers towards civilian employment. The report makes recommendations in each of these areas, which agencies within government (principally the Ministry of Defence and Office for Veterans Affairs) have since taken up as part of efforts to improve the management of transition.

Aside from the policy detail, the report also constructs a narrative of transition which, articulated in the official language of state policy, seeks to establish itself as authoritative. This 'state transition narrative', as I refer to it, constitutes the state's preferred version of transition, the officially sanctioned version, the story it wants and expects to hear veterans telling. 'The state' is relevant here mainly because, as the sovereign power with the ability to 'make live or let die',[4] it is the state that bears responsibility for sending troops to war and the state that is held to account (e.g., by the media, academia, the public) for preserving and caring for veterans' lives. One way in which the state manages this responsibility – or, perhaps, the *impression* of responsibility – is by seeking to exercise control over public narratives of veterans. The *Veterans Transition Review* was the state's first major attempt (in the contemporary post-9/11 sphere of government and military policy) to construct a narrative of transition. It does so, first, in the report's opening section titled 'Why good transition matters', whereby Ashcroft as the state's representative provides a precis of the narrative with the claim that 'most service leavers already make a successful transition ... Despite the widespread public belief to the contrary relatively few experience serious problems.'[5] The essence of the narrative follows shortly thereafter. In what was to become the report's most resonant proclamation, Ashcroft states that:

> Public perception of Service Leavers needs to be changed. Though a small number do have problems and need special provision, Service Leavers as a whole begin new careers, enjoy good health and are no

more likely to suffer PTSD, become homeless, commit suicide or go to prison than the rest of the population. Yet there is a widespread public perception that veterans are likely to be physically, mentally or emotionally damaged by their time in the Armed Forces. This in itself constitutes an unnecessary extra hurdle for Service Leavers, restricting their opportunities by lowering expectations of what they can do. There is a good story to tell.[6]

Ashcroft's expectation is that this good story will be told, and that state representatives will work harder to tell it, ensuring that 'bad' stories are displaced by the good. In the report's key recommendation on public perceptions, Ashcroft calls on the Ministry of Defence to champion this good story of transition:

> ... the MOD and the single Services should aim to promote a more positive picture of Service Leavers, and be bolder in countering information in the media and elsewhere that presents an unduly negative impression. The purpose here is not PR for its own sake or to cover up failings. The more prevalent the impression of veterans as victims who struggle to lead normal lives, the harder it will inevitably be for them to find good jobs and contribute to civilian society – and the harder it will be to recruit into the Regular and Reserve Forces.[7]

As introduced in the *Veterans Transition Review* (and subsequently developed elsewhere; see below), the state transition narrative presents a clear value judgement over veterans' stories of transition by casting those it regards 'unduly negative' as marginal and problematic. The key function of the state narrative – as McGarry's analysis of the 'victimised state' also demonstrates[8] – is protecting the state's interests and identity from the impression of vulnerability, negligence or malfeasance. McGarry argues that the image of the vulnerable victim-soldier is considered by those in power as a fundamental threat to the operational equilibrium of the British military, and the state accordingly has to manage this sense of vulnerability by distancing itself from negative stories and by 'mystifying' from public view the harms that veterans can encounter as a result of their service. Indeed, as the Review further asserts, 'Those who have problems are largely in the same proportion as their civilian peers, and these problems are *not commonly a direct result solely of their Service career.*'[9] Some of the interests the state is seeking to protect are referenced explicitly here; notably, recruitment into the regular and reserve forces, and thereby the ability to maintain a military force that can be relied upon to wage war on the state's behalf. Implicitly, the reputation – and therefore also the *power* – of the military and the government is at stake. 'Failed' transition not only results in veterans becoming a burden on society, but it also undermines the authority of the government on matters of war and the military.[10] That is, there are serious political costs to failed transition, too.

Sanna Strand's work on the 'invention' of the Swedish war veteran shows that similar processes of state narrative construction are at work in other neoliberal economies with a strong military presence in society.[11] Her analysis is useful here because it reveals the same market logics by which the British state's narrative aims to secure a more positive and more 'accurate' representation of veteranness. Strand argues that a programme of policymaking and political speech-making by the Swedish state has been working to re-script Swedish veterans as responsible, valued neoliberal citizens, who are both uniquely competitive in the civilian labour market and uniquely valued by the country for their altruistic service to others. 'The recognized veteran', Strand writes, 'is scripted as a self-sacrificing and yet self-fulfilling individual, for whom war deployments have brought about personal and professional growth. These constructions render veterans competitive and employable in civilian labour markets and represent the military institution as a career stepping-stone for young, responsible individuals,'[12] Soldiering, along with military employment more broadly, thus becomes re-branded as a social and economic 'good' which enables personnel to develop 'characteristics, skills, and ethics broadly considered to be valuable and appealing within the "enterprise culture" of neoliberal democracies'.[13] The Swedish state thereby seeks greater recognition for the value of military work and workers, in a bid to promote the military institution in society more generally.

This desire for recognition is a key feature of the British state's transition narrative, too. The state narrative is framed as a deliberate counter to the 'damaged veteran' narrative which is assumed to be far too prevalent in British society. Echoing Strand's analysis of the Swedish veteran, it is a market logic which provides the fundamental counterpoint to the idea of the damaged veteran in the state's narrative. This logic is succinctly captured by Ashcroft in this extract towards the end of the Review:

> There is a good story to tell. As I have said in the introduction to this Review, the Armed Forces offer what amounts to Britain's biggest and best apprenticeship scheme. The opportunities available in terms of

education and training, life experience and social mobility cannot be matched by any other employer. The Forces do a remarkable job for the nation and nearly all Service Leavers settle into civilian life and become valuable contributors to society.[14]

The state narrative thereby seeks to offer recognition to veterans in terms of the economic value they represent; they are to be seen as 'net contributors' to society, rather than detractors.[15] The market logic which supports the state's version of veteranness as *entrepreneurial* rather than troubled is visible in the stories chosen to evoke it, and in how these stories are framed, such as the example with which this chapter began of one veteran's transition from the army to Amazon by virtue of her military training. In this story, qualities such as people skills and teamwork – which in the grammar of such stories are framed as uniquely *military* qualities – become usefully deployed in service of profit-driven big tech companies like Amazon. Further examples include the 'Life after service' campaign ran by the British Forces Broadcasting Service, designed to 'tell some of the many fantastic stories of what ex-servicemen and women go on to achieve with their lives and careers after leaving the armed forces'.[16] The stories used to illustrate such achievements include 'Army ex-serviceman turns multi-million-pound entrepreneur', 'Adventure-loving veteran creates kids' outdoor product range', 'How a former army officer rose to lead the health and safety profession', and 'Former RAF pilot builds construction firm for veteran tradesmen'.[17] These stories re-create the veteran as an enterprising, entrepreneurial figure, sculpted by the military into 'responsible and resourceful citizens of neoliberal society'.[18]

Driven by the fear of veterans being cast as 'damaged', and military service itself as 'damaging', the state transition narrative has since the launch of the *Veterans Transition Review* been taken up by numerous advocates in the media, in veteran culture, in academia, and especially within government and the Ministry of Defence. For instance, the state's preferred narrative prominently shaped the launch of the 2018 'Veterans Strategy' by the Office for Veterans Affairs under the slogan 'Valued. Contributing. Supported'.[19] Four years later, the OVA's update on the Strategy, the 'Veterans' Strategy Action Plan' released in January 2022, attested to a shift in public perceptions beginning to occur, while continuing to warn against the so-called negative stories:

> Although the wider public generally believe that veterans make a valuable contribution to society and that military service instils

positive values such as self-discipline and loyalty, negative and incorrect stereotypes of veterans as being psychologically impaired can be damaging to veterans and their families, and in turn can feed public misconceptions. These incorrect stereotypes result from a focus on stories of veterans in crisis rather than the vast majority who transition successfully and happily into civilian life.[20]

Each time the state narrative is reiterated, it thereby emphasises the marginality of stories that do not conform to its preferred account of transition. Veterans and others are reminded that certain kinds of story are not to be told, that they represent 'incorrect stereotypes', and that we should not be focusing on them. The state narrative thereby seeks to exercise narrative power over veterans' stories: it authorises the 'positive' stories it wishes to amplify, while encouraging scepticism and doubt over the stories it wishes to downplay. The state demands that 'negative' stories be heard 'in their proper context',[21] which is a disclaimer never attached to the 'positive' stories it designates as representative. The state narrative puts pressure on individual veterans to become advocates for veterans as a whole; it calls on them not to become detractors from the state, and certainly not to dissent from the message it is attempting to convey. It also seeks to assign blame for 'failed' transition to individual veterans and whatever vulnerabilities or character flaws they might be presumed to have had *prior* to military service. Accordingly, the state narrative serves the interests of power by deflecting attention from the problems that military service – indeed, the process of transition itself – can create. It reinforces the image of a strong national military by marshalling veteranness in line with its core message of resilience and success.

As Plummer argues, 'deep infrastructures shape narrative power'.[22] In relation to veterans, the institutional power of the state along with its mechanisms of governance are central to its exercise of narrative power. Such mechanisms are evident (as above) in the policy discourse of the *Veterans Transition Review* and the Office for Veterans Affairs. The state produces its key storytellers, such as Johnny Mercer MP, in his capacity as the Veterans' Minister, to champion the transition narrative in public life. It also shapes the discourse of other actors outside the infrastructure of the state and 'recruits' them to promote the preferred narrative. Influential members of veteran culture, such as the host of the 'Declassified' podcast, Michael Coates, can be powerful storytellers in this regard; as Coates proclaimed on the podcast, 'I'm the biggest advocate, what I do in my work time, I advocate why veterans and reservists, spouses, partners are a national asset, especially in business.' As I will examine in the next chapter, the state narrative also sustains an industry of transition research, with researchers and charities working together to promote the government's core narrative about veterans. In this sense, the state transition narrative is also *well funded*: government-sponsored research reports frequently appear asserting the normativity of success and the marginality of failure regarding veterans' transition, amassing evidence in support of the narrative's core proclamations about veteranness.

The state transition narrative is, in essence, quite straightforward: most veterans transition successfully into civilian life, and we are working hard to ensure those who do not receive the right support. The simple structure renders it a 'good' story, in the sense that it is highly communicable, easy to understand and distils the complexity of transition into a manageable soundbite, which especially aids the transmission of the narrative in our digital age. Inevitably, then, the narrative obscures much about transition, too. The state narrative is, first, a gross oversimplification of what 'transition' entails, with all the social and identity-related challenges that can ensue for veterans avoided entirely.[23] Secondly, in claiming representativeness, it denies the realities of many veterans whose stories do not fit the mould, rendering these stories marginal and deviant. Thirdly, it also assumes a homogeneous White male veteran population as the default. Neither the 2014 *Veterans Transition Review* nor the 2018 *Veterans Strategy* makes reference to female, ethnic minority or LGBTQ+ veterans, and in the 2022 *Veterans Strategy* update there simply exists a commitment to funding future research into the needs of these veterans. My aim, then, in the next part of this chapter is to complicate this picture by considering stories which contest the state's transition narrative.

'Failed' Transition and Veteran Disenfranchisement

My argument does not engage with the question of whether veterans *are* (in statistical terms) transitioning successfully into civilian life. This question frames debate about transition on the terms defined by the state, for on these terms the state can easily steer the debate in the direction of the evidence it sanctions and towards the conclusions it favours. That is, when the only important question to ask is whether 'most' veterans are transitioning successfully, the state narrative has already stolen the limelight, and narrow criteria used to define 'success' come to stand in for a much deeper engagement with the notion of transition itself. This question is thus a political trap, the avoidance of which is important for a critical cultural politics of veterans' narratives. Rather, my argument concerns the *narrative struggle* playing out over transition, for where there is narrative power, there is also struggle and resistance.[24] Narrative power does not simply act *on* veterans, compelling them to tell stories which conform to the expected transition narrative. Veterans also resist the imposition of narrative power by telling stories which contest the state's transition narrative. In the dynamic interplay between contrasting narratives of transition is a core site of struggle animating the cultural politics of veterans' narratives.

In contrast to the stories of successful, entrepreneurial veterans channelling their military life-skills into the needs of business are stories of disenfranchised veterans grinding out an existence 'on the fringes of society'.[25] Stories of the disenfranchised veteran show him homeless, suffering mental health problems, lonely, isolated, suicidal, unable to access support from the government or healthcare providers, and lacking political representation. As I argued in Chapter 2, such stories have a longer historical provenance, recurring throughout history as a prominent literary and media representation of the veteran in British society. As such, the state transition narrative can be read as a deliberate *counter-narrative* to this long-established notion of veteran disenfranchisement. In the grammar of the state narrative, disenfranchisement is problematic because it unduly portrays veterans as 'mad, bad and sad',[26] and therefore representations of madness, sadness and criminality within veteran communities ought to be suppressed. In the academic and policy spheres which govern transition, 'mad, bad and sad' is a byline for all that is ignorant, inaccurate and unwanted about veterans' stories. Stories which can be placed into this reductive epithet provoke disdain; I have seen policy types and academics alike wincing at the mention of such stories. Absent from this dismissive construction of the disenfranchised veteran, however, is the anger which forms a key constitutive component of disenfranchisement. The disenfranchised veteran is *angry* at the way he has been treated, and anger is personally and politically different to madness (as in mental illness), badness (as in criminality) and sadness (as in malaise or depression).

Stories of the disenfranchised veteran continue to circulate, representing the anger veterans feel and also calling forth anger in response to the poor treatment of veterans in society. Disenfranchisement is expressed in various forms and through various channels, including mass media, social media and in the military charity sector. One prominent representation of disenfranchisement is the sense of 'alienation' from civilian society that veterans report. Disenfranchised veterans feel that society has become an alien world since their return from the military, or that they have themselves been made aliens to society. This sense of alienation was captured by one of Britain's largest and longest-running military charities, the Soldiers, Sailors, Airmen and Families Association (SSAFA), in a research report published in 2018 titled 'The Nation's Duty: Challenging Society's Disservice to a New Generation of Veterans'. The report states:

> One of the most striking findings of our research was the overwhelming sense of alienation from society. SSAFA veterans feel undervalued. They do not think that civilians understand them, and they do not believe they are treated fairly by employers or state agencies.[27]

This finding is illustrated by stories like the following from army veteran Walter Richardson:

> My problems started pretty much straight after I was discharged. We couldn't get social housing, even though we had four kids, and had to rent privately instead. I got into financial difficulty, and I was using my Army pension to pay the rent, council tax and bills. I thought I would leave the Armed Forces, have that on my CV, be vetted and go on from there. But it was the complete opposite. I put my references as 'HM Armed Forces', but got frustrated because I wasn't getting calls. I removed it and put 'references on request' and got six or seven phone calls in a week. When people ask me what I did previously I no longer say that I was Armed Forces. Out of ten people there will be two that are pro-Army, the rest are against them for some reason. I was so proud when I left the Army, but times have changed. I don't go out of my way to tell people that I served. People ask why I'm not working, people don't believe you. I was stuck with the stigma that I was trying to claim dole money.[28]

The key elements of disenfranchisement are starkly presented in this story and many others like it: veterans are discriminated against by employers and housing agencies, the people are 'against them', 'people don't believe you', and veterans are left with the stigma of claiming benefits. Stories like Walter's contest the state's claim that transferable skills from the military are a passport to success in civilian life. Instead,

Walter finds that labour opportunities and the goodwill of others are alienated. He faces animosity and antagonism from the civilian other. It is 'us', or now, rather, 'me' against 'them'. The tendency of the state narrative is to blame the teller of the disenfranchisement story for his own misery. The disenfranchisement story is a 'negative and incorrect stereotype', and the route out of disenfranchisement is the telling of more positive stories. We might consider this a form of *narrative gaslighting*; that is, emotional abuse of the downtrodden veteran by coercing him into questioning the reality of his disenfranchisement, or by placing the blame on his flawed character developed prior to, or in spite of, military service. The narrative struggle here is whether the claim that military service is an apprenticeship for later success can establish itself against the *opposite* claim – that military service is a harbinger of future failure occasioned by the ignorance of a society determined to misunderstand and misrepresent the veteran. From the state's perspective, it is a struggle for the hegemony of its transition narrative. From the veteran's, it is a struggle to be recognised and respected, rather than 'gaslit' and denied.

Like other genres of veteran narratives, there is a gendered dimension to disenfranchisement stories which ought to be addressed. While the state transition narrative simply ignores the gendering of veterans' post-military experiences, disenfranchisement stories seem primarily concerned with the male veteran's alienation from society. It is *his* isolation, *his* mental health, *his* homelessness – *his* struggle – which forms the dominant media and public representation of the disenfranchised veteran. He is the one who is *expected* to be employed following his release from the military, and therefore, it is *his* unemployment which is considered egregious. A scoping review of British women veterans' health and wellbeing, 'We also served', captures this notion of female service as an afterthought.[29] The report found that female veterans are more likely to be unemployed than their male counterparts, and that they were also more likely to have left the military early due to childcare or family-related issues. Where female veterans' stories do feature as representations of disenfranchisement, it is clear that they can face additional gender-specific challenges.[30] As one unnamed female veteran told the authors of the SSAFA 'Nation's Duty' report:

> There are lots of jobs out there that do like ex-Forces, but, hand on heart, I can tell you when you are a woman and you say you are ex-Forces, they get scared of you. Shaven head and tattoos everywhere –

that's the image they have of us. When I tried to get a job at a clothes shop, I was told ex-Forces are too brash, too direct in dealing with customers. I stopped putting Army on application forms, I just said HGV driver. I'm proud of what I achieved in the Army, I loved HGV driving and I loved the logistics. But when I spoke to one company the bloke looked at me and said: 'We tend to take on blokes, do you know what you are doing?'[31]

Given the dominant societal impressions of veteranness – 'Shaven head and tattoos everywhere' – it can be difficult for female veterans to be recognised as veterans at all; to claim and express a veteran identity. Moreover, gendered expectations about how women should present in a civilian workplace (i.e., not 'brash', not 'direct', not driving trucks) meant that female veterans could struggle to find acceptance by employers. As Bulmer and Eichler therefore suggest, 'It is perhaps not so much military gender norms but civilian gender norms that make the experiences of female veterans invisible.'[32] As such, disenfranchisement often takes on differently gendered forms. For male veterans, it represents an aggrieved, weakened and sometimes ridiculed position of masculinity while simultaneously enabling a masculine display of anger in response. For female veterans, it constitutes invisibility, in society generally as in the cultural politics of veterans' narratives.

Closely tied to alienation is the belief that 'there is no support out there for veterans', which is an accusation frequently levelled at the government, the Ministry of Defence and the military charity sector. The 'no support' accusation is integral to disenfranchisement stories and to the political work these stories seek to accomplish. 'No support' is a regular and prominent theme of media headlines, claiming, for example, 'Veterans forced to food banks after being told they don't qualify for DWP support',[33] 'Thousands of military veterans "let down by medical discharge failures",[34] 'New troops "not getting help for mental health"',[35] and 'Top military charities sitting on £277m – while veterans struggle'.[36] The aforementioned SSAFA report similarly admits that 'in some instances, we are failing to support those who have been willing to make the ultimate sacrifice on our behalf'.[37] 'No support' reverberates throughout veteran communities online, further reinforcing the image of disenfranchised veteranness. As one veteran, calling out Veterans UK and Johnny Mercer MP tweeted, '@VeteransGovUK and @JohnnyMercerUK promoting that they are doing all they can for the veterans community, whilst guys and girls are taking their lives, I can honestly say that in my opinion this is not what I and others are seeing, we need a national change', and further, 'Veterans questions are ignored Veterans on the streets are ignored Veterans committing suicide with PTSD are ignored Veterans facing persecution & prosecution are ignored and anyone who dares mention it gets blocked.' Narratives of disenfranchisement can be pieced together through 'fragments' such as these – brief outpourings of anger vented into social media that invoke a larger narrative – or they can appear as fully formed narratives, setting the veteran's proud history of service in stark contrast with his forlorn civilian existence. Each form works to reinforce the image of the British veteran as abandoned by the government and by an uncaring and ungrateful civilian public.

The 'no support' claim is also interesting to consider in light of a large military charity sector which exists to cater to veterans' needs, and which far exceeds the type of welfare support available to any other former occupational group in Britain.[38] The sector incorporates a diverse range of organisations and forms of veteran support and has benefitted from substantial public generosity particularly during the wars in Iraq and Afghanistan. For example, a review of armed forces charities published in 2014 revealed that the sector's combined annual income was £872 million in 2012 alone.[39] However, the sector has been criticised by veterans for being overly complex and difficult to navigate.[40] It has also been accused – as per one of the above-cited headlines – of hoarding resources while putting bureaucratic processes in front of veterans trying to access support. This latter claim again filters through into online communities, becoming a focal point for anger, as one veteran took to posting on Twitter 'The reason why we need help is because the top six charities have over £890 million in their bank accounts, in property portfolios, in five-and-ten-year-long plans, and in investments and reserve accounts.' Scepticism towards the 'big' charities is by now a familiar feature of veteran cultures. That those charged with helping veterans are seen to be selfishly withholding funds from those in need is a major source of resentment and a further expression of veteran disenfranchisement.

Disenfranchisement stories carry out what Alice Cree and I have previously described as 'emotional–political work'; that is, 'the manner in which narratives are scripted to evoke particular emotions' together with 'the political effects of this emotional conditioning'.[41] By drawing on the capacities of stories outlined in Chapter 1 (e.g., 'truth-telling', 'inherent morality', 'point of view'), disenfranchisement stories invite an emotional response, working to create an emotional identification with the storyteller. 'No support' suggests that injustice is occurring and that anger is the appropriate response. Listeners may either accept this emotional identification and thereby share in the veteran's anger and feelings of abandonment or reject it by responding with disdain or indifference. To the extent that the emotional identification succeeds, stories of the disenfranchised veteran are politically powerful because they muster opposition towards state elites.[42] These elites might attempt, cynically, to harness disenfranchisement for their own ends, for example, when Prime Minister Boris Johnson described veterans being abandoned as a 'stain on our national conscience'.[43] Yet such attempts also risk further alienation and disenfranchisement if the promises made to veterans are not kept. Stories of the disenfranchised veteran thus embody the capacity of 'speaking truth to power', undermining the state's transition narrative and contesting its attempt to assert narrative control over transition. Disenfranchisement also contains a more potent emotional script than does the state's narrative, in that the anger of injustice compels attention more effectively than the state's facile assertion that 'everything is fine'. The state's refusal to acknowledge disenfranchisement – moreover, its *denial* of the disenfranchised veteran – guarantees that feelings of anger and betrayal will persist among veterans who feel alienated.

Despite offering the veteran a political voice of anger, however, the disenfranchisement narrative also restricts the possibilities veterans have for exploring new identities as a 'civilian'. Disenfranchisement is what Frank described as a 'deprecated identity'.[44] To be disenfranchised is to be downtrodden, outcast and alienated. It is an embittered veteranness, humbled and reduced from a once-proud status of belonging to a respected institution. Disenfranchisement thus confers an unwanted and stigmatised identity, yet, as Frank suggests, 'Stories that interpellate the character or listener into a deprecated identity are hard to walk away from, because at least they offer some identity.'[45] Following Frank's suggestion, the dilemma this creates for the disenfranchised veteran is that 'by accepting being in a story, a person at least provisionally accepts being what the story casts him or her to be, its interpellation'.[46] The character of the disenfranchised veteran, then, is one that veterans can readily inhabit as a means of coming to terms with misfortune or betrayal, and of expressing anger. While arguably not a 'good' story, in the sense that its outcomes are normatively undesirable, the story of the disenfranchised veteran at least *makes sense*. It provides an explanation for the struggles veterans face in civilian life and it offers a communal identity with other veterans who share the same fate. Or, at least it does so for those who are able to claim and express an identity *as* a veteran.

Conclusion

The idea that service personnel 'transition' from the military into civilian life, where they at once become 'veteran' and again 'civilian', has become popular in recent decades. Transition is now an organising concept for a great deal of academic research, government policy-making, and programme delivery in the military charity sector. Much of this work is driven by the concern that, as Bulmer and Eichler put it '"bad" or failed transition will result in veterans being a burden on society, alongside other "non-productive" individuals'.[47] My focus in this chapter on 'success' and 'failure' is not intended to create an artificial classification of veterans' narratives into binary opposing camps. Rather, it calls attention to the way in which narratives of veterans in society are organised by the state, by the media and by veterans themselves. My aim is to show how archetypal veteran narratives of 'transition' are constructed, how they oppose each other, and the politics at stake in this narrative power struggle. In particular, I have identified how the state transition narrative creates public representations of veterans which bolster the impression of a strong national military and which assert the value of military service, thereby aiding recruitment and reflecting positively on the state which sends the troops to war. I have also identified how stories of the disenfranchised veteran offer a political voice to veterans who feel betrayed by their government or their society and who are angered by the alienation and marginalisation they face in civilian life.

While stories can be effective means of communicating the nuances of people's characters and experiences, *transition stories* always seem to oversimply and elide the complexity of veterans' lives. I argue that *both* archetypal transition narratives – the disenfranchised veteran and the go-getting entrepreneurial one alike – are insufficient, in that they both fail to grapple with the lived complexity of 'transition' and everything that entails. Both reinforce a progressive linear temporality, moving from 'military' to 'civilian', 'war' to 'not war', which ignores the blurring of military and civilian spaces and forms of existence as veterans work through a process of shifting identities, norms and experiences. Indeed, the idea of transitioning *from* the military *to* civilian life suggests that the former is left behind while the latter is neatly embraced, and that some kind of 'orderly progression' has taken place.[48] The very language and concept of 'transition' thereby demarcates the military and the civilian into separate spheres, preventing us from thinking through the temporo-spatial continuities and discontinuities that might be involved.

Moreover, both archetypal narratives can arguably be understood as 'veteranising' the veteran, in that they essentialise 'veteranness' as the most or only significant feature of veterans' character and identity.[49] In both the state transition narrative and the disenfranchisement narrative, 'success' and 'failure', respectively, are attributed directly to this veteranness. In the former, success in civilian life is achieved *because* of the unique and special qualities that veteranness imbues. In the latter, failure and marginalisation are endured *because* veteranness cannot be accommodated in civilian life. One of the principal dangers of transition narratives, then, is that they trap veterans in veteran identities. Nothing else about their interests, backgrounds, personalities or relationships really matters; it is their veteranness which counts. Veteranness is to be celebrated, and veteranness is to blame. Archetypal transition narratives constitute a failure of what Molly Andrews termed the 'narrative imagination'; that is, our ability to create novel meanings and stories by imagining the 'not-yet-real', by imagining different possible futures.[50] By trapping veterans in their veteranness, both archetypal transition narratives fail to reimagine what transition 'is' or might be. They create 'flat' characters with fixed motives and desires attributed solely to their veteranness. Stories are needed that allow veterans to become rounded and varied characters, that allow them to become *more than* veterans. In the next chapter, I will consider how academic stories also constrain what can be said about veterans – and the military more generally – and how this ought to change.

Notes

1. British Army, 'Army veteran Jessica Masterman MBE on her successful transition to Amazon UK'.
2. SSAFA, 'The new frontline'.
3. Plummer, *Narrative Power*.
4. Foucault, *Society Must be Defended*, p. 239.
5. Ashcroft, *Veterans' Transition Review*, p. 8.
6. Ibid., p. 14.
7. Ibid., pp. 177–8.
8. McGarry, 'Demystifying the "victimised state"'.

9. Ashcroft, *Veterans Transition Review*, p. 178 (my emphasis). The claim that problems veterans experience are 'uncommonly' a result of military service is misleading, given research has not properly explored (and would likely struggle to disentangle) the extent to which issues encountered by veterans either 'pre-exist' their enlistment or developed afterwards but from causes unrelated to the military.
10. Bulmer and Eichler, 'Unmaking militarized masculinity'.
11. Strand, 'Inventing the Swedish (war) veteran'.
12. Ibid., p. 23.
13. Ibid., p. 28.
14. Ashcroft, *Veterans Transition Review*, p. 178.
15. Ibid., p. 8.
16. Forces Net, 'Life after service'.
17. Ibid.
18. Strand, 'Inventing the Swedish (war) veteran', p. 25.
19. HM Government, 'The strategy for our veterans'.
20. HM Government, 'Veterans' Strategy Action Plan 2022–2024', p. 32.
21. Ashcroft, *Veterans Transition Review*, p. 25.
22. Plummer, *Narrative Power*, p. 31.
23. See, for example, Cooper et al., 'Transition from the military into civilian life'; Bulmer and Eichler, 'Unmaking militarized masculinity'; Albertson, 'Relational legacies impacting on veteran transition from military to civilian life'; MacLeish, 'Churn'.
24. Plummer, *Narrative Power*.
25. Mercer, *We Were Warriors*, p. 326.
26. Royal British Legion, 'UK household survey of the ex-service community', p. iv.
27. SSAFA, 'The Nation's Duty', p. 26.
28. Ibid., p. 22.
29. Godier-McBard, Gillin and Fossey, 'We also served'.
30. Bulmer and Eichler, 'Unmaking militarized masculinity'; Eichler, 'Add female veterans and stir?'
31. SSAFA, 'The Nation's Duty', p. 15.
32. Bulmer and Eichler, 'Unmaking militarized masculinity', p. 172.
33. Barker, 'Veterans forced for food banks after being told they don't qualify for DWP support'.
34. Sabbagh, 'Thousands of military veterans "let down by medical discharge failures"'.
35. BBC News, 'New troops "not getting help for mental health"'.
36. Bunkall, 'Top military charities sitting on £277m – while veterans struggle'.
37. SSAFA, 'The Nation's Duty', p. 3. From the foreword by His Royal Highness Prince Michael of Kent.
38. It is worth mentioning that within state-funded services such as the NHS there also exist a range of specially tailored services for veterans such as 'OP COURAGE' launched in 2021 to encourage veterans to seek support for their mental health.
39. Pozo and Walker, 'UK armed forces charities'.
40. Herman and Yarwood, 'From warfare to welfare'.
41. Cree and Caddick, 'Unconquerable heroes', p. 261.
42. Bulmer and Eichler, 'Unmaking militarized masculinity', p. 165.

43. HM Government, 'PM creates new Office for Veterans Affairs to provide lifelong support to military personnel'.
44. Frank, *Letting Stories Breathe*, p. 51.
45. Ibid., p. 51.
46. Ibid.
47. Bulmer and Eichler, 'Unmaking militarized masculinity', p. 166.
48. MacLeish, 'Churn', p. 205.
49. In a separate context, there are parallels here with Edward Said's argument in *Orientalism*, whereby all supposed character traits and cultural forms of 'Oriental' people are fixed and attributed to their 'Oriental' ways.
50. Andrews, *Narrative Imagination and Everyday Life*, p. 5.

CHAPTER 5

Narrative Politics and the Militarised Academy

The Ministry of Defence (MoD) main building in Whitehall, central London, is a colossal grey stone edifice. Imposing by design, it is located in the beating heart of UK government power and surrounded by the symbolic gravitas of bronze statues like that of the equestrian-mounted Field Marshal Haig memorial, as well as other statues of former generals, and the solemn figure of the Cenotaph. Curiously, there are also two large stone statues of nude figures on plinths above the north entrance, apparently representing 'earth' and 'water'. After passing along the Whitehall corridor, past the statues and the Cenotaph, I used to walk beneath the odd stone statues and into the building itself for project meetings with MoD civil servants. I had to be security-vetted in order to do so, and even then I was only permitted to walk through the building escorted by my host. Being there made me feel important and gave me a feeling of validation as a young academic fresh out of postgraduate study. Although I was treated with the caution and suspicion of an outsider, I felt connected to power and authority; that I had privileged access where other academics did not, and that my work was sure to produce 'impact'. I always wore a smart suit and tie for these meetings.

The meetings were for a project I worked on evaluating the MoD's 'Spouse Employment Support Trial' funded by the Forces in Mind Trust (FiMT). As the name suggests, the trial aimed to support military spouses to develop their employment prospects, or, in the MoD's terms, 'to help spouses optimise access to employment and to help them find better employment at a level that is commensurate with their skills, knowledge and experience and/or in accord with their aspirations and ability'.[1] The trial was a response to well-known issues arising from spouses having to sacrifice their own careers and aspirations to support their partners' military careers, and the knock-on effect this problem has on the retention of military personnel.[2] It was the first project I worked on after starting as a Research Fellow at the Veterans and Families Institute at Anglia Ruskin University and I was eager to demonstrate my value as a new member of the team.

The project meetings were tense, especially at the outset. Aligning our 'research' agenda with the MoD's interpretation of the project strictly as a 'service evaluation' proved difficult. During one forthright exchange, an MoD civil servant with whom we were working offered us a stark reminder of the trial's purpose. 'Let's not forget why we're doing this,' he reminded us, 'We're not doing this to be nice to spouses, we're doing this ultimately so we can be more effective at making holes in the Queen's enemies.' I recall my own nervous laughter at this, probably appearing every bit the 'squeamish' ivory tower academic I was trying not to be perceived as. On the face of it, the trial was a laudable attempt by the MoD to improve the conditions of military spouses and could even be considered progressive; a conscious effort to address the disadvantages encountered by a largely female population who support the institution by shouldering the burdens of childcare and emotional labour for their families, all while sacrificing their own career opportunities. And yet here I was confronted by the brutally instrumental logic of the institution towards spouses who, in reality, required nothing more than appeasement in order to retain service personnel for *making holes in the Queen's enemies.*

I bit my tongue. We had just been awarded substantial funding for this project and I was a junior academic starting out on my research career. I acceded to this logic in order to smooth our collaboration and avoid jeopardising the relationships we were building. Our evaluation celebrated the trial as a success, our principal finding being that spouses had become more 'confident', and that they felt 'valued' and 'supported' as a result of the MoD's investment in them.[3] In our project report, we discussed spouse employment as a 'retention issue',[4] following the MoD's investment logic, but in the apolitical register of 'staff turnover', as opposed to the more political register of the institution's capacity to carry out violence. As academics committed to a social justice agenda – and to weaving a good 'impact story' – our hope was to encourage the MoD to continue supporting spouses and accordingly the story we told was about how beneficial the trial had been for the women taking part. Our choice of framing hid from public view – and, arguably, from ourselves – the militarist politics of the 'retention' issue as well as the MoD's instrumental treatment of spouses. We handed the MoD an opportunity to demonstrate its progressive credentials by showcasing its commitment to creating opportunity for spouses; a reading of the trial confirmed by the words of Lieutenant General Richard Nugee (Chief of Defence People) in the foreword to our report:

> The clear message that this trial contributed to the overall sense of value that the MOD places on spouses reinforces our strongly held view that spouses and families are of significant importance to the health, wellbeing and confidence of Service Personnel, and thus the Armed Forces as a whole.[5]

It is this 'taming' of academic research by the military institution – and by militarising power relations more generally – that forms the basis of my critical reflection and discussion in this chapter. I argue that interwoven dilemmas of funding, access and impact serve to 'militarise' researchers (if they were not already militarised) and lead to predictable academic narratives which echo the institutional preferred narratives about soldiers, veterans and their families. Systemic pressures on academics to secure funding, negotiate access to research participants, and demonstrate impact collectively exercise control over the kind of stories that can be told through research. Following Plummer, such control can be understood as *narrative power* which 'disciplines' academics by moulding them into predictable storytellers: subjects able to speak in privileged voices on behalf of others, but who are themselves tightly positioned by the institutional demand for certain stories.[6] I trace the dominant narrative emerging from this disciplining process as a 'liberal progress narrative', whereby military service is constituted as a fundamental benefit to society, and academics act in support of government and the armed forces by making incremental progress towards a better-supported veteran population. In this narrative, 'impact' is the prized outcome, academics and policymakers are the key protagonists, and the plot itself is perpetually sustained by collective efforts at tweaking the neoliberal 'system' to make it less violent and more beneficent for veterans and their families in exchange for their service to the nation. By examining the part that academics like myself play within this narrative, I argue that the institutional politics of academia also plays a formative role in the cultural politics of veterans' narratives.

To be clear, support for military spouses is a good thing. Arguably, it is the right thing to do for the military to compensate spouses for the sacrifices they have made through being forced to relocate so frequently and to live in remote places where jobs are scarce. Improving their employment prospects empowers spouses and may even prove self-defeating for the military's retention logic if their careers end up being more lucrative for their families than remaining tied to the military. However, the 'martial politics'[7] driving such efforts – along with the academic research which underpins them – are either disguised or wilfully unacknowledged by those involved. On the scale of academic research which enables militarism, the issue of spouse employment is likely towards the 'low impact' end.[8] Yet, as my example demonstrates, it can be difficult for academics to disentangle their work from the political projects that underpin research and drive funding agendas. Moreover, as I will argue throughout this chapter, much academic work on veterans and the British military is premised on a far more overt and uncritical acceptance of 'support' for the armed forces which, while presented as 'objective' and free of ideology, is fundamental to upholding military power and authority, making the institution appear benign or even empathic. I therefore argue there is a need to contest this depoliticised view of British military research by highlighting the political projects it serves.

Academics, too, are storytellers. We tell stories about the people whose lives we research, working these stories up into a refined analytical narrative which illustrates the points we wish to make. Often the stories we tell through our research projects align with the stories told by other academics, and our collective efforts feed the broader overarching narratives of our field of study and academic discipline. As I've demonstrated elsewhere in this book, we are also constrained by these narratives, 'disciplined' by them, and pressured to reiterate and retell them. In academia, too, there are preferred narratives; ways of talking and writing about veterans' lives that are accepted, common to those who share this field of study, and considered to represent empirically validated truth. Academics feel a responsibility to articulate, defend and promote these narratives by telling the right kind of story through their work. Yet seldom do we reflect on the relationships of power and influence – cutting through and extending beyond academia – which elevate certain narratives to the status of 'knowledge' while working to prevent other narratives from taking hold. The notion of 'narrative politics' provides a way of thinking about how power is exercised and resisted in the stories we tell through research.[9] It plays out on grant funding committees, at conferences, in academic departments, the peer review system, the Research Excellence Framework (REF), on Twitter, and in the relationships academics are expected to cultivate with government and industry partners. Ultimately, narrative politics is an important means by which the 'militarised academy' reproduces itself, and by which academia intersects with the cultural politics of veterans' narratives.

My own academic career has been conditioned by the forces of both militarism and anti-militarism, with no clear means of disentangling the relations of power and influence which infuse my work and my thought with conflicting political priorities. I am immersed in professional relationships that constitute and reinscribe militarism whilst simultaneously finding myself drawn towards an anti-militarist logic of inquiry and a search for radical alternatives. As a political and academic subject, I am conflicted – as are all subjects, to some degree – and pressured to inhabit multiple competing narratives simultaneously. From this conflict has arisen two distinct strands in my work: one 'mainstream' strand funded largely by the Forces in Mind Trust, and the other 'critical' strand, consisting mainly of my own unfunded work and writing.[10] A lesson I have had to internalise in order to succeed in my role is that I can be 'political' in my critical military studies work, as long as my more mainstream work on veterans and the British military does not rock boats or raise political questions. Yet even in my critical work there is no 'pure' space of inquiry devoted to emancipatory anti-militarist ideals, for as Chris Rossdale reminds us, the work of anti-militarists is 'frequently shaped and conducted by those very social relations which constitute militarism'.[11] These constitutive relations of force include institutional frameworks and funding structures which demand what has been described as 'functionalist' or 'instrumental' research output which speaks to and serves the needs of military policy development.[12] Throughout this chapter, I aim to reveal – with my own conflicted academic CV as a springboard for critical reflection – how the field of British military and veterans' studies research is shaped by these relations in line with the entangled politics of militarism and anti-militarism.

Funding for Forces

Since 2012, much of the British research on veterans and the military has aligned itself with the interests and priorities of the Forces in Mind Trust (FiMT). Brought into existence by a £35-million endowment from the National Lottery Community Fund, FiMT is a grant-giving organisation funding research on veterans and their families, with a stated mission of enabling 'successful sustainable transition'. To understand the ideological framing of veterans' research, it is worth examining the role that FiMT has played within the military and veterans' studies research community since its creation. The availability of funding naturally creates an incentive for researchers to submit grant applications in the hopes of securing research income, thereby keeping themselves above water in the hyper-competitive grants culture of British universities. Pressure to generate funding – closely bound up with career progression and, increasingly, survival – means that academics will adjust their work to fit the agendas and priorities of organisations willing to fund their research. It is when these agendas conceal militaristic policy projects behind a depoliticised framework of 'support' that academics become co-opted in service to military power. FiMT's policy goals are framed as supporting vulnerable or misrepresented members of the ex-service community, but are rarely, if ever, subjected to critical scrutiny. As a result, the liberal progress narrative succeeds in carrying out a great deal of political work unnoticed.

The idea of liberal progress is tied to an implicit belief in liberal democracy as the best available means for promoting a nation's prosperity. In liberal democratic states, the market is understood to guarantee the 'freedom' of the individual, while state policy is designed to create the conditions of security, democracy and human rights which enable freedoms to flourish.[13] Under a 'liberal progress narrative', then, liberal democratic government is naturalised as the ideal, while progress is achieved by refining or 'optimising' policy in line with the needs of citizens, particularly those whom the government wishes to enfranchise. Policy thus functions as a means of softening market conditions for certain groups, such as veterans, while 'policy change' – slow and bureaucratic as it is to deliver – is understood as the primary mechanism for the progressive advancement of society in conjunction with the market; of making society more habitable. This is the narrative within the confines of which I understand most of the funded research on veterans to be operating. According to the liberal progress narrative, state institutions such as the Ministry of Defence are reformed *gradually* based on policies designed to make them more effective and efficient, and the role of academia is to support this process. Achieving 'policy impact' is the key element of struggle within the liberal progress narrative and it is how academics, funders and policymakers demonstrate success and for which they are rewarded.[14] In line with this narrative, research which prioritises 'impact' upon military institutions and decision-making processes has been described as 'functionalist' in nature,[15] and this functionalism is reinforced by the normative ideological belief that 'support for the armed forces community' constitutes an important rationale for academic research.

The notion of a liberal progress narrative as the guiding framework for research crystallised for me during my years of toiling within a localised 'knowledge economy' formed at the interface of the Forces in Mind Trust, the Ministry of Defence, military charities and the university.[16] Through years of working on FiMT-funded projects (and bidding unsuccessfully for others), I came to understand how my own efforts along with those of other academics and the Trust itself were being organised by an impact-driven agenda which (rather fancifully) privileges incremental policy change as the crucial mechanism for making a difference in people's lives. The idea of a liberal progress narrative, as I have described it above, captures the logic at play here. Aside from my years spent working within this knowledge economy, there was a serendipitous element to my identification of this narrative logic; a moment that brought into focus the fantastical optimism of the liberal progress narrative and its futility in the face of real-world events. It occurred during the evacuation of the remaining troops and foreign citizens from Afghanistan during the Taliban takeover in summer 2021. A time of chaos, fear for the people of Afghanistan, and anxiety for the veterans who had fought there who watched helplessly as their efforts over the past two decades unravelled in weeks. In the midst of this unfolding chaos, one of the board members of the Office for Veterans Affairs (OVA), 'quote tweets' the OVA proclaiming 'A really productive meeting MOD, OVA, NHS, Devolved Administrations, Charities and veterans and families voice. Great partnership and collaboration'. I do not know what was discussed at this meeting or what the outcome was, but what struck me was how the OVA were congratulating themselves on a 'productive meeting' while veterans – and the people of Afghanistan – were in genuine crisis. The liberal progress narrative is nudged onwards by many such productive meetings, strategies, research findings and policy initiatives, each marking a degree of 'progress' in the ever-unfolding plot. Although only one small instance among many that can be chosen to represent this narrative (see below), for me this example captured the ignorance and sheer banality of the liberal progress narrative.

* * *

In order to ensure the wider societal impact of my work, I have worked with funders (e.g., Forces in Mind Trust) and key stakeholders (e.g., Ministry of Defence, military charities) to disseminate findings and support social and policy change. Examples of this include meetings with the Ministry of Defence (MoD) following completion of the VFI's spouse employment research (in which I played a substantial role), discussing how our recommendations could be implemented. This work led directly to the MoD's introduction of a new Partner Career Support Programme, and our findings were discussed at length in a 2020 government-commissioned review into the needs of Armed Forces families (*'Living in our shoes'*), which stated 'this was an important study as it provided a wealth of information about the views of partners who took part'. (Excerpt from my application for promotion to Associate Professor, January 2021, p. 110)

* * *

Examining the activities of Forces in Mind Trust helps to reveal how the liberal progress narrative develops through academic research, as well as how it connects to the state transition narrative I discussed in the previous chapter. As a result of its ability to decide which proposals receive funding, FiMT can shape the field of military and veterans research in line with its political agenda. While the Trust's frequent claims regarding the 'objectivity' and 'credibility' of its research suggest the absence of any discernible agenda, I argue that its work is embroiled in both the politics of militarisation specifically and in the neoliberal policy project of welfare governance more generally. FiMT's agenda can be understood as a functionalist policy project designed to enhance the reputation of the British military by elaborating a progressive impact story told through its activity reports, the research reports authored by its grantees, and by its other public communications. FiMT's capacity to impose this agenda on universities is strengthened by virtue of its position as the only 'independent' UK funder specialising in military-connected research, with other research being funded through more general sources such as UKRI.[17] In accordance with its agenda, FiMT will not fund critical research *about* the military, rather it will only fund research carried out *for*, or *in service of*, the military. There are, therefore, limits on what can be said about the military, or militarism, in work funded by the Trust.

FiMT-funded research is subdivided into seven core programmes, corresponding to the six 'outcomes' it seeks to influence along with an 'enabler' programme described as 'Improving the capability of organisations that work with the Armed Forces Community by generating better understanding and enhancing capacity.'[18] As at the time of writing, the six outcomes (i.e., outcomes of transition for the veteran and his or her family) encompass housing, health, employment, finances, relationships and criminal justice. Each outcome is associated with a set of policy goals whereby the Trust aims to use the research it funds to create impact. By basing their programme of activity around these outcomes, FiMT can compartmentalise and distil the problem of transition into distinct areas whereby progress is measured against quantifiable metrics which lend themselves to a positive impact narrative. Compartmentalising makes transition measurable in a way that conceals the imminent complexity and politics of veteran experience and allows FiMT to present itself as an influential agent of change. The words of FiMT Chairperson, Hans Pung, express the policy project at the heart of the Trust's agenda:

> I am convinced that our efforts, working through a varied programme of activities and supported by strong partnerships, move us closer to our ultimate vision that all ex-Service personnel and their families lead fulfilled civilian lives. Of course, this is very ambitious, and the Trust only plays a small part in working with a range of stakeholders – from our Cobseo military charities to government departments to wider third sector partners – to deliver this goal. Our distinct role in this challenge is to bring knowledge and evidence to bear in order to inform and influence the challenges of transition, while working in collaboration with others in the sector and building capacity to allow them to transform in order to achieve greater impact.[19]

The altruistic tone of FiMT's vision arguably elides the militarising logic underpinning this project of impact and policy improvement. The logic at play is that of liberal progress – promoting military improvement as a *social good* to be incrementally pursued on behalf of the nation, with military service likewise positioned as honourable and enriching. I suggest that this logic can be identified through a critical reading of the research reports published by FiMT. Forewords to the reports function as FiMT's narrative framing of the research. Many of the forewords are written by the Trust's (now former) chief executive, high-ranking former RAF officer Ray Lock, with some also written by charity or business partners, or (as with our spouse employment work), by the Ministry of Defence.[20] A pervasive commitment to the state transition narrative is evident in these forewords, which consistently emphasise what the individual veteran has *gained* from his or her service. Introducing one report 'Improving transition out of the Armed Forces', Lock writes, for example:

> It is a truth worth repeating that most Service personnel and their families enjoy a successful transition from military to civilian life, their time spent working and living within the serving community having been rewarding and enriching in equal measure. For certain, civilian life presents challenges, and these have been well identified in the myriad of publications the last few years' focus on transition has spurred, many of them of course funded by Forces in Mind Trust. And there is a spectrum of success in meeting those challenges: some settle easily, a few struggle badly, and the majority succeed, but not entirely without facing up to some adversity.[21]

These comments are a typical illustration of FiMT's framing of the research it funds, which constantly reiterates the normativity of success and the marginality of struggle in transition.[22] The message is often even more explicit, as in Lock's foreword to another report which proclaims 'The evidence presented in this report is compelling and usefully draws attention to the positive value of military service as well as to the negative effects suffered by some.'[23] In essence, FiMT's research promotes the state transition narrative discussed in the previous chapter. Moreover, Lock's comments highlight the crossover between the state transition narrative and the liberal progress narrative examined here. Both share the assumption that military service is a personal, social and economic good. Both, therefore, are part of a broader militarist worldview – 'liberal militarism' – which considers military service to be an honourable undertaking on behalf of the nation. As I introduced it in Chapter 2 (i.e., as the defining character of British militarism), liberal militarism is 'the commitment by liberal democratic states and societies to maintain and use military force',[24] and is an important tool by which liberal progress is pursued internationally. Indeed, liberal militarism is seen as *defence* of liberal progress. Both the state transition narrative and the liberal progress narrative share the ethos of this liberal militarist ideology. In the cultural politics of veterans' narratives, these two narrative frameworks are closely intertwined and are promoted by the same storytellers.

They each serve a different yet complementary purpose. What distinguishes them is that while the state transition narrative seeks to define the reality of veterans' transition, the liberal progress narrative functions as the organising framework for research and policymaking in the militarised academy and in government. It is the latter which identifies the appropriate goals of policy and research, and which designates the appropriate object of intervention as the individual veteran whose wayward trajectory must be realigned with the state transition narrative.

The liberal progress narrative, then, is a shared understanding about how change happens, what kind of changes are desirable, and who the key actors are in bringing about these changes. In this narrative, change happens *through* and *within* the frameworks of liberal democracy and liberal militarism. By making small changes to policy, veterans can be incrementally better supported while keeping the overarching structures of liberal militarism and government firmly intact. Government policymakers are the key actors, the ones we are striving to influence. The narrative promotes the idea that policy will lead to improved conditions for veterans and their families while ruling out the more radical idea that liberal militarism itself may be at issue. A section of FiMT's 2020 Impact Report titled 'Impact through influence' demonstrates the narrative logic at play here. Examples used to demonstrate influence include: 'Convened a seminar for Labour Friends of the Forces on Mental Health in the Ex-Service Community'; 'Created policy statements on Housing, Health and Criminal Justice, outlining our evidence-based recommendations – each resulting in meetings with policymakers'; 'Shared our 2019 report Sanctions, Support and Service Leavers with the Department for Work and Pensions, to be used in the development of its Armed Forces support strategy', and; 'Submitted evidence to the Health Select Committee on Delivering Core NHS and Care Services during the Pandemic and Beyond.'[25] Each of these meetings, policy statements and strategies are naively assumed to create change, without ever acknowledging that a more effective and radical change could be achieved by dismantling militarism and by addressing the classed, raced and gendered harms that veterans – as well as others in society – encounter daily.

* * *

Its December 2019 and I'm in a Westminster pub with colleagues at a charity who provide respite breaks to military families. We are meeting to discuss the consultancy project I'm working on for them:

a literature review on the benefits that holidays provide to families' wellbeing. I like these people, and it's close to the Christmas break so there is an air of festivity to our conversation. I'm far less enthusiastic about the project, however. I'm working on it because it provides income to the research institute, and we are in a 'funding drought' which means I have no big project to occupy my time with more engaging work. Our conversation turns to the paper I will write and how to frame a rationale that will appeal to the military journals I will target for publication. The notion of 'operational effectiveness' is suggested as central to my argument. Respite breaks for military families are worth supporting because they will lead to better adjusted service personnel who are more capable of carrying out their military duties. I know this argument well; I've encountered it before in the spouse employment work. I know the politics embedded in it,[26] but I also know that raising objections would be antithetical in the context of our meeting and would only serve to alienate me from this pleasant company. So I don't. Once again, I accede to the logic of 'operational effectiveness' because this is how my paper will get published, and how I will fulfil my obligations to the charity who are paying for my time as a consultant.

* * *

The liberal progress narrative 'militarises' researchers by defining the parameters of research and by keeping critical research questions off the table. By concentrating its inquiries on how military service benefits the individual veteran – or, conversely, on how those who 'fail' to transition may be remedied – FiMT designates the *individual* as the proper subject of inquiry and intervention. The politics of the military itself, or militarism, or state policy, are therefore considered inappropriate, making research intended to scrutinise military power essentially unfundable. In this sense, the FiMT research agenda discreetly evinces the neoliberal ideology of the military and governmental elites whom it supports. Indeed, if neoliberal ideology is understood, in essence, to represent the primacy of 'the individual' as sovereign master of his or her fortunes, alongside the denial of 'society' and its institutions, then focusing on the success or failure of the individual to transition bears clear resemblance to the currently hegemonic neoliberal mode of governing.[27] That FiMT's back catalogue contains numerous works concerned with veterans as welfare claimants,[28] and that the work of the Trust is supported by establishment figures such as Lord Ashcroft,[29] further supports a reading of the FiMT project as driven by militarised neoliberal government.

In order to preserve their access to funding, academics funded by FiMT are made complicit in militarism through quiet acquiescence to the concerns of military bureaucracy and public relations-style image management. The stifling of critique, and adherence to a 'policy improvement' logic of inquiry, is upheld by a pre-eminent concern with what the Trust regards as 'objective' and 'credible' research. As declarations in numerous forewords illustrate – 'this report presents a credible and contemporary picture of reality'[30]; 'For the first time, it will now be possible for those working at all levels in this area to base their decisions upon an independent and credible source of information'[31]; 'The objective and thorough research conducted by DSC will support evidence-based policy development'[32] – notions of objectivity and credibility are frequently invoked, yet without reference to specific qualities of the research which might justify these claims.[33] Yet their repeated use by the Trust enhances the authority of its research while insulating their depoliticised agenda from critical scrutiny and avoiding more overtly political questions about British militarism.

Do We Care? Navigating Care, 'Support', and Liberal Progress

I have worked closely with the military charity sector ever since I entered the field of veterans' studies in 2011. During this time, I have witnessed transformational and empowering work carried out by people with a deep-seated empathy and passion for helping others. The smaller charities with whom I have worked labour tirelessly on behalf of their beneficiaries, restoring purpose and human connection among people who have become isolated as a result of trauma or transition. These organisations sometimes take considerable risks in supporting people whose behaviour can be volatile, and these risks are integral to the ethic of care the charities practice. Yet the ethic of care that drives the transformational work of the sector also conflicts with – in big and small charities alike – the political imperatives of the liberal progress narrative. Charities work hard to raise funds and justify their continued existence, and to do so they must maintain boundaries over *who* and *how* they help, in line with the expectations of funders, government and the militarised academy. As Herman and Yarwood put it, relations of care become 'entangled in broader networks of market forces and inter-agency politics'.[34] Care is vulnerable to liberal progress; they occupy competing ethics and rationalities, diverting effort from one another.

Veterans are attentive to situations where the institutional demands of liberal progress are prioritised over relations of care, and it leads towards stories of disenfranchisement as identified in the previous chapter. I have personally encountered many veterans who felt 'processed' by military charities, as though they were 'just a number' moving through a system akin to the military itself. As it wends its way through the military charity sector, the liberal progress narrative affords a bureaucratic approach to case management together with a policy-driven ethos which puts relationships with the state at the forefront of charities' concerns.[35] Through agencies such as the Armed Forces Covenant Fund Trust, which in 2020/21 awarded over £25 million in grants to charities,[36] military charities are centrally involved in realising the state's ambitions. They help to enact government policy by plugging the gaps in veteran care that the state cannot fill directly. To receive the funding they need, charities have to demonstrate 'progress' in their beneficiaries; that veterans are becoming productive, contributing individuals. Charities also need to show that their efforts align with government policy (e.g., the Veterans' Strategy) and with the state transition narrative. They need to tell the right kind of story, and this means that beneficiaries become *indicators of progress* as well as recipients of care.

Through partnerships with the charities, the militarised academy plays a key role in telling this story. Universities enable the co-opting of charities into the ideology of liberal progress in two ways. One is the primacy of a 'service evaluation' logic of inquiry within the 'charity–academic research nexus'.[37] In order to measure progress, the charities' programmes and services have to be evaluated, so universities market their capacity to carry out evaluation. To the extent that beneficiaries' testimonies and questionnaire scores indicate progress, researchers congratulate the charities on their work and/or teach them how to improve. As one such evaluation concluded, 'The Poppy Factory pilot service was effective in achieving positive employment outcomes and improvements to wellbeing and quality of life.'[38] Services and programmes then become policy and the liberal progress narrative perpetuates itself on the glossy front covers of project reports. Meanwhile, researchers gain a compelling impact story that plays well in the REF. As I wrote, for example, in an 'impact case study' for the 2021 REF exercise, our research 'made an impact on government policy, commerce, charity policy and practice, GP training and practice, and the health, well-being, professional development and quality of life of soldiers, veterans and their families'. The second mechanism is through 'strategic direction' provided by academics sitting on the boards of organisations such as Cobseo (the umbrella organisation for military charities), and as trustees or advisers to individual charities. In my experience, these boards and the meetings through which they coordinate action are far removed from the charities' beneficiaries. They discuss 'strategic objectives', alignment with government policy, programme delivery, oversight, and the implementation of findings and recommendations. They provide academics with an opportunity to demonstrate influence while elevating bureaucracy, prioritising policy impact, and diverting attention further away from relations of care.

* * *

I've been asked to attend an advisory board meeting for a research project being run in collaboration with the military charity sector. The project isn't ours; it belongs to academics at another university, and since I possess similar expertise, I have been invited to assist in the governance of the research. I turn up to the meeting in central London and sit through the prosaic updates, listening to questions from other advisory board members but saying little myself. It's not a project that will provide tangible benefit to anyone, and it's fair to say my heart isn't in it. Afterwards there's a buffet lunch, so I stick around for a while, milling about and making polite conversation. I'm asked by one of the board members what my field of research is. This seemingly simple question has become fraught with tension for me lately. I've clocked the questioner as ex-military, probably quite senior. I missed his introduction at the start of the meeting, but the tell-tale signs are all there: tall, solid build, cleanly shaven, smartly suited, and that distinctive combination of deep vocals and upper-class accent which announces senior officer standing. Opting for a balance of risk and conformity in my answer, I respond by telling him that my field is 'military sociology' (leading with this half-truth to garner respectability) ... 'and critical military studies' (the more accurate, if antagonistic answer). 'Critical military studies', he echoes, with a furrowed brow and ponderous head tilt. I hesitate for a moment, unsure how to proceed. At this point my colleague steps in having overheard our exchange. Recognising I am at risk of undermining the governing ethos of this space by breaking with militarist terms of reference, he kindly explains that 'It's about critical thinking to help create a better policy environment for the military and working together for change.' I am being apologised for. Feeling awkward,

I smile and nod for the rest of the conversation, making the most of the free sandwiches and planning a swift exit.

* * *

Whether care or liberal progress occupies the everyday reality, the governing ethos of the military charity sector is about 'support' for the military and the armed forces community. Charities support military effectiveness by supplementing the welfare of personnel and their families, and they support the wider armed forces and veterans' community by playing a leading role in care. To place themselves in a supportive position, organisations must align themselves with the values and priorities of the armed forces. They must acknowledge – even if they do not exactly share – the same motivations and desires. Moreover, and by legal requirement, they must remain 'apolitical', avoiding interference with or criticism of government policy.[39] 'Support' is an ethos which welcomes some stories, relationships and priorities while keeping others fenced off outside its physical spaces and narrative environs. So pervasive is this ethos, it becomes an embodied disposition; a way of being and operating within the charity–academic nexus that compels respect and admiration towards armed forces personnel and veterans. Performing a supportive disposition is necessary to gain and sustain access, particularly at the sector's 'strategic' or governing level. In most cases, such a performance is easily maintained. For me as a young White male academic with a middle-class accent and normative gender presentation, it is easy to blend in among the type of people I encounter in the bureaucratic charity spaces within which I am required to operate.[40] All it usually requires is for me to adopt a business-like appearance and demeanour (donning the smart suit) and keep quiet about the critical perspective I take in the 'other strand' of my academic work. Against this disposition of support, critique of the military is positioned as disrespectful. Understood as hostility, critique is considered anathema to the governing ethos – the 'doxa', in Bourdieusian terms – of these spaces.

Support for 'the troops' – or the armed forces, or war – is an inherently political position,[41] yet the posture of support erases and denies politics by casting it out as inappropriate. In other words, support is *depoliticising*. The screening out of critique ensures that politicised voices are kept out of the narrative environment created among the charities. Gatekeepers, such as the charity CEOs, grant or deny access to academics and thereby ensure that the right kind of stories continue to be told. Demonstrating support, for example, by advocating the ideals of service and respect, builds familiarity and trust. It smooths the pathways of interaction and collaboration. Absent a supportive disposition, the cooperation of gatekeepers can easily be withheld or withdrawn. Academics without a reputation for 'safe' or non-political research can find themselves excluded.

The requirement of gaining access means that academics who do not share the charities' apolitical outlook must adopt (at best) a neutral posture on broader political questions of militarised violence. Faced with this reality, I have been forced to consider what I will surrender to gain access to research participants and to work my way onto boards and committees that allow me to demonstrate 'influence'; both of which help to sustain my professional, promotion-oriented self-narrative as an influential, impact-driven researcher. Upon reflection, it transpires that I have been willing to forfeit much in order to succeed. Often, I have had to forfeit the ability to position my work politically and have traded my critical curiosity for compliance with the standard view that 'most veterans do well' upon leaving the military. I have also accepted that ascertaining the extent to which veterans *are* 'doing well' is the right question and the only question worth asking in research governed by the narratives outlined in this chapter. In short, I have had to set politics aside in order to get on with the business of doing research. The stories which emerge from this research are cleanly sanitised, disavowing the realities of militarised violence, undermining care, and positing 'support' as the unquestionable moral imperative of the charity–academic nexus.

Given these entrenched pressures, I argue that academics ought to do more to resist the depoliticising of research under the dominant ethos of liberal progress. There may be several avenues for resistance, or at least avoiding or reducing complicity with liberal progress in the militarised academy. One option may be to avoid submitting grant applications to organisations that adhere to a clearly neoliberal agenda with defined policy goals in support of the military. As I make clear earlier in this chapter, however, this option may be less viable for early career researchers (as I was then) needing to establish their research and funding credentials. Another may be to critique the funding structures we are part of, as I have done in this chapter, and as other colleagues have done in relation to different funders.[42] Finally, one mode of resistance that might be more widely available to colleagues across institutions and career stages is to be more critical of 'impact' and to jointly pursue a healthier impact culture.[43] Not all forms of impact are 'good', and we need to be more critical of impact produced solely to feed the demands of institutional approval and research governance (e.g., REF). As Reed and Fazey suggest, 'Healthy impact cultures underpin their impacts with rigorous and ethical research. Without relevant safeguards, it is possible for research to have seriously negative impacts.'[44] Seeking forms of impact that directly support marginalised communities while resisting co-optation into liberal progress ideologies should thus become a priority, as should the telling of impact narratives that rely on grassroots support rather than institutional policy change as the key marker of success.[45] To confront the militarised academy, we need to find alternative narratives in which to position our work. We need to tell better stories.

Conclusion

The spread of opinion and research within British military and veterans' studies is more diverse than I have perhaps suggested in this chapter. There are critical dissenting voices as well as those who choose to speak in tune with the liberal progress narrative.[46] Nevertheless, I have argued in this chapter that research with veterans and other military-connected groups is entangled with militarism in a manner that few academics working in the field have acknowledged. In recognition of the basic facts about my professional needs for funding and access, it is impossible not to conclude that my research career has been 'militarised' by the demands placed upon me. This is a situation from which I have been attempting to disentangle myself by seeking more radical alternatives and by adopting an increasingly critical anti-militarist stance in the work I produce. Yet I am also aware that such efforts are always partial, and that just as it is impossible to extricate oneself entirely from the social relations that militarism imposes, I will likely remain embedded in academic structures that underpin militarism along with situations which undermine my ability to position myself and my work in ways that I deem politically necessary.

The liberal progress narrative, together with the knowledge economy it supports, requires me to operate as a 'professional' in Edward Said's sense of the term. For Said, the intellectual as professional is one who does not rock boats or stray beyond the accepted limits and narratives of a narrow field of expertise, who desires to remain 'marketable and above all presentable, hence uncontroversial and unpolitical and "objective"'.⁴⁷ The professional is given over to 'serving and winning rewards from power',⁴⁸ principally by working towards the policy goals of the governments and organisations he or she is funded by. In Said's eyes, the professional attitude kills off critical thought and the exercise of independent judgement and analysis which ought to be the domain of the intellectual worker. The liberal progress narrative is a thoroughly 'professional' story. I am paid by the Forces in Mind Trust to tell it through my research and I am rewarded by militarised academia for doing so. This is not how I desire to operate in my career as an academic. In contrast to professionalism, I desire what Said described as 'amateurism'; that is, 'to be moved not by profit or reward but by love for and unquenchable interest in the larger picture, in making connections across lines and barriers, in refusing to be tied down to a speciality, in caring for ideas and values despite the restrictions of a profession'.⁴⁹ Said's vision of the intellectual sustains me and motivates me ever more urgently at times when the stifling imperatives of professionalism constrain my freedom to tell better, critical stories through my work.

The larger substantive claim here is, of course, that the structural politics of academia intersect with the cultural politics of veterans' narratives, so that only certain kinds of academic stories about veterans are considered 'tellable' and 'fundable'. Backed by academia's institutionalised authority to legitimise and delegitimise claims to knowledge, research about veterans affirms certain narratives as truthful while casting doubt on others it deems 'mythical'. In doing so, it works to shift the political terrain of veterans' narratives rightwards, to a zone in which veteran storytelling is marshalled in support of militarised policy projects and neoliberal rationales of government. Academic research actively seeks to intervene in cultural politics, promoting depoliticised stories about veterans which portray the military institution and its supporting third sector apparatus in a positive light. The liberal progress narrative which organises vast amounts of research activity presents an illusion of meaningful change without ever really changing anything. It serves power by muting curiosity of its actions and beliefs. Stories which reclaim the political significance of veteran experience in ways which might upset the dominant narratives, or which focus attention on the harmful impressions of military power, tend not to be recognised within this narrative domain.⁵⁰ Since such stories refuse the patriotism which infuses the dominant culture of veteran storytelling, they are routinely marginalised. The culture of veteran storytelling is all the more political precisely because of attempts by academia and mass culture alike to deny politics as a suitable framework for understanding and critiquing veterans' stories.

Notes

1. Ministry of Defence, 'Spousal employment – the way ahead'.
2. In the annual 'Armed Forces Continuous Attitudes Survey' (AFCAS), issues related to spouse employment are consistently cited as one of the main reasons personnel will consider leaving the military.
3. Godier-McBard, Caddick and Fossey, 'Confident, valued and supported'.
4. Caddick et al., 'Evaluation of the Ministry of Defence Spouse Employment Support Trial'.
5. Ibid., p. 5.
6. Plummer, *Narrative Power*.
7. Howell, 'Forget "militarization"'.
8. Particularly, for instance, when compared to weapons manufacturing and military technology research. For an overview of the harmful connections between academia and the military, see Stavrianakis, 'In arm's way'; Jenkings et al., 'Military occupations'; Bourke, *Wounding the World*.
9. Plummer, 'Narrative power, sexual stories and the politics of storytelling'.
10. There is, of course, a further concern regarding the difficulty of getting 'critical' work funded, particularly where such work does not immediately lend itself towards easy utilisation by external partners or governments.
11. Rossdale, *Resisting Militarism*,
12. Catignani and Basham, 'The gendered politics of researching military policy in the age of the "knowledge economy"'; Jenkings et al., 'Military occupations'; Stavrianakis, 'In arm's way'.
13. For example, Rose and Miller, 'Political power beyond the state'; Gilbert, *Twenty-first Century Socialism*; Somers, *Genealogies of Citizenship*.
14. Stavrianakis, 'In arms way'.
15. Jenkings et al., 'Military occupations'; Higate and Cameron, 'Reflexivity and researching the military'.
16. For a critique of the knowledge economy and its relation to the gendered politics of research into military policy, see Catignani and Basham, 'The gendered politics of researching military policy in the age of the "knowledge economy"'.
17. The trend towards functionalist research is also evident in military-connected research funded by larger bodies such as the Economic and Social Research Council (ESRC). See Catignani and Basham, 'The gendered politics of researching military policy in the age of the "knowledge economy"'.
18. Forces in Mind Trust, 'Impact Report 2019', p. 11.
19. Forces in Mind Trust, 'Activity Report 2017', p. 2.
20. Lock was chief executive of the Forces in Mind Trust from its inception in 2012 until June 2021, when he was replaced by fellow veteran Mike Ellicock. Ellicock resigned, under unclear circumstances, within a year of taking up the post.
21. Halkiopoulos, Makinson and Heal, 'Improving transition out of the Armed Forces'.
22. Ross McGarry makes a similar point in his critical essay on military mental health research; that mainstream research consistently problematises the

'minority' of veterans considered to struggle with transition whilst celebrating the successful 'majority'. See McGarry, 'Demystifying the "victimized state"'.
23. Armour, McGlinchey and Ross, 'The health and wellbeing of armed forces veterans in Northern Ireland', p. 2.
24. Basham, 'Liberal militarism as insecurity, desire and ambivalence'.
25. Forces in Mind Trust, '2020 impact report', p. 13.
26. Long, 'Maximising operational effectiveness'.
27. Gilbert, *Twenty-first Century Socialism*.
28. See, for example, Burdett et al., 'Veterans and benefits'; Scullion et al., 'Sanctions, support and service leavers'; Howarth, Doherty and Cole, 'Armed forces charities' financial support'.
29. For example, Ashcroft has previously addressed conference sessions organised by FiMT and served as the founding Patron of the FiMT Research Centre at Anglia Ruskin University.
30. Burdett et al., 'Veterans and benefits', p. 2.
31. Pozo and Walker, 'UK Armed Forces Charities', p. xi.
32. Cole, Robson and Doherty, 'Armed forces charities', p. ix.
33. Moreover, these terms are deployed uncritically, lacking an appreciation of the thorny philosophical issues plaguing concepts such as 'objectivity'. See, for example, Levitt et al., 'The meaning of scientific objectivity and subjectivity'.
34. Herman and Yarwood, 'From warfare to welfare', p. 2641.
35. Ibid.
36. Figures obtained from Armed Forces Covenant Fund Trust website.
37. To adapt and mirror the term 'military–academy research nexus' coined by Jenkings et al., 'Military occupations'.
38. Thomson, McKenzie and Vaughan, 'Evaluation of the Poppy Factory's NHS-embedded employment support pilot for veterans'.
39. Herman and Yarwood, 'From warfare to welfare'.
40. Harriet Gray makes a similar point about allowing herself to be read as 'unthreatening' based on her appearance and style of self-presentation in military settings. See Gray, 'Researching from the spaces in between?'
41. For example, Millar, *Support the Troops*; Stahl, 'Why we "support the troops"'; Herman and Yarwood, 'From warfare to welfare'; Woodward et al., 'The possibilities and limits of impact and engagement in research on military institutions'.
42. Catignani and Basham, 'The gendered politics of researching military policy in the age of the "knowledge economy"'.
43. Reed and Fazey, 'Impact culture'.
44. Ibid., p. 6.
45. Harman, *Seeing Politics*.
46. Critical work on veterans is largely the purview of academics who situate their work within critical military studies, such as McGarry, 'Visualizing liminal military landscape'; Higate, 'Proud to "fly a desk" and wear a medal?'; Higate et al., 'Militarization, stigma, and resistance'; Clarke et al., 'The good, the bad and the rebels'; Bulmer and Eichler, 'Unmaking militarized masculinities'; Cree and Caddick, 'Unconquerable heroes'.
47. Said, *Representations of the Intellectual*, p. 74.
48. Ibid., p. 86.
49. Ibid., p. 76.
50. But see, for example, Schrader, *Fight to Live, Live to Fight*.

CHAPTER 6

Intertextual Narratives and the War in Afghanistan

Veterans' stories stake authoritative claims to the truth of war. They possess the qualities of 'ground truth'[1] and 'flesh witnessing'[2] which give veterans the rhetorical power to narrate war persuasively. Since veterans have mustered the courage to serve and to fight, their stories acquire a moral – and deeply gendered – form of persuasiveness that we rarely associate with other stories and storytellers. We look to veterans' stories, their memoirs in particular, for 'real' accounts of war, untainted by political objective or reporting bias that are assumed to contaminate the war narratives of politicians and journalists. When it comes to the war in Afghanistan, Britain's longest and most arduous twenty-first-century war, there has been no shortage of memoirs written by veterans offering their version of events 'on the ground'. These stories seek to educate wider publics by conveying factual information about the war in Afghanistan, and to compel the reader's attention by placing the personal, human encounter with war at the heart of the narrative.[3] In this chapter, I engage with a small and carefully selected subset of Afghanistan war memoirs in order to consider what these stories might tell us about 'failure', and indeed about Afghanistan itself. When the Taliban swept back into power in July–August 2021, many in the West finally conceded that the war in Afghanistan had been a failure. Some veterans saw it coming. Their memoirs, published while the war was still ongoing, spoke of failure or warned of it virtually from the beginning. My argument in this chapter is that the *reasons* attributed to failure in Afghanistan matter deeply not only because they tell us what went wrong, but also because they suggest different *responses* to failure in ways that reinscribe, or alternative undermine, British militarism.

Veterans are motivated to write their memoirs because they have a story to tell, often because they intend to form part of, or to correct, some aspect of the public record on war.[4] Their stories call for a response; indeed, they hold the reader accountable *to* respond. As Woodward and Jenkings put it, 'There is a morality to military memoirs, about consciousness-raising and the sharing of responsibility for a military experience with the reader.'[5] Their stories also offer a script. If failure in Afghanistan was due to 'x', then fix 'x', and you fix Afghanistan, or war or Britain and its military reputation. I am interested in the kind of responses that veterans' stories call for, either implicitly or explicitly, through their writing. For example, should our response to a failed war be about developing better strategies for military intervention, or developing anti-imperialist politics? I am interested, then, in what *kind* of failure was the war in Afghanistan, and how do veterans' stories guide us to respond?

A growing scholarly literature asserts the value of studying memoir as a form of veteran storytelling.[6] Military memoirs are important cultural artefacts which can be understood as 'vectors of militarism', but through which we can also 'see the disruptions they bring to dominant discourses which prioritise military solutions and interventions'.[7] Discussing the study of autobiography more generally, Smith and Watson argue that life narrative is best approached as a 'moving target',[8] involving acts of self-representation that engage with the past according to both identity in the present and imagined futures. As well as grappling with memories that 'change colour' and shift over time, memoirists write with specific rhetorical intentions to testify, to persuade, to justify, to craft identities and uphold reputations. While such intentions likewise underpin other forms of storytelling, they are amplified in memoir. Indeed, as Frank suggests, 'Memoir may be the most self-conscious work of nonacademic narrative analysis.'[9] Added to these observations are issues such as self- and state-censorship which, Woodward and Jenkings contend, influence the ways in which readers are invited to engage with the military memoir.[10] Such concerns have generated anxieties for historians and other readers about the authenticity of military memoirs; the very feature upon which memoirists depend to assert the importance and urgency of their stories.[11] Like Woodward and Jenkings in their extensive study of military memoirs, I wish to take these accounts seriously and on their own terms. That said, I am not concerned primarily with the 'accuracy' of the memoirs I draw upon as source material. In keeping with the book's aims, my focus is rather on how these stories are situated within the cultural politics of veterans' narratives, focusing on the plot and language of the memoir, how the narrator positions himself in relation to others, and what happens to our understanding of war and militarism as a result. Even while claiming to accurately represent historical experience, a story need not be strictly 'true' in order to be powerful.

The stories veterans tell through their memoirs also form influential representations of Afghanistan itself. Through memoirs emerge stories of the Afghan people and their 'deeply conservative' social values,[12] of the hot and dusty terrain; 'a very uncivilized part of the world' and 'a place of extreme terror blended with supreme beauty',[13] and of the corruption inherent to the Afghan government's 'narco state'.[14] War memoirs form part of what Manchanda calls the 'imagination' of Afghanistan.[15] That is, how Afghanistan 'forms' as a social construction in the minds of Western publics depends at least in part on the stories veterans tell of fighting there. These stories in turn draw upon a long history of imperial knowledge and narratives which provide veterans with resources to narrate their own war stories. Social imaginaries of Afghanistan are incredibly influential because of the politics they enable towards Afghanistan. Manchanda asks, for instance, 'how is Afghanistan thought about in a way such that it is possible to invade and bomb it?'[16] To the extent that narrative, or in Said's terms, 'The power to narrate, or to block other narratives from forming and emerging',[17] constitutes a key mechanism of imperialism, veterans' memoirs can be read as part of the imperial knowledge process which denotes Afghanistan as an 'intervenable' space. Crucial to this chapter's argument, then, is that while telling of military failure in Afghanistan, veterans' stories 'imagine' Afghanistan itself in politically significant ways.

In seeking to understand failure in Afghanistan, my aim is to place in dialogue with each other stories which offer different perspectives on the war. To do this, I rely upon Fairclough's notion of 'intertextuality' and relatedly Bakhtin's concept of 'heteroglossia' to consider how these stories speak to one another. According to Fairclough, intertextuality refers to 'the dependence of texts upon society and history in the form of the resources made available within the order of discourse'.[18] Just as narratives are relational and historical (see Chapter 1), texts are related to one another and to the socio-historical contexts in which they are produced. Intertextual analysis bridges the gap between text and context, conceiving of a dialectical relationship between the two. Texts are highly sensitive to the wider conditions under which their production takes place, and they also constitute a form of social action back upon those conditions. Afghanistan war memoirs, for instance, are deeply influenced by the historical and political circumstances of the war just as veterans seek to influence these circumstances in some way through their writing. Individual veterans' stories are also part of a wider 'library' of stories about the war in Afghanistan. Bakhtin's notion of 'heteroglossia' shows how stories within the library are interrelated. Frank, whose work on narrative is heavily influenced by Bakhtin, explains that 'Heteroglossia emphasizes how every story is assembled from multiple codes of language usage and genre.'[19] Veterans' stories share codes including professional jargon, tropes, codes for emotional expression and expectations of plot progression. These stories are heteroglossic in that the voices of individual authors merge and diverge in a manner that is clearly evident when their memoirs are read side-by-side. They 'talk' to each other; they are in dialogue.

The four stories I juxtapose in dialogue each have something different to say about the war in Afghanistan. They are all written as memoir and their authors are positioned very differently in relation to the war. One is a General, one is a junior officer and frontline soldier, one is a junior soldier who turned publicly against the war, and one is an Afghan civilian whose life was uprooted and transformed by the war. Three are White and British, one is Afghan Pashtun; all are men. All discuss 'failure' in Afghanistan, but in markedly different ways. Since Afghanistan is routinely spoken *for* and *about* – in veterans' stories as in Western politics generally – I consider it necessary to contrast the veterans' stories to a seldom-listened-to Afghan voice on the war. The comparison is not direct, as Qais Akbar Omar's memoir *A Fort of Nine Towers* predominantly covers the period of civil war followed by Taliban rule which immediately preceded the international military intervention in Afghanistan after 9/11. Yet since Omar's position in relation to the war is so different to that of the veterans, intertextual comparison nonetheless reveals much about how these stories are so fundamentally interwoven despite their lack of synchronicity. My intertextual and heteroglossic argument is that we learn more from these stories when reading them in dialogue than we could by reading them in isolation. In seeking to understand failure in Afghanistan through narrative, I am also therefore asking how the meaning of one story can be amplified, or re-contextualised, when read in light of another?

Political failure: *'Leading From the Front'*

As a former Chief of the General Staff (CGS) who held the highest level of command over the British Army's mission in Afghanistan between 2006 and 2009, General Richard Dannatt has a unique perspective to offer on the war. Published in 2010, his book *Leading from the Front* is a career autobiography rather than a memoir dedicated specifically to the war in Afghanistan, though it does contain several long chapters about the war and the political process by which it was organised and funded.[20] Dannatt was outspoken during his time as CGS in a manner that attracted severe criticism from media and political elites. The book is a continuation and an example of his outspokenness about the irresponsibility of government in times of war. Dannatt is self-reflective about his critique of the government, noting throughout the memoir that he viewed his own task as moral advocacy on behalf of the soldiers being asked to fight the nation's war. Upsetting the conventional wisdom of civil–military relations – that is, that military command operates under civilian political leadership – Dannatt would ultimately claim that 'if war is too important to be left to generals, then the funding of war is too important to be left to politicians'.[21]

Leading From the Front reads as a stark warning that failure of political leadership and commitment would lead to military and policy failure in Afghanistan, all the while expressing a resolute determination to avoid such an outcome. Dannatt speaks of his fervent attempts to persuade senior political leaders to adequately resource the war, and of his frustration at their furtive reluctance to grant his requests due consideration. As a General, Dannatt was never deployed to Afghanistan. Instead, we read of him shuttling backwards and forwards between visits to deployed troops, army camps, and ministerial meetings, trying to build support for the war being fought in Afghanistan. As Dannatt claims:

> The Army was being expected to achieve success on operations with a 'make and mend attitude' that ignored the seriousness of our mission. Without the proper equity and adequate trained manpower in the short term, we risked long-term failure. It was hard, however, to persuade either politicians or Treasury civil servants of the dangers into which they were forcing us. Resourcing the armed forces in Afghanistan appropriately was not the same as some of the other spending priorities for the Government: it was life and death for the young volunteers out on the ground. We could not let them down.[22]

Stories apportion blame. That is one of their core functions linked to the idea of stories' inherent morality; their capacity to inform our sense of what counts as good and bad (see chapter one). Dannatt's memoir seeks to apportion blame for failure in Afghanistan to the politicians, or rather to ensure the blame would land on their shoulders should failure transpire. He explicitly accuses Tony Blair, the Prime Minister under whom he first served during his tenure as CGS, of lacking the "moral courage"[23] to demand the Treasury department properly fund the army's requirements. Moral argument is the primary "code of language usage and genre" (in Frank's terms) which brings meaning and coherence to *Leading from the front*. The book's title and plot are organised around the compelling theme of moral leadership, which works to convince the reader of the rightness of Dannatt's position. One means by which Dannatt does this is contrasting the morality of the soldier with that of the politician, drawing on the historical trope of war as being declared by old men, while young men fight and die. Dannatt writes:

> I was deeply frustrated that while our young men and women were fighting and dying on the front line of two of our country's wars, those of us who understood what needed to be done were still failing to bring sufficient attention to resolving even some of the most minor issues that would enable us to succeed, and bring the troops home. The phrase that came to mind was 'spoiling the ship for a ha'pennyworth of tar'. I often asked my staff what the problem really was – was it money, industrial capacity, leadership or energy? I invariably concluded that while more money would help, the real lack was in leadership and drive at the highest levels.[24]

Moreover, Dannatt explicitly contrasts his own morality to the politicians' – whom he accuses of 'parsimonious wishful thinking'[25] – by appropriating the media's depiction of him as 'A very honest General'. The mainstream British media construed Dannatt's outspokenness as honest and heroic, and Dannatt's shrewd use of this characterisation calcifies its opposite; the miserly and deceitful politician. Notably, Dannatt's and the media's main concern is that *the troops*, rather than Afghanistan, are being failed, with the emotive 'troops' moniker designed to bring additional moral weighting to the issue. The juxtaposition of characters creates a forceful moral effect: the responsibility for deaths on the battlefield and for failure in Afghanistan is to be laid at the feet of unscrupulous politicians.

Leading From the Front is a call to arms. As well as defending and justifying his actions during his time as CGS, Dannatt's story of moral leadership behoves politicians to strengthen their commitment to war. Dannatt addresses them directly:

> Where military intervention is required, it must be strong, robust and timely. Where a fractured state needs help, the international assistance needs to be broadly based and to cover not just the military lines of operation, but governance, the rule of law, justice, human rights and economic support.[26]

Towards the end of the memoir, Dannatt then refines these general sentiments on military intervention into the specific case for robust war in Afghanistan. Turning his attention to the lessons that we as a nation should learn from Afghanistan, Dannatt argues:

> What is required now – indeed, has been required, but lacking, since 2006 – is the need for Britain to conceive of its involvement in Afghanistan as what it is; namely, to accept that the country is at war. This requires of us a degree of seriousness of intent and commitment that I believe for years has been absent from our Government. The current situation requires the same sort of War-Cabinet-type commitment that Margaret Thatcher established during the Falklands War.[27]

In setting out the case for war, Dannatt calls for a stronger commitment to the liberal militarist politics which paved Britain's road to Afghanistan in the first place. The story Dannatt tells, and the failure warnings he adjures, put liberal militarism – done better, firmer, bolder – as the solution to Britain's moral weakness in war. Liberal militarism, as Basham reminds us, normalises the expansionist, interventionist use of military power to solve the problem of 'illiberal' states and the threat they pose to liberal order.[28] War, and the willingness to wage war in defence of liberal values, is a key pillar of the modern liberal democratic state. The ringing concern in Dannatt's memoir is that this pillar is in danger of crumbling. The core principles of liberal militarist politics are clearly evident in his proclamations: military intervention needs to be 'robust' and 'timely', and Britain needs a war cabinet that demonstrates a 'seriousness of intent and commitment' to war. A faltering commitment to war would suggest that Britain is neglecting its international role as 'masculinist protector', both of its own citizenry and of oppressed peoples overseas.[29] By returning to Thatcher-era militarism, when the British state was viewed as robust and masculine in its response to the threat from illiberal states, war can thus be salvaged as a means of fulfilling our international duty. Afghanistan emerges from this scenario as 'fractured', incapable of governance and in need of military intervention. Afghanistan is a security problem that needs fixing,[30] and the tragedy is that Britain lacks the political commitment to do what is required of it.

Dannatt is an elite storyteller. As head of the army, his was an integral role on behalf of the British state. He attracted significant media attention due to his unconventional outspokenness, and his lofty interlocuters included defence ministers and prime ministers. His story marshals a degree of credibility and legitimacy that is unavailable to most storytellers, even despite the authority others might derive from 'frontline' encounters with the war in Afghanistan. The pages of *Leading From the Front* carry traces of the cultural capital he embodies, and his story of the war in Afghanistan as political failure therefore carries clout. Yet it is not the only possible story of failure and nor is it the most vociferous condemnation of the war.

Strategic failure: '*Spin Zhira*'

A former officer in the regular British Army, Chris Green re-enlisted later in life as a reserve soldier to go in search of adventure in Afghanistan. The title of his memoir, *Spin Zhira*, purportedly means 'old man' in the Pashto spoken in Helmand Province where Green served one tour as an infantry officer. His story chronicles the strategic failures he witnessed first-hand in Afghanistan, as a means of casting critical judgement on the war as a whole. Green's journey to Afghanistan began with a gnawing dissatisfaction with his life of comfortable consumerism and a failing marriage. The personal failures of his unfulfilling life and deteriorating relationship come to mirror the wider failures of Britain's efforts in Afghanistan. Green is erudite, entertaining and self-deprecating. Early in the memoir he channels the words of philosopher John Stuart Mill whose thoughts about 'war to protect other human beings against tyrannical injustice'[31] being a means to regeneration provides Green with his own motivation to go to Afghanistan. As Green writes, 'I was looking for regeneration and Mill seemed to offer the solution. A war to protect other human beings against tyrannical injustice was just what I now needed to restore my self-esteem.'[32] He would later return to these words as his disillusionment with the war mounted and it appeared to Green as though he had instead *preserved* tyrannical injustice.

Whereas Dannatt expressed a resolute determination to avoid the failures to which Britain seemed destined, Green is unequivocal about failure having transpired. Indeed, *Spin Zhira* is framed as a failure narrative from the beginning, as a prelude of the story to follow:

> I was privileged to witness the incredible bravery and devotion to duty of the young men and women of the British and Danish Armed Forces as they fought a counter-insurgency campaign for which there was little popular mandate in their home countries. It is a war which, for all their extraordinary efforts, I have no doubt history will judge them to have lost by almost any measure other than body count.[33]

Despite the ironic humour and sarcasm (a code of language usage largely absent from Dannatt's more 'serious' reflection), there is a biting sense of anger in Green's memoir. It is a sense that his own and others' commitment to duty – to fighting honourably for an honourable cause – was betrayed by those in charge of conducting a mission doomed to fail. As a memoirist, Green looks for comedic relief in the daily absurdities of the war. Yet his story is as ultimately tragic as his own hopes for regeneration along with the dutiful commitment of others are trampled by actors both malign and incompetent. Green emerges from Afghanistan jaded and cynical, with a dismal view of international forces' accomplishments there. The anger seeping through the pages of *Spin Zhira* reflects the bitter truth that, as Green puts it, 'I had seen men killed and others grievously wounded in the pursuit of these [war] aims.'[34] These dead soldiers, along with the living veterans whose ideals of duty had been thwarted, and along with the people of Afghanistan, had been betrayed. It is not simply that the war had failed, but their efforts and in some cases their lives, had been failed too.

Once deployed, Green quickly arrived at the view that *strategic failures* on multiple simultaneous fronts were underpinning the disaster unfolding in Helmand. As Green recalls a moment of reflection early in his tour, 'Everything I'd seen over the last two months had convinced me that the UK strategy in Afghanistan was deeply flawed.'[35] He then develops his analysis of these strategic flaws:

> The breathtaking hubris of DfID's [Department for International Development] nation-building ambitions, combined with the superficial resources at their disposal and an absence of competence with which to execute the plan, were a recipe for disaster. Unfortunately, there was no plan B, and no one brave enough to put the brakes on this particular runaway train. By 2012 the international community were pinning their hopes on a corrupt Karzai regime in Kabul while

failing to take into account the influence of the international opium black market.

> *Joint Doctrine Publication 3-40 Security and Stabilisation: The Military Contribution* broke the mould of verbose British doctrine when it simply and bluntly stated: *Failed states fail their people.* There was no doubt in my mind that the GIRoA [Government of the Islamic Republic of Afghanistan] government was failing its people. Propping up this dysfunctional administration was at best prolonging the failure, at worst it was amplifying the catastrophe.[36]

According to Green's analysis, sources of Britain's failure to bring security and stabilisation to Helmand were multiple, including the delusional nation-building ambitions which the British state was ill-equipped to fulfil, the corruption of the Afghan government, and widespread complicity in drug cultivation and trafficking. In the face of such strategic miscalculations, the military effort was destined to fail from the beginning, with the only vague notion of 'success' being measured in body counts. Green is fiercely critical both of the British military approach and of Afghan attempts at governance, though his criticism carries a different inflection in each case. The British he accuses of failing to plan for and resource the objectives they had set themselves for nation-building and democratising Afghanistan. He also bemoans the military for undermining its own strategic effort through wanton disregard for collateral damage to people's lives, homes and livelihoods. The Afghans, on the other hand, are accused of rather more fundamental character failures, including perpetuating a 'dishonest administration' which was 'corrupted beyond redemption',[37] and of empowering 'incompetent' and 'narco-compliant' officials whose 'sole interest was personal gain'.[38] He also views the local population as stubbornly resistant to change by virtue of their 'deeply conservative rural values',[39] 'absurd practice of gender segregation',[40] and their rejection of Western-style democracy and religious tolerance. There is more than a hint in Green's criticism, then, that *our* failure is ultimately because of *theirs*.

Throughout his story, Green paints colourful portraits of his Afghan interlocuters whom he meets throughout his tour of Helmand. These include Haji Jalander, the 'wise old Muj'[41] (Mujahideen) fighter who now mentors young Afghans taking up arms against the invaders; Mirajdin the 'accidental insurgent'[42] whom the British suspected of detonating a fatal roadside bomb; Balool Khan the chairman of the Nahr-E-Saraj District Community Council, a 'wise old bird' who saw the Council as existing simply 'to part the infidel with his money'[43]; Salim Rodi the corrupt 'dipsomaniac'[44]; Nahr-E-Saraj district governor in the pay of the opium trade; and Haji Gul, the dependable Hawala-dar (money lender) whom the British Special Forces arrested on suspicion of 'aiding and abetting the Taliban'.[45] Unlike many Afghanistan war memoirs, whereby Afghan interlocuters are either thinly described or else are absent from the narrative,[46] Green turns these people into rich and roundly defined characters, writing several long reflections imaginatively projecting himself into their lives. In doing so, Green shows empathy with these people and their struggles, but he also cannot help but orientalise them, for example, by attributing to them simplistic motivations of revenge and tribal rivalry. The picture of Afghanistan which emerges from Green's memoir is of a severe people with a mistrustful nature, bound by ancient tribal codes. The narrative thus feeds the popular image of Afghans as 'an unruly, backward and fundamentally untameable people'.[47]

Green's closing comments on the war and his personal contribution show a clear sense of hopelessness and futility:

> In the nine months I've been here nothing much has changed in MOB [Main Operating Base] Price. I've passed through it's fortified walls almost unnoticed. My presence has done little, if anything, to alter the daily rhythms of the place as I'd hoped it might when I first embarked on my journey. With the benefit of hindsight I now know better. Nothing much has changed in Nahr-E-Saraj in half a millennium.[48]

Ultimately, Green's story of strategic failure leaves us with a return to the politics of distancing and disavowal which have characterised Western engagement with Afghanistan for centuries. Afghanistan is constructed as immutable and hostile, destined to remain an ungovernable 'tribal' space. Failure is pre-determined by Afghanistan's 'medieval' nature: attempts to modernise and democratise the country are pointless and the British should have known better. Green's personal view on departure from Helmand follows a wider disavowal of complicity with regard to Afghanistan.[49] Foreign actors such as the British military enter and leave Afghanistan with impunity. Due to Afghanistan's fundamental pre-modern 'otherness', the British are justified in their withdrawal from and abandonment of its people, leaving them to their own ungovernable mess. Such disavowal also negates the damage that the British have inflicted on Helmand. They are purportedly leaving it in much the same state as they found it – no better and no worse – but with their own trail of blood and lost treasures to mournfully reflect on. In contrast to Dannatt's call for stronger British militarism, Green's story thus gives us a perspective on the futility of war, but one which denies (or at least avoids) responsibility for Afghanistan and British intervention there.

Moral failure: *'Soldier Box'*

Joe Glenton is a former lance corporal (junior enlisted soldier) who achieved public notoriety, or acclaim, for turning against the war in Afghanistan. Glenton's memoir, *Soldier Box*, tells how his tour of duty in Afghanistan led him to question the war and gradually to disagree with it on moral grounds.[50] Rather than return to Afghanistan for a second tour, as he was obligated to do under orders from his superiors, Glenton chose to become a 'deserter' and fled the country with the knowledge that he would be charged with going 'AWOL' (absent without leave) if and when he returned to the UK. After spending time in Southeast Asia and Australia reflecting on his experiences and his options, Glenton returns to the army to face his AWOL charge and to use the ensuing legal battle to mount a public campaign against the war in Afghanistan. Despite facing up to a decade in prison, ostensibly for his desertion, Glenton ultimately serves four months in military prison before being released from the army, his position on the war vindicated by the military's hapless failure in refuting his anti-war arguments. In contrast to Dannatt and Green's stories, which give vehement condemnation of political or strategic failure, but which do not question the underpinning ideology of war, Glenton's story seeks to undermine the edifice of imperialist war itself as morally wrong.

Soldier Box describes Glenton's gradual moral and political awakening as his tour of duty in Afghanistan progressed. Prior to enlisting, he describes himself as naive and politically unaware. In Glenton's words, 'I held a dangerous view that a government was some kind of benign, impartial organization that looked after its citizens. I was a chump ready-made for the army, indifferent, apolitical and working class.'[51] Yet his questioning attitude towards the war began shortly after his arrival in Afghanistan. Glenton was deployed as a logistics specialist based in the huge American airbase at Kandahar. The reports coming to him from 'outside the wire' suggested that there was little logical coherence to the war being fought. As he recalled:

> We had daily briefings reporting the deaths of 'armed men'. They were assigned different names like Taliban, militia or insurgents, but most often it was just armed men. I started to think about the vagueness of it all, though I kept it to myself... 'Just get on with it,' was the mantra we had been given. And curiosity was out of my pay scale.[52]

Despite being discouraged from thinking about or questioning the war, Glenton began to critically unpick the logic and morality of the war. He describes this as a gradual process of political awakening:

> I didn't just become a radical overnight. Lots of others seemed to think the war was stupid or at least dubious. My staff sergeant, my troop commander, some of the other privates had all seemed to think along similar lines at various points. I was responding to what I was learning, and no contract in the world could restrain me. I saw no justness in the war.[53]

Glenton's story shares much in common with Green's, in that they both conform to a well-worn narrative script of war turning idealistic young men (or in Green's case, an old one) into jaded and cynical (older) men. In this sense, both stories resonate with the wider canon of Afghanistan war memoirs which give an overwhelming sense of being 'disappointed by war'.[54] Yet where Glenton's story differs from Green's – and most others – is that his disillusionment eventually mounts into active resistance against the war whereas others' do not. In an act of passive resistance, Green resigns from the army following his tour in Afghanistan. But the narrative of strategic failure does not provide the same thundering condemnation that stories of war as moral catastrophe level against the military and political establishment.

Although his tour of Afghanistan becomes the basis for his act of protest, the story Glenton tells in *Soldier Box* ultimately appears more concerned with his own struggle against the army than it is about Afghanistan or Afghans. The character he portrays is of a lone hero fighting doggedly against the system trying to destroy him. As with other stories told by anti-war veterans,[55] the codes of language usage and genre which make this characterisation possible bear a striking resemblance to the norms of militarised masculinity which underpin stories of war-making in the first place. That is, the privileged persona of the militarised masculine soldier becomes the very basis for dissent, thereby complicating the relationship between dissent and its object.[56] Glenton makes this tension explicit in the memoir's opening pages when he claims that 'They don't know what to do with me, because I am attacking them with the same bloody-mindedness they instilled in me and I am doing it well.'[57] The talk of 'attack' and 'bloody-mindedness' focuses the reader on Glenton's heroic resistance as a feature of the archetypal masculine soldier hero. This position is further reinforced by the 'hardening' of Glenton's stance against the government. As he writes:

> I would state my views and go at them as hard as I could. I doubted I would win in the sense of a final submission but I was not a deserter. Cowards don't stake their liberty on anything, or take on governments and bruise them. If it was going to be prison, I wanted it known exactly why: because I had refused to return to war.[58]

The characters portrayed in veterans' stories are never morally neutral: stories guide reflection on the moral character of characters.[59] In stories of resistance such as *Soldier Box*, the opposite side of moral failure is moral triumph for the individual (anti)war hero.

At the end of the book, however, Glenton connects this individual triumph to the wider politics of which he is becoming conscious. In contrast to Dannatt, who calls for *more* liberal militarism, Glenton identifies the actions of liberal democratic military force as the central problem:

> My own politics have gone from zero to very distinct and I do not pretend that I can divorce politics from the world around me anymore. I am still told that the society I live in is liberal and democratic and that this is 'lucky' and that I should be thankful that I don't live somewhere awful like Afghanistan. What they forget to tell you is that Afghanistan is as awful as it is today *because* of the actions of 'democracies'. Whatever may have been liberal or democratic about liberal democracy seems to have died in the wars it started. This is not lucky at all. The fact is liberal democracy makes a poor case for itself by militarising young men and women in the name of security or progress and sending them to kill people just like themselves for profit, or influence or whatever. This is the Civilian Box. After all, my government put me away for refusing to help dominate and kill people.[60]

War as moral failure begets a stronger challenge to British militarism than do stories of war as political or strategic failure. Indeed, it is the only story that guides us towards anti-war politics, which loses faith in war itself – or at least the 'war on terror' – as something of moral value. Even though resistance to war is never complete and is often articulated through the terms of militarism itself, stories of veterans turning against war can contribute to 'projects of peace' through the moral awakenings they exemplify.[61] At the end of the book, Glenton fleetingly names imperialism as the moral and ideological offense, while rejecting the view that the war in Afghanistan was simply a case of 'humanitarian intervention being executed poorly'.[62] He would later go on embrace anti-imperialism along with class struggle as part of a more developed form of resistance to militarism.[63] The kernels of this anti-imperialist politics are traceable in *Soldier Box*, albeit in a way that avoids stating what Britain's responsibility to Afghanistan should now entail following the moral failure of imperialist invasion. What Glenton's story ultimately tells us, when read in dialogue with others' such as Dannatt and Green's, is that the war in Afghanistan not only failed in its conduct or execution – that is, that it failed to achieve aims that were in principle legitimate – but that the very idea of the war was morally perverse and that all such war should be resisted.

The Triumph of Madness: '*A Fort of Nine Towers*'

Qais Akbar Omar, whose memoir *A Fort of Nine Towers* I first discussed in Chapter 1, was a young boy when war broke out in the Kabul neighbourhood where he lived with his parents and siblings, his cousins and their families, and his beloved grandfather.[64] His story begins with the arrival of the 'holy warriors' who began fighting for control of Afghanistan, destroying Omar's family home in the process. The 'fort of nine towers' is a large house on the other side of the city where Omar and his family take refuge from the fighting. When even the fort becomes too dangerous, Omar flees the city with his parents and siblings, leaving the rest of his family in Kabul. As factional conflict engulfs more and more of the country, the family journey all over northern Afghanistan relying on distant relatives and on the kindness of strangers to shelter from the war. When word reaches them that Kabul is safe again, the family return only to face further destruction followed by the cruel and oppressive Taliban regime which took hold in 1996. Omar's story tells of his family's struggle for survival against the devastation that befell Afghanistan, and of his determination to avoid the pain of separation from his loved ones. The book is a testimony to the losses he suffered while coming of age in a war. As he begins:

> Uncertainty hangs thick like the dust in the air. I cannot see where the path of life will lead me. It is not in my nature to sit and wait for something to happen. For the moment, though, unable to look forward, I have settled for gazing backward, to chronicle what I have witnessed in these few strange and turbulent years I have known.[65]

Rather than war as a kind of failure per se, Omar defines war in Afghanistan simply as evil, or as a victory for evil men bent on plunder and destruction. 'The triumph of madness' is the title for the section of his memoir about life under the bizarre cruelty of Taliban rule. Another section, 'In the time of Shaitan' (the devil) tells of Omar's brutal encounter with a factional commander who tortured him, and of the death of his favourite cousin Wakeel caused by a rocket attack in Kabul. War is the result of killers and thieves in pursuit of power and riches, and Omar and his family bear the cost of their greed and of the Taliban's fanatical obsession with a perverse form of piety. Early in the memoir, Omar scorns the hypocrisy of these people: 'Our country was being destroyed more every hour, by factions whose leaders slaughtered thousands during the day, then talked like holy men on their broadcasts during the night.'[66] The war is senseless, a 'storm of ignorance'.[67] As well as making Omar a witness to rape and mass slaughter, and a victim of torture and bereavement, the war keeps him separated from his family, his education, and from the joys of flying kites with his cousins on the rooftops of their houses. In Omar's story, war is about the brutality and criminality of others and the grief of his family as they became refugees in their own country.

Omar loves Afghanistan, its people and its culture. He implores his reader to 'become curious about the many layers of Afghan culture that so unexpectedly and for so many of the wrong reasons have become the focus of the world's attention'.[68] Despite the incredible pain in his story, Omar hopes to educate a Western audience accustomed to viewing Afghanistan through a prism of death and depravity. He writes about the beautiful carpets that his family bought and sold, and that he later learned to weave. He writes also about his family's love of literature, their nomadic heritage, and about the kindness and respect of strangers who helped them survive the war. The book is full of lovingly attentive descriptions of the people and places that became part of his journey, like the following portrait of his cousin:

> Wakeel's voice was deep. Like Grandfather's, it was always calm. He always spoke very clearly in a way that made even grown-ups pay attention to what he said. And he always chose his words very carefully. His face was like a fast-changing sky and revealed his thoughts even before he expressed them in words. His eyes would grow large one moment and tight the next. His mouth changed shaped with his emotions.[69]

To read such descriptions in dialogue with veterans' stories is to read of people full of love and character, in contrast to the typically reductive portraits of Afghans as backward villagers with simplistic feuds and medieval practices. Indeed, to seek out Afghan voices on the war helps to resist the orientalist narratives that veterans' stories perpetuate – inadvertently or otherwise – through the half-formed impressions they are prone to offer of and on behalf of the Afghan people.

At the end of the book, the dialogue with veterans' stories becomes more direct when Omar shares his view on foreign intervention in Afghanistan. As he writes:

> My mother was right. The foreigners were more interested in their own politics than in our country. They chased the Taliban away for a while. But they brought back the same factions who had claimed to be Mujahedin and who had destroyed our country ... Many of the foreigners who came here claiming to help us left very rich. We are waiting to see what they will build, besides their military bases.[70]

His story identifies the failure of international solidarity that enabled the destruction in Afghanistan, along with the cursory nature of engagement with Afghan history and politics which led Western politicians to empower the 'warlords' in the wake of the former's invasion.[71]. War in Afghanistan, for Western powers, is about their own politics, or about adventure, self-renewal or self-righteousness. For Omar and his family, it is simply about survival. Yet Omar's story still leaves open the question and problem of what should be done about the violence in his country. His vivid descriptions of rape and of sadistic torturers might, for example, be read as just cause for 'humanitarian intervention' by Western militarists. Stories possess 'interpretive openness', and as such they allow differently positioned readers to view their responses as directly informed by the story being told.⁷² Stories are – as Frank puts it – 'out of control'.⁷³ In labelling the war as evil, and the Taliban as mad, Omar risks depoliticising the conflict in ways that legitimise a military response from the invading imperialist countries. Indeed, these are the very same labels that the American-led coalition used to justify their war against the Taliban and to evade responsibility for the damage they caused in the process. Dialogue, then, is multi-layered; discordant voices are sometimes curiously resonant with one another, even while they speak of war from radically different perspectives. Without therefore wishing to draw false equivalence between Afghan condemnations of 'evil' terrorists and similar pronouncements by Western imperialists, it is sometimes necessary to view the dialogue between their stories as complexly interwoven.

Conclusion

The cultural politics of veterans' narratives cannot avoid Afghanistan. So central is it to Britain's twenty-first-century encounters with war, the 'problem' of failure in Afghanistan haunts veterans' stories and the politics that encircle them. Afghanistan forms the setting, subject, and often the villainous and/or damsel-in-distress character in these stories. As I have shown in this chapter, failure in Afghanistan looks different depending on the story being told. Failure unfolds differently in each case, with different actors, events and decisions held to account, and different lessons to be learned. Some in Britain attempt to square the circle of failure through what we might call the 'heroic caveat'; that is, the belief that whatever the political circumstances of the war, the soldiers who fought in Afghanistan did so with immeasurable pride and commitment to duty. For example, even as the Taliban swept back into power in July–August 2021, General Dannatt was able to write in *The Telegraph* that 'for us, even if the strategic objectives were wrong and the operational paths flawed, the British soldier on the ground did all that was asked of him or her, and more'.⁷⁴ The heroism of the individual solider thus redeems the failure of the war itself. Meanwhile, the British government has never apologised for the damage inflicted on Afghanistan, its territory or its people. Some British politicians have issued calls for apology, but with only British veterans and bereaved families as the parties deserving recompense, and no mention of an apology owed to Afghanistan itself.⁷⁵

Reading these stories through the dual notions of intertextuality and heteroglossia, it is possible to hear how different voices on the war in Afghanistan overlap and diverge. Each of the veterans' stories share codes of 'language usage and genre'[76] – such as militarised masculine language and a knowledge of military operations – making them resonate. All four of the stories discussed in this chapter share different perspectives on Afghanistan, making them part of a broader 'library' of Afghanistan war memoirs. What kind of failure story each memoir tells matters because different kinds of failure afford different political responses. Some of these responses are explicit in the narrative (e.g., Dannatt, Glenton), others are implicit in the conclusions drawn by the author (e.g., Green), and others are left open (e.g., Omar). While allowing for the possibility that failure in Afghanistan was multi-faceted, comprised simultaneously of political, strategic, ideological and human failings, I argue that *narrative* is integral in persuading us that different faults and thus different resolutions lie at the heart of the matter.

Moreover, responses are not equal in terms of the political and material consequences they entail for Afghanistan. A liberal militarist response which posits political weakness as the central failure, and stronger intervention as the solution, bears obvious flaws in that it legitimises racialised violence towards Afghanistan as the cost of pursuing security for the West.[77] Likewise, war as strategic failure exacerbated by a mixture of Afghan intransigence and British arrogance leads us towards isolationist non-interventionism, which is problematic insofar as it disavows Western complicity in Afghanistan's problems and shrugs off ongoing commitment and solidarity. Viewing the war's founding premises as ideologically harmful comes closer to building a just foundation for political relations with Afghanistan, but here also lies the risk of privileging heroic opposition in the West as the main ingredient of change. Responses which centre Afghan agency and which respect the role of Afghan politics and culture in Afghanistan's future are therefore to be sought.[78] At the end of his memoir, Omar quotes the words of a cousin with whom he shares such a vision of Afghan agency. The cousin tells him:

> Somebody has to have the guts to step in. We know that no country is here to help us. They are here to help themselves. We have to tell the world that Afghanistan has a new owner, and that owner is our generation.[79]

Interpretive openness in Omar's memoir is, here in the story's coda, poised against the affirmation of Afghan agency as the necessary fulcrum of change. Western responses to the war in Afghanistan ought now to practice an engaged, respectful solidarity which both renounces militarism and acknowledges Afghan agency in the struggle Afghanistan faces today. As Manchanda suggests, 'Our task, as academics, activists and those invested in a more just global order, is to stop living under the illusion that we can be non-partisan bystanders. We are both implicated and capable – good starting points to initiate change.'[80] Veterans' stories of fighting the war in Afghanistan have a role to play, but they must ultimately be decentred and heard alongside – in dialogue with – Afghans' own stories. Moreover, and to reiterate a key premise of a cultural politics of narrative, we must consider what kind of politics their stories enable, what ethical possibilities they lead us towards, and what worlds they create.

Notes

1. Tidy, 'The gender politics of "ground truth" in the military dissent movement'.
2. Harari, *The Ultimate Experience*.
3. Woodward and Jenkings, *Bringing War to Book*.
4. Ibid.
5. Ibid., p. 115.
6. See, for example, Woodward and Jenkings, *Brining War to Book*; Dwyer, 'Making sense of the muddle'; Kleinreesink, 'On military memoirs'; Kleinreesink and Soeters, 'Truth and (self)censorship in military memoirs'; Bourke, 'Bodily pain, combat and the politics of memoirs'; Dyvik, '"Valhalla rising"'; Dyvik, 'Of bats and bodies'; Chouliaraki, 'From war memoirs to milblogs'; Wasinksi, 'When the war machine produces its enemies'.
7. Woodward and Jenkings, '"This place isn't worth the left boot of one of our boys"', p. 495.
8. Smith and Watson, *Reading Autobiography*, p. 1.
9. Frank, *Letting Stories Breathe*, p. 16.
10. Woodward and Jenkings, *Bringing War to Book*.
11. Dwyer, 'Making sense of the muddle'.
12. Green, *Spin Zhira*, p. 184.
13. Mercer, *We Were Warriors*, p. 84.
14. Ledwidge, *Investment in Blood*, p. 175.
15. Manchanda, *Imagining Afghanistan*.
16. Ibid., p. 5.
17. Said, *Culture and Imperialism*, p. xiii.
18. Fairclough, 'Discourse and text', p. 195.
19. Frank, 'Practicing dialogical narrative analysis', p. 35.
20. Dannatt, *Leading From the Front*.
21. Ibid., p. 243.
22. Ibid., p. 302.
23. Ibid., p. 243.
24. Ibid., p. 384.

25. Ibid., p. 370.
26. Ibid., p. 229.
27. Ibid., p. 428.
28. Basham, 'Liberal militarism as insecurity, desire and ambivalence'.
29. Ibid., p. 36.
30. Manchanda, *Imagining Afghanistan*.
31. Quoted in Green, *Spin Zhira*, p. 58.
32. Ibid.
33. Ibid., p. xi.
34. Ibid., postscript, p. 16.
35. Ibid., pp. 262–3.
36. Ibid., p. 263.
37. Ibid., p. 178.
38. Ibid., p. 307.
39. Ibid., p. 184.
40. Ibid., p. 186.
41. Ibid., p. 398.
42. Ibid., p. 392.
43. Ibid., p. 298.
44. Ibid., p. 178.
45. Ibid., p. 203.
46. Woodward and Jenkings, '"This place isn't worth the left boot of one of our boys"'.
47. Manchanda, *Imagining Afghanistan*, p. 40.
48. Green, *Spin Zhira*, p. 416.
49. Manchanda, *Imagining Afghanistan*.
50. Glenton, *Soldier Box*.
51. Ibid., p. 8.
52. Ibid., p. 42.
53. Ibid., p. 61.
54. Woodward and Jenkings, '"This place isn't worth the left boot of one of our boys"', p. 505.
55. See, for example, Tidy, 'The gender politics of "ground truth" in the military dissent movement'; Cockburn and Enloe, 'Militarism, patriarchy and peace movements'.
56. Bulmer and Eichler, 'Unmaking militarized masculinity'.
57. Glenton, *Soldier Box*. p. xi.
58. Ibid., p. 103.
59. Frank, *Letting Stories Breathe*.
60. Glenton, *Soldier Box*, pp. 167–8.
61. Messner, *Guys Like Me*, p. 1.
62. Glenton, *Soldier Box*, p. 166.
63. Glenton, *Veteranhood*.
64. Omar, *A Fort of Nine Towers*.
65. Ibid. p. 6.
66. Ibid., p. 56.
67. Ibid., p. 169.
68. Ibid., p. 396.
69. Ibid., pp. 54–5.

70. Ibid., p. 375.
71. Manchanda, *Imagining Afghanistan*.
72. Frank, *Letting Stories Breathe*.
73. Ibid., p. 35.
74. Dannatt, 'The West has squandered its early success in Afghanistan'.
75. Scott, 'Johnson should apologise to troops and families over Afghanistan, says Tory MP'.
76. Frank, 'Practicing dialogical narrative analysis', p. 35.
77. Basham, 'Liberal militarism as insecurity, desire and ambivalence'.
78. Manchanda, *Imagining Afghanistan*.
79. Omar, *A Fort of Nine Towers*, p. 388.
80. Manchanda, *Imagining Afghanistan*, p. 225.

CHAPTER 7

Trauma Stories, Surfing and Undoing the Residue of Militarism

Not long after I first joined, I got into a fight with somebody and strangled him, and nearly actually flippin' killed him, right. I was like 'Fuckin' hell, I've gone over the top here', 'cos I just totally fuckin' lost it. And this NCO [Non-Commissioned Officer] come running over and said, 'What's up Graham, what you done?' And I said, 'I think I've killed him'. And he run over and gave him the kiss of life and all that, and then he came back round. And then he [NCO] went 'Fuckin' hell, mate', he says, 'Keep this fuckin' quiet or you'll be in court'. And they just brushed it all under the carpet. And I was like 'For fuck sake', you know, really they should have done something about it then and I would have had the help back then.

Graham began his life in the army with an all-too-familiar story of childhood trauma from a violent upbringing. As we sat opposite one another, in the office of the veterans' surfing charity at which he was now a beneficiary and a volunteer in equal measure, Graham told me how he'd experienced PTSD – post-traumatic stress disorder – in one form or another, for most of his life. As he put it, 'I can't remember being at peace with myself, having a nice fuckin' time, ever.' He'd then spent his entire army career fighting, not simply, or even predominantly, with 'the enemy', but because fighting was normal. Any notion of a threat – a glare, an off-handed comment, a punch thrown in his direction – would unleash a torrent of violence. The abuse he'd suffered as a child had taught him that trust in others was misplaced and had made aggression a habitual response to hostility. The army then provided an environment whereby aggression was tolerated, cultivated even, and where incidents of extreme violence would be 'brushed under the carpet'. In 2008, many years after he left the army, Graham was diagnosed with 'chronic severe PTSD with comorbidity . . . and all that sort of stuff', which according to his clinician derived 50 percent from his childhood and 50 percent from his army career. To Graham, diagnosis came as a relief because it offered an explanation for his behaviour, for his anger, and for the feeling of chronic anxiety that wracked his body up with a frenzied desperation.

Whether or not the clinical PTSD diagnosis continued to provide Graham with a useful framework for self-understanding, it was clear that he carried inside him a legacy of trauma. Or rather, a lifetime of responding in kind to violence and aggression – together with the traumatic 'incidents' which clinical trauma language packaged into neat time-bounded parcels – had left deep imprints in Graham's psyche and on his body. He felt it as a tightness in his chest, 'horrible . . . like heartburn', when going about his daily routine. He felt it as a tearfulness that came over him when he sat alone 'going over the same things in your head'. He felt it in his 'fuckin' terrible' concentration, like in the interview we were recording, 'I'm having problems with it now; like I'm not sure if that's me meds and that, but it's just; you get like a real anxiety, really high levels of anxiety, which is what I've got now.' Not to mention his sleep, his loss of self-confidence and, as Graham summed it all up, 'I just have problems, you know, on a day-to-day basis really.'

In this chapter, I focus on stories – like Graham's – of the traumatised ex-military body, of the body's 'unlearning' of trauma and violence by going surfing and spending time in nature, and on how such stories depart from institutional narratives which define 'trauma' as a particular psychological illness to be treated via individual, clinical therapies.[1] I read trauma as a direct consequence of British militarism; it is the embodied residue of time spent inhabiting a violent, hyper-masculine institution and of being required to enact violence on behalf of the nation. This chapter narrows the analytical lens from the cultural narratives through which politics unfolds in the domain of veterans and militarism more generally, to a more intimate analysis of veterans' personal stories of healing from the effects of trauma. In rounding out the book's empirical contribution, I therefore wish to consider how veterans themselves might 'pick up the pieces' of a life project dismantled by trauma. Still within focus, however, are the institutional-level narratives which seek to govern how trauma or 'PTSD' is represented, and how it is treated, for it is against this narrative backdrop that veterans' individual healing journeys are realised (or not). There is much at stake for cultural politics in terms of how trauma is narrated, and the institutions central to British militarism (including the Ministry of Defence, and in the context of PTSD, the psychiatric profession) have invested a great deal of money and research attempting to ensure that the 'official' story of trauma – its conceptualisation, prevalence, and treatment – remains dominant. I explore these stakes in this chapter while seeking to show how veterans' stories of surfing and PTSD might advance our understanding of trauma's role in the cultural politics of veterans' narratives.

The chapter returns to interviews I conducted in 2012–2013 as part of my PhD research on the role of surfing for veterans diagnosed with PTSD. By re-examining these interviews, I have sought to explore and construct additional layers of meaning which were less apparent to me in the original study.[2] I consider how three veterans' stories of surfing and PTSD enact a politics of trauma which promotes compassion, which emphasises the body – rather than the 'disordered' mind – as the location of both trauma and healing, and which highlights the inadequacy of institutional trauma narratives to chart the course of 'post-traumatic' suffering and the movement away from it.[3]

At the level of public awareness, trauma stories often crowd out other stories about veterans. They come in many forms: newspaper exposés about 'tidal waves' of PTSD flooding out of the military, shock documentaries about our 'broken heroes', charity features calling for more support for traumatised veterans, and autobiographies revealing the chaotic realities of post-war suffering. As numerous authors and commentators have remarked, PTSD is the dominant and sometimes the only available narrative of post-war suffering.[4] Historical and cultural analyses of the PTSD diagnosis have charted its cultural ascendency following the Vietnam War, with several scholars discussing the political controversies sparked by widespread application of PTSD to understanding the psychological damage of war.[5] The notion of PTSD as a framework for categorising and explaining post-war suffering is further reified by the vast body of academic research on the subject. Much of this research, it has been claimed, 'routinely objectifies veterans and their experiences' by abstracting, categorising and pathologising the state of being in which veterans find themselves after war.[6] 'PTSD' thus leaves veterans' stories *over-invested* with meaning, without attending to the materiality and complexity of their experiences.

Trauma stories exemplify another of Frank's story 'capacities': the capacity to create 'trouble'. Frank writes that 'Socio-narratology's interest in trouble is twofold: first, how do stories present models of dealing with different kinds of trouble, and second, how do stories themselves make trouble?'[7] 'Trouble', in narratives terms, is about the capacity of stories to help us make sense of life when things go wrong, and to articulate a means of resolving the trouble. Speaking to the first of these twofold interests, PTSD manifests as a particular kind of trouble: a pathology that must be dealt with. PTSD is trouble not only for the individual veteran and his or her family, but also for an army of clinicians, researchers, charities, policymakers, psychiatrists and military personnel who attempt to deal with this trouble on veterans' behalf. Stories about PTSD, from institutional narratives to personal trauma stories, present different models, first, of conceptualising, and then dealing with, the damage of war. As this chapter unfolds, I will show how veterans' use of surfing to understand and deal with trauma challenges the orthodoxy of clinical trauma discourse, and that these veterans' stories therefore have an important role to play in the cultural politics of veterans' narratives.

Concerning the second interest – 'how do stories themselves make trouble?' – it is important to consider how trauma stories are *contested*, and have been so ever since psychiatrists, researchers, military officers and others began arguing over how to conceptualise the trauma of war: from 'shell-shock', to 'battle fatigue', 'soldier's heart', 'post-traumatic stress disorder', and, contemporarily, 'traumatic brain injury' and 'moral injury'.[8] Of all these constructions, PTSD has been the most enduring and the most generative in terms of debate, intervention, financial compensation and research. The ubiquity of trauma stories is itself considered a source of 'trouble'; that PTSD becomes the *expected* narrative from soldiers returning home from war, thus turning trauma into a self-fulfilling prophecy. The cultural prevalence of trauma, together with its close association with wartime combat, raises concerns among disparate actors. For military psychiatrists, the rise of a 'culture of trauma' in Western societies inflates the 'problem' of PTSD such that, in the words of psychiatrist Simon Wessely, 'we may not face an epidemic of PTSD, but we have experienced an epidemic of stories about it'.[9] Meanwhile, for critical scholars and anti-war activists, the dominance of PTSD displaces alternative post-war stories, and for returning veterans, 'virtually inoculate[s] them against a political interpretation of their own experience'.[10]

Much of the 'trouble' with trauma stories can be attributed to the *constructed* nature of the PTSD category. 'Diagnoses are invented, not discovered', writes Alison Howell, meaning that they come into being under particular historical and political circumstances as a means of explaining psychological suffering as a particular *kind* of pathology.[11] One of the primary effects of the PTSD diagnosis is to medicalise and individualise post-war suffering. Rather than Harari's 'flesh witnesses' – those who have collectively witnessed and experienced the destruction of war – PTSD turns veterans into the pathological *victims* of war. Veterans become 'ill' rather than 'angry', their thoughts 'disordered' rather than accurately reflecting the traumatic reality of things. As Howell continues, 'Treating trauma as a medical problem has meant that it is approached as something to be cured, safely sequestering the experiences of, for example, war, in the private realm, and removing them from political scrutiny and action'.[12] PTSD thus takes something that is at heart a social and moral affliction – war and its deadly consequences – and turns both the explanation and the cure for it into something private and individual.[13]

The notion of PTSD as an individual medical problem is a core component of the 'institutional trauma narrative'; that is, the formal institutional story of PTSD elaborated over many years, through diverse media, and by many 'tellers' within (primarily) the military and the medical establishment. Tracing the architecture of the institutional trauma narrative, Molendijk and colleagues write that 'In this narrative, the cause of post-traumatic problems is a stressful event, and the impossibility to integrate this event into one's mental system. The event is abnormal, and the resulting mental health problems are normal.'[14] Trauma is defined in terms of the psychological symptoms to which it gives rise, with other potential meanings – such as moral and political ones – thereby displaced. The institutional narrative also identifies the appropriate response to trauma as *integrating* it into one's psyche as a means of restoring normal functioning. As Molendijk and colleagues continue:

> The answer is then redeveloping a functional 'mindset' or cognitive scheme that is effective in integrating the event as much as is possible. In this narrative, the meaning of PTSD is a-moral and a-political. Neither the soldier nor anyone else is to blame for PTSD. It is an individual illness, which consists of dysfunctional thoughts and behaviors.[15]

For the military and for the medical profession, the institutional trauma narrative is useful because it fixes trauma into a clear narrative logic of event, diagnosis and treatment. In this sense, PTSD diagnosis and 'cure' can function as a means of disciplinary control; as a way to 'control and subjugate' veterans' memory.[16] Scholars such as Ken MacLeish and Zoe Wool criticise the institutional trauma narrative for distorting veterans' experiences of life after war. For MacLeish, PTSD 'makes a single object out of a whole range of experiences' in that it gathers together a broad range of causes, violent exposures and symptom types into a single explanatory framework.[17] Indeed, it *makes* experience *into* symptoms, whereby routine features of soldiering – such as preparing the body to commit and be exposed to violence, through the use of violence itself – suddenly become pathological. Likewise, for Wool, PTSD 'stands in for a vast and subtle array of experiences', such that feelings of sadness and melancholy, anger and bitterness, violence and aggression, together with suicidal urges, alcoholism, and transformations in veterans' ways of being in and moving through the world all get bundled into the same 'condition'.[18] Veterans with completely different life experiences and afflictions come to be understood under the same reductive label and offered the same psychologised remedies.

While numerous critiques of the institutional trauma narrative have identified the social and political problems with dominant conceptualisations of PTSD, less well explored in the critical trauma literature are veterans' stories of actually living with the legacies of trauma and militarised violence, of attempting to manage it and to deal with it on their own terms. Veterans' stories show the complexities of living with trauma and they centre modes of dealing with trauma which do not conform to the institutional narrative's template of individual psychological treatment and recovery. The stories of surfing veterans emphasise being in nature and the reformulation of trusting relationships with others as the central methods of coming to terms with trauma's legacy and seeking a liveable existence. In doing so, these stories introduce compassion to the cultural politics of veterans' narratives, though not necessarily in a utopian sense that extends compassion to all others or even all veterans.

I encountered these veterans and their stories as part of the research I conducted with a UK-based veterans' surfing charity. The original aim of the research was to explore the impact of surfing in the lives of veterans diagnosed with PTSD.[19] To do this, I interviewed sixteen members of the charity (some on multiple occasions) to listen to their stories at length. I also spent time hanging out with the group at their drop-in centre, surfing with them at their weekly 'beach clinics', and living among them during three residential weeks at remote guesthouses along the English coastline. The latter were often the most intense and the most intriguing spaces within the group's environment and subculture. The residentials incorporated numerous activities including surfing, yoga, meditation, group-based art therapy and coastal walking. These were intense and intimate spaces, with around eight veterans, two members of staff, a psychotherapist and me, living together, sharing meals together and taking part in the activities together for a week. These spaces were a haven for the veterans, an escape from the intensities of day-to-day life with a 'mental illness', and an opportunity to reflect and work on their wellbeing in the company of supportive others. As with the weekly beach clinics and the interviews I carried out (some during the residential weeks) I learned much about the veterans, the group and their subculture by spending this time with them. In this chapter, I have chosen to zoom in on three of the veterans' stories, each of which illustrates a different layer of trauma, surfing and the aftermath of British militarism. In particular, I focus on their experiences with surfing and how compassion unfolded within the group environment, including moments where compassion seemed to fail.

Graham

In his late forties, and with knee and back injuries stemming from his time in the army, Graham never imagined himself as a surfer. Yet there was something about the physical sensations of going surfing that took hold of his body and imbued the experience with an array of pleasant, sometimes 'magical' qualities. Best were the days when the sea shone crystal clear and took on a 'lovely turquoisey-blue' appearance and when the waves were calm but crisp, unlike the murky blue-grey of a blown-out winter surf. Then, of course, there was the fresh salty smell of the ocean air which invigorated Graham and gave him the feeling of a 'massive high'. These two qualities alone helped to empty his mind completely: 'That's what it's like when I'm in the water, you're not thinking about anything else, it's just sometimes you're almost daydreaming and thinking "this is great".' Beyond this, there was another feeling – that of 'weightlessness' – which for Graham was even more compelling in terms of the bodily sensations it generated:

> After it, I'm tired like you can only be tired when you've been in the ocean if you know what I mean . . . you don't realise you're getting

tired do you? Everything's weightless, its good on me back, good for me knees, all that sort of stuff. And you come out and you get that really – where you sit down and you feel all warm and you start draining don't you, and just fall asleep. It's that nice feeling. Well, that's a good day for me; because it's a whole day, and it's a night's sleep.

Graham described this weightlessness primarily as a physical sensation, and he linked it to the deep physical feeling of calm and relaxation he experienced in the post-surf period. The more experienced surfers (in the group, as in surf culture generally), described this feeling as 'stoke', as in 'being stoked', which referred both to the thrill of catching a wave and to the warm 'glowing' sensation of the after-surf. Yet there was another sense in which this 'weightlessness' was deeply psychological, too. As with Graham's comments about 'day-dreaming', the mental weightlessness was about being completely unburdened from anxiety while out surfing. For Graham, these feelings endured beyond the time he spent in the sea, bringing him a rare peaceful sensation throughout that day and – importantly – at night.

Surfing was a *practice* for Graham, both in the sense that it required effortful repetition in order to learn, and in the sociological sense of being a regular activity that was imbued with meaning derived from the social sphere in which Graham was situated. The meaning of surfing as a practice was as much social as it was personal. It was in the context of the group, the way the veterans talked to each other about surfing and the particular – boisterous, playful, slapstick – manner of doing surfing that the practice took on special meaning. A well-worn phrase in the group environment was that surfing was about putting 'smiles on faces', and often the biggest cheers and hollers were for the most spectacular 'wipeouts' rather than mastery of surfing techniques. Flying surfboards and tumbling headlong into the waves were standard fare. 'Elation' was how Graham described it. Surfing made Graham feel 'a lot more laid back' too, and this was tied to an embrace of the relaxed, carefree ethos of surf culture; perhaps the furthest away he could travel, culturally speaking, from the discipline and aggression of a military lifestyle.

Surfing as a practice was, for Graham, a different way of *being in* and *using* his body. It was about the unique physical sensations stimulated in his body by being in the ocean and the different register of emotions this experience awakened inside him. Through gradual repetition, surfing seemed to help Graham 'unlearn' violence and aggression and feel his way into a more relaxed state of being:

> Its [surfing] made my life different, it's made me think calm, it's made me realise that being aggressive isn't acceptable and it isn't flippin'– it isn't right. And that actually, underneath all this, I'm not really an aggressive person, I'm quite a sensitive person who just wants to have a life, who wants to be normal – whatever normal is.

Graham described himself as being 'in a better space. I feel quite laid back; I don't feel aggressive anymore'. Surfing seemed to do for Graham something that years of therapy couldn't quite accomplish: it was teaching his traumatised body to let go of aggression and relieving it from the grip of tension and anxiety. In this sense, surfing was a means for the body's unlearning of trauma. Just as Graham had been conditioned – from childhood onwards – to respond to threat with aggression, surfing provided his body with a different exposure, one that produced a new pattern of peace and calmness. Through immersing himself in the physical environment of the ocean and in the social atmosphere of the group, Graham had begun to unravel the lifelong impact that trauma had had on him. This movement away from trauma, violence and aggression, and towards a calmer, more laid-back pattern of existence was the key emotional script of the story Graham told me. It was about putting himself in a better place, where living with the aftermath of trauma was more manageable. It was not, Graham was adamant, about 'cure'. The very notion seemed illusory. I asked Graham about 'recovery' and he defined it as being able to manage his mental health, including by learning to recognise the signs of a 'bad day' and reaching out to others for help lifting his spirits: '. . . and if you're asking me if I'm like that, yeah I am like that . . . I'm definitely in that place. But it doesn't make it any less emotional or whatever, you know'. Graham was articulate and nuanced about what surfing could do for him in his attempts to come to terms with a traumatic past. He was deeply critical of the 'brutality' of army life and at the same time proud to have served. He was also insightful and reflective about the legacy of trauma in his life and, in the one tearful moment during our interview, expressed his deepest longing: 'Life's been pretty shit, and I just wanna be happy. That's what I want, mate.'

Samuel

Before he joined the surfing group, Samuel had already done a lot of work in therapy unpicking his past and his relationship with alcohol. He'd spent ten years in the Royal Navy, although it was never a deliberate career choice; more like avoiding the kind of rural occupations he'd grown up around like fishing or farming. There had been several incidents during his career that Samuel would (much later) identify as having been traumatic, but for the most part, drinking in the Navy was simply a habitual activity and a means of dealing with boredom. After he left, life had no structure, 'like suddenly I had an endless leave-pass'. Plans that he'd made, like going to college and eventually getting a job and a mortgage, never materialised. From the Navy, Samuel 'went straight in the pub . . . and stayed there for about three years'. He'd been isolated from civilians (whom he often resented), had periods of homelessness, and was getting into trouble for causing fights and for being drunk and disorderly. At the root of his problems, there seemed a gnawing feeling of apathy and withdrawal. As Samuel described it, 'I had no real interest in even having a life really', though in an 'indifferent' rather than an actively suicidal manner. In the seventeen years between leaving the Navy and the two interviews I did with him, Samuel had cycled through periods of alcoholism, time in a rehab facility, as well as periods of relative success and stability. It was following his latest relapse (two years ago, at the time I spoke with him) that he was referred to the surfing charity by the local alcohol rehab centre.

Samuel had never been diagnosed with PTSD. Through talking to other veterans in the group he'd begun to associate aspects of his experience with the concept of PTSD, although he never fully applied it to himself; partly, it seemed, in deference to those who *had* been diagnosed. His deference prompted kindness from the other group members, keen for him to share the same story. As Samuel put it, 'they'll tell me I have [got PTSD] even if I say I haven't'. Still, his trauma experience was qualitatively different from that of Graham's, for instance, and different still from other members of the group. For Samuel, the key problem – the organising project in his life – was about developing a meaningful idea of a self which had for a long time been drowned out by alcohol. His was the never-finished project of staying sober, which went hand-in-hand with searching for meaning and purpose. Yet no less for Samuel than for the other veterans, surfing and the relationships he'd established through the group were a deep well of meaning and connection.

Surfing for Samuel was again a practice, but a more intimate one than it was for Graham. The boisterousness of the group surf sessions – the shouts and hollers – while enjoyable, were often a distraction. Samuel's best surfing experiences were meditative, even spiritual, and about feeling a connection with the ocean. This was not necessarily (or not yet) an ecological sensibility but was rather about creating a meaningful connection with something that he could relate to a sense of self. I asked Samuel what the difference was between surfing in the group and surfing – as he often did – by drifting apart from the others:

> *Samuel*: Its hard to explain really. You know like sometimes if there's loads of messing about, sort of catch a wave and fall off and go in or whatever, I don't really remember it. I don't really notice anything while I'm doing it. But sometimes if I'm on my own, suddenly its almost like in slow motion sometimes; you can see the spray and hear the surfboard cutting through the wave. And suddenly everything kind of slows down. It's a weird experience really, and it doesn't happen very often, but when it does – that's really amazing
>
> *Nick*: So you wouldn't tend to have that sort of experience with the group then?
>
> *Samuel*: No, I don't think so. I think that's more of an external kind of enjoyment, whereas . . . and I'm not saying I'm on my own, but when I sort of cut myself off a bit more from the group and focus more on myself, it's more of a kind of internal thing. And *that* kind of feeling is something I can take home with me and feel good about, you know . . . rather than having a hoot and a holler, and then come down off it.

Surfing was a more 'complete' experience when he focused on it as a personal practice. His senses awakened and the world around him came into sharper focus. Psychologists call this sensation 'flow', characterised by a genuinely satisfying state of consciousness and deep 'internal' enjoyment.[20] Samuel practised surfing alongside daily meditation, and together these two practices were helping him to experience an enriched present, and life as 'full' rather than 'empty'. He no longer felt indifferent about life. Samuel credits surfing with helping him 'find out who I am'. As he put it, 'I think that's what a lot of this stuff that I've been doing has been about this past couple of years. I think a lot of it got lost . . . I think the Armed Forces take away a lot of your identity and that's why when I came out I didn't really know who I was.' Rather than 'unlearning', for Samuel, surfing was about learning to experience life in a way that felt more genuine and more complete. In this sense, it was really about learning a sense of self.

Outside the practice of surfing itself, the connection Samuel felt with other veterans in the group was also important to him. I had witnessed the care and compassion he talked about when the group hosted art therapy sessions, where the veterans shared their struggles with each other. Despite the progress he'd made in recent years, Samuel still struggled sometimes and still had bad days. Yet unlike his previous attempts at living sober, he was now part of a group with an ethos of mutual care and responsibility. The others were well attuned to the signs of sadness and apathy and would recognise often before Samuel did when he was having a bad day, and would show concern:

> There has been times when I've really not wanted to come along, but its good because if I don't come, someone's always gonna ring me up. And that surprises me, 'cos I sort of think 'If I don't turn up, no-one's even gonna notice'. And then I get like three or four phone calls, asking me if I'm alright, which, you know, takes a bit of getting used to.

Care and compassion manifested in numerous ways among the veterans, although its expression was always carefully managed so as not to upset the ideals of masculinity they still navigated around. Samuel's story revealed how the dynamics of masculinity – the accepted norms around maintaining a manly posture and identity – complicated the space of communal healing and care the veterans had created.[21] Even though help was never more than a phone call away, for Samuel the hardest thing was to pick up the phone and ask for it. This was despite the fact that he would encourage others to talk about their problems and would support them in doing so. As Samuel explained, 'It's almost like pride killing you, you know, I'd rather die of pride than ask someone for a hand. That's quite a strong thing, quite a hard thing to get over.' Translating this into an ocean metaphor, Samuel felt he would sometimes prefer to drown beneath the waves than reach his hand above the surface to signal for help. He pondered aloud the absurdity of such a situation, but he knew all too well that pride could continue to be his downfall; so potent was the gendering of 'help' and the feeling of being observed by others in a position of weakness.

Freddie

For all the veterans I spoke with at the surfing charity, their ability to trust in others had been harmed in various ways by their encounters with the military. Much of what they gained through being around other veterans and sharing their stories was about rebuilding bonds of trust with other people. If, as Edkins argues, an essential feature of trauma is a betrayal of trust, then regaining trust can be considered an essential feature of healing.[22] This was clearly the case in Freddie's story, as was the damage that a breakdown in compassion had done to his fragile trust in others. Freddie had been bullied by others all his life. It started with a violent upbringing and an abusive father and continued in the army, where the bullying and the violence got worse. As a result, Freddie suffered with an absence of self-esteem; 'dumb shit, low as I can be', was how he described himself. He was frequently depressed and had no motivation. While he had never received a formal PTSD diagnosis, Freddie's therapist believed he had suffered the effects of trauma and betrayals of trust throughout his life. He often felt invisible, let down by others who were supposed to be helping him, and as a consequence found it hard to trust.

I interviewed Freddie shortly after we'd both taken part in a residential week. His reflections on the experience were mixed. He'd taken steps to open up to others and by telling his story during the art therapy sessions had made progress in developing some confidence and self-respect. However, because he approached the social dynamic of the group differently, he was accused of 'being negative', and this hurt Freddie and undermined the trust he was slowly developing. As Freddie told it:

> *Freddie*: I'm a bit of a loner, I don't mix with anyone anyway. I don't know if you noticed that while we were there, I was a bit more stand-offish. I had the odd word to say, but most of the time I'd just stand back and watch and listen. And apparently, it turned out I were being negative. When they [staff] gave everybody a debrief on the last day, I was told I was being negative.
> *Nick*: That's how it was seen maybe, was it?
> *Freddie*: Mmmm – because I didn't stop at the dinner table after I'd eaten my meal and chat like everybody else – I had my meal, and sat there for a little while then I'd bugger off, go off into my own little world and sit in the bedroom or whatever. I mean that's me, that's the way I am, even now that's the way I am . . . If I wanna be negative, I'll be negative – that is part and parcel of PTSD. But because I voiced my negativity, it didn't go down very well.[23]

The dinner table chats that Freddie refers to were a key feature of the group's social dynamic. Loud and lively, these occasions were filled with laughter, joking and sexualised 'banter'. For Freddie, however, the noisy din of mealtimes was difficult. He struggled to follow and to engage with the raucous banter, preferring a quieter atmosphere and, often, his own company. The dinner table thus emerged as another gendered space within the group where conforming to the style of hyper-masculine banter functioned as a means of integrating oneself into the dynamic of care and camaraderie. For those who were unwilling or unable to engage in it, it could also therefore function as a means of exclusion.

The dominant ethos of the group – exemplified in Graham and Samuel's stories – was about 'positivity', which was achieved by demonstrating a commitment to dealing with PTSD and by being an enthusiastic participant in all the group's activities. Actions read as contrary to this dominant ethos, at least from Freddie's perspective, were met with confrontation and challenge, rather than care and understanding. When I interviewed Freddie for a second time several months later, he'd stopped going to the charity, having attended infrequently since our initial interview. As he explained, 'I don't think my face fit to be honest. I think it were a case of "if your face fits".' As such, he never received the kind of calls Samuel talked about above:

> They should have at least made an attempt to contact me and find out *why* and what I were doing, and what were wrong, instead of just leaving me to it. I mean they used to phone other people and look after other people and make attempts with them, but me they never seemed to . . . I feel if nobody gets in touch with me to find out why I haven't been, then I feel neglected, not wanted and all that sort of thing. And I just think, 'If that's their attitude, bollocks to them'.

Trauma, Surfing and Cultural Politics

Into the contested terrain of trauma narratives, I present these stories of surfing as movement towards healing. What 'healing' looks like varies for each veteran and often it is a never-finished journey. Some of the changes veterans experience after trauma – a 'knowledge of evil', for instance – are irreversible.[24] There is no going back to a prior time of innocence and contentedness. This is why the cliché that healing is a 'journey, not a destination' resonates strongly with veterans. I have argued that surfing provides a means of unlearning the violence and aggression that encircles the traumatised body, and precipitates movement towards a calmer, more peaceful way of being. I also suggested that surfing as a practice provides an embodied and sensory connection with nature that can help to rebuild a sense of self, particularly where prior notions of self had been lost to trauma, alcohol and to life in the military more generally.[25] Both of these aspects of surfing as a movement towards healing take away the institutional narrative's emphasis on treating *symptoms*. Surfing stories show how healing is fundamentally embodied and communal. Neither trauma itself nor healing can be boxed into the mind of the individual veteran. As Shay argues:

> The essential injuries in combat PTSD are moral and social, and so the central treatment must be moral and social. The best treatment restores control to the survivor and actively encourages communalization of the trauma. Healing is done *by* survivors, not *to* survivors.[26]

Surfing stories restore this communal – and, I have argued, embodied – character of healing. Surfing as both an 'unlearning of trauma' and a 'learning of self' makes healing a project over which veterans can take ownership, which is a far more autonomous version of healing than the institutional narrative makes available. The contribution these stories make to the cultural politics of veterans' narratives is, I suggest, more about displacing the institutional trauma narrative than it is about counteracting it or challenging it directly. The stories of the veterans I interviewed were not overtly political and did not set out to undermine the institutional narrative and its method of 'governing' trauma.[27] Rather, these stories exemplify an alternative means of dealing with trauma which emphasises the importance of nature and of rebuilding trust in others as the core components.

While not-yet-realised in the context of the surfing charity, healing from trauma through surfing could also prefigure a more radical political project. In Graham and Samuel's stories, there is a movement away from aggression and emptiness and towards the peace, tranquillity and sensory 'fullness' that surfing promotes. For these veterans, the movement is towards *inner* peace, with the communal aspects of healing extending mainly to other members of the surfing charity itself. A more radical healing project would therefore entail a stronger politicisation of trauma and a movement towards *outer* peace, too. One example of healing as a more radical project of transformation is provided in the work of Ben Schrader, who advocates veteran activism after war as a means of demilitarising both the self and one's wider community.[28] Schrader emphasises how communalising trauma through environmental, anti-war and class-based forms of activism can help veterans to heal by repairing the damage war and militarism have done to the self and to the world. This makes healing more agentic for the veteran and simultaneously more outward-looking as well. With greater emphasis on communal healing, and on the role of nature in the healing journey, surfing could likewise become a more radical healing project. Indeed, immersing oneself in a surfing subculture can precipitate environmental activism, as the long-running UK-based campaign Surfers Against Sewage demonstrates.[29] By linking the healing journey with its dependence on the natural world, and by broadening out the communal ethos embedded in the veterans' stories, surfing stories could yet make a stronger intervention in the cultural politics of veterans' narratives.

Yet to do so would also entail addressing the gendering of veteran spaces such as the surfing charity. Just as inclusion within military environments is often predicated on one's ability to conform to masculine norms of behaviour and expression, so too can veteran spaces such as charities reinforce gendered logics of interaction. The ritualised, hyper-sexual banter which formed the typical style of group interaction was an influential means of gendering the group culture. There was a contradiction here, in that the group was also characterised by genuine care and compassion for others, and sharing distress with others was viewed as a sign of masculine 'strength' rather than as feminised 'weakness'.[30] However, it was also true that being able to engage with the banter was a key marker for acceptance and thus being able to access the benefits of care and camaraderie.[31] Those who were reluctant to engage in the banter could therefore find themselves excluded or accused of harbouring a negative attitude which detracted from the dominant ethos of 'positivity'. This form of exclusion was subtle, but powerful, nonetheless. It was not, I suggest, the result of any deliberate or overt hostility, rather it was a failure to accommodate different ways of being and of expressing oneself into the cultural logic of the group. Such failure to accommodate difference may also explain why the surfing charity – as with many other veteran groups and support services – was not a diverse environment, with no women and few non-White veterans taking part.

Conclusion

Talking about trauma is fraught with challenges. The concept of PTSD is so prevalent that finding a neutral or non-stigmatising way of discussing veterans' mental health is not easy. In this chapter, I have preferred the term 'trauma' as a means of signalling the traumatic occurrence, rather than the diagnostic label. Movements to de-stigmatise PTSD (e.g., by dropping the 'D', or by prefixing with 'combat-related') have been led by veterans suffering the effects of trauma and by the charities and media organisations who support them. Such efforts seek to re-position PTSD from a stigmatised mental illness to an 'invisible' war wound; as something more reflective of the heroism and sacrifice traditionally associated with 'physical' combat injuries.[32] The de-stigmatisation of PTSD is usually framed as a means of promoting help-seeking, allowing veterans to present for treatment without the shame attached to declaring oneself 'mentally ill'.[33] However, de-stigmatisation is charged with a political affect which influences how cultural politics unfold from the telling of trauma stories. This is because veterans' stories of *heroic* trauma, in line with the militarised patriotism encircling veterans' stories more broadly, also perform another kind of political work. The valorisation of trauma as a form of sacrifice imbues PTSD with a sense of pride and nobility just as surely as it promotes the need for timely and effective care. Herein lies a further depoliticising move, inoculating PTSD from any sense of political anger or betrayal and shifting the cultural politics of trauma narratives further into the domain of militarised patriotism. Whereas PTSD once functioned to depoliticise trauma by medicalising it,[34] it now *also* depoliticises trauma by celebrating it as bravery. While destigmatisation can therefore be viewed as a necessary *response* to the institutional trauma narrative, it can also be considered *useful* from an institutional or establishment perspective.

What story to tell about trauma is a political choice. It depends on the view we take on conflict and our position vis-à-vis the institutions whose narratives govern the way trauma is conceptualised and treated. As Wibben suggests, 'although there may be several possible narratives, which one is told and which ones are deemed acceptable scientific knowledge, is political'.[35] The institutional trauma narrative maintains that there are specific, validated clinical therapies (e.g., trauma-focused cognitive behavioural therapy) which are to be used to treat the symptoms of PTSD, thereby inserting trauma into a linear clinical narrative of treatment and response. The institutional narrative makes no space for alternative approaches. Indeed, I have attended conferences where well-known military psychiatrists have publicly scoffed at the notion of surfing being used as an approach to dealing with trauma. The stories I present in this chapter enact a different, more elementary truth about trauma: that grounding oneself in nature and building trust in others can bring about a powerful healing response. Surfing demonstrates how healing can be about the body gradually learning a different, perhaps 'demilitarised', way of being in the world. Through literally immersing oneself in nature, it is about learning to feel and respond to the world differently, loosening trauma's grip on the body, practising a feeling of calm, awakening the senses, and developing a sense of self.

In centring these stories in this chapter, I too have made a political choice, in that I have chosen to privilege the trauma stories of male 'combat' veterans. While I have deliberately attempted to emphasise the 'non-combat' features of these stories – such as the violence endemic in military life and the feeling of emptiness that life after the military can bestow – it is also possible that I have reified the association between trauma and 'front-line' combat roles. The notion of trauma gains a deeply unwarranted glory from this association, giving it the gloss of noble sacrifice and patriotism. As the veterans whom I interviewed know well, there is no glory whatsoever in the daily realities of life after trauma, except the *illusory* glory of a forlorn heroism that culture has come to attribute to 'combat' PTSD. Furthermore, the centring of male 'combat' veterans' stories pushes other stories to the margins of traumatic legitimacy, including the stories told by survivors of military sexual violence, for example, and the even more seldom-heard stories of those in the Global South who become caught up in wars that create mass trauma but without the infrastructure of support available to Western war veterans. These stories too are greatly in need of amplifying.

To end this chapter, and the book's empirical contribution, there is one further political choice worth discussing; that is, the choice to listen to a trauma story in the first place. For veterans trying to navigate confusing and male-centred healthcare systems, there is often little choice but to tell their trauma story over and over in the hope of being heard.[36] But to really *listen* to veterans' stories, we must start with close attention to the experiences they recount without seeking to pin diagnostic labels on their stories. This can be difficult to do. Shay commented that the 'Trauma narrative confronts the normal

[sic] adult with the fragility of the body. These stories bring mortality into view. Trauma narratives cause normal adults to imaginatively identify with one or more of the characters in the narrative. The feelings this arouses are almost all unpleasant.'[37] Thus, the political choice is to practice narrative empathy in relation to trauma stories, which is an uncomfortable yet necessary responsibility for citizens in whose name the violence is perpetrated.

Notes

1. Molendijk, Kramer and Verweij, 'Conflicting notions on violence and PTSD in the military'.
2. Ethical approval for the original study was granted by Loughborough University, with approval for the re-examination of this data set granted by Anglia Ruskin University. That the interviews were amenable to additional layers of meaning construction I attribute both to the extraordinary richness of the veterans' stories and to my own evolving analytic concerns and perspectives developed since the original research was conducted.
3. In thinking through the embodiment of trauma and the inadequacy of clinical PTSD discourse to capture and reflect this dimension of veterans' experiences, I am indebted to the work of Zoe Wool and Ken MacLeish. See Wool, 'On movement'; MacLeish, *Making War at Fort Hood*.
4. Molendijk Kramer and Verweij, 'Conflicting notions on violence and PTSD in the military'; Lembcke, *PTSD*; MacLeish, *Making War at Fort Hood*; Wool, 'On movement'.
5. Lembcke, *PTSD*; Edkins, *Trauma and the Memory of Politics*; Howell, 'The demise of PTSD'; Young, *The Harmony of Illusions*; Kienzler, 'Debating war-trauma and post-traumatic stress disorder in an interdisciplinary arena'.
6. Bulmer and Jackson, '"You do not live in my skin"', p. 29.
7. Frank, *Letting Stories Breathe*, p. 28.
8. Lembcke, *PTSD*.
9. Wessely, 'Risk, psychiatry and the military', p. 461.
10. Lembcke, *PTSD*, p. 17.
11. Howell, 'The demise of PTSD', p. 215.
12. Ibid., p. 216.
13. Shay, *Achilles in Vietnam*, p. 187.
14. Molendijk, Kramer and Verweij, 'Conflicting notions on violence and PTSD in the military', p. 348.
15. Ibid., p. 349.
16. Edkins, *Trauma and the Memory of Politics*, p. 16.
17. MacLeish, *Making War at Fort Hood*, p. 120.
18. Wool, 'On movement', p. 404.
19. See Caddick, Smith and Phoenix, 'The effects of surfing and the natural environment on the well-being of combat veterans'.
20. Csikszentmihalyi, *Flow*.
21. I have explored this issue in detail previously in Caddick, Smith and Pheonix, 'Male combat veterans' narratives of PTSD, masculinity, and health'.

22. Edkins, *Trauma and the Memory of Politics*.
23. Quote first appeared in Caddick, Smith and Pheonix, 'Male combat veterans' narratives of PTSD, masculinity, and health'.
24. Shay, *Achilles in Vietnam*.
25. A growing body of work now attests to the 'healing power of nature' for veterans dealing with physical injury and psychological trauma. This is a diverse body of work ranging from cognitive psychology to more sociological investigations of being in nature and the meaning attributed to it by veterans. See, for example, Dietrich, Joye and Garcia, 'Natural medicine'; Havlick, Cerveny Derrien, 'Therapeutic landscapes, outdoor programs for veterans, and public lands'; Hawkins, Townsend and Garst, 'Nature-based recreational therapy for military service members'; Berman, Jonides and Kaplan, 'The cognitive benefits of interacting with nature'.
26. Shay, *Achilles in Vietnam*, p. 187.
27. Following Edkins, the institutional narrative can be read as domestication of trauma by inserting it into a linear narrative of event–trauma–treatment, thereby exerting control over veterans' experiences and stripping them of political potential; that is, of 'governing' them in the Foucauldian sense.
28. Schrader, *Fight to Live, Live to Fight*.
29. Wheaton, 'Identity, politics, and the beach'.
30. I have written previously about how the typical gendering of distress as 'weakness' was inverted within the charity context by drawing on a discourse of masculinity which framed sharing problems – and dealing with them – as proactive and masculine. See Caddick, Smith and Pheonix, 'Male combat veterans' narratives of PTSD, masculinity, and health'.
31. Green et al., 'Exploring the ambiguities of masculinity in accounts of emotional distress in the military among young ex-servicemen'.
32. Lembcke, *PTSD*.
33. The conversations with veterans on the 'Declassified' podcast discussed in Chapter 3 are a key example of this de-stigmatisation discourse.
34. Howell, 'The demise of PTSD'.
35. Wibben, *Feminist Security Studies*, p. 34.
36. Whelan, *Going Crazy in the Green Machine*.
37. Shay, *Achilles in Vietnam*, pp. 193–4.

Conclusion

> Veterans tell war stories for any number of reasons: to satisfy the expectations of comrades and civilians; for catharsis; to set the record straight; to cover up the truth; to memorialise; to forget; to shock; to entertain; to focus attention; to distract attention . . . the list could go on. And the age of mass warfare reinforced the connection between veterancy and storytelling; indeed, made veteran identity and existence foundational upon it and so produced in excess a figure apt to convey its own excesses.[1]

The cultural politics of veterans' narratives calls for a healthier relationship with veterans' stories. Healthy relationships are characterised by honesty, openness and respect. They are built on familiarity and trust, and require a willingness to know and embrace the other. We must be willing to *know* veterans and their stories. It is not enough to simply acknowledge their existence once a year and henceforth absolve ourselves from the discomfort of war and its aftermath. True respect for 'our' veterans is not something that is shown from a distance, it must be *practised* up close by relating to them, striving to understand the struggles they are facing and acting in solidarity. As a veteran I met during a recent project put it, transition to life as a civilian is about belonging to a community, 'So we become more like them, and they become more like us.' A healthy relationship means that veterans' stories are not viewed abstractly as 'part of the furniture', providing a stable bedrock of heroism and moral certainty to our national culture. Instead, they must be allowed to become part of *us*, fully human with all the joy, struggle and conflict that entails. Moreover, healthy relationships are peace-seeking ones. Key to the argument for a cultural politics of veterans' narratives is that we need to relate and respond to veterans' stories in ways that build peace and that reject the politics of militarism which always lead towards violence. To reiterate Plummer's call, we need 'better stories told in better ways for a better world for all'.[2]

Importantly, 'better' sometimes demands ruthless honesty and always requires critical dialogue. Within healthy relationships, critique emanates from friendship and operates in both directions – so that veterans too can critique the 'civilian' cultures they find themselves part of. In this book I have written critically about veterans' stories and the politics they enact. Yet I must be clear that my critique, along with a cultural politics of veterans' narratives more generally, should not be read as in any way 'anti-veteran'. On the contrary, it is fundamentally *pro*-veteran, in that it strives to treat veterans' stories with the care and attentiveness they deserve as narratives of human experience, and in that it seeks to contest the abstracted, dominant narratives which leave the veteran figure over-represented and which precede and prefigure their individual stories. Despite my criticism in Chapter 3, for example, of the work that 'values talk' does to elevate veteran personhood, I am impressed and humbled by the commitment veterans espouse towards living by values such as solidarity and being in service to others. I remain sceptical, however, of the way these enduring values get overlaid with a form of national patriotism that is, in my view, wholly unworthy of such strong attachment. Veterans deserve better from their country, and until their country – their government in particular – begins acting in line with *its* supposed values, patriotism will always ring hollow.

What we currently have in our national culture is the antithesis of a healthy relationship with veterans' stories. Veterans' stories are not *known* in any meaningful sense. Rather, they are held at a comfortable distance out of fear and out of ignorance masquerading as 'respect'. Too often we are afraid to ask questions, either because we fear the answers or because we fear we will ask the wrong questions. Why not simply ask veterans what it is like to live as a 'civilian', or how they feel their service has been reciprocated by their government, or, perhaps more sensitively, whether the war was worth it? Instead, our culture treats younger veterans as victimised heroes and elderly ones as gods, but it does not know their stories. In the media and the public eye, veterans' stories are more or less interchangeable with the image of a red poppy, or of the Union Jack flag. They are filtered through until all we are left with is a familiar collection of dehumanisations: bravery, courage, trauma, violence, service and sacrifice. On the basis of such dehumanisations, veterans' stories *act* to repeat and reinforce the moral authority of military service. Veterans' stories are active in this way even before they have been told. When members of the public ask me about my work, the two most common responses I receive are 'that must be such rewarding work' and 'those guys go through so much'. Yet, as I hope to have illustrated in this book, veterans' stories have the capacity to act in varied and creative ways provided we are willing to lift away the patriotic camouflage webbing that overlays them.

Our national culture poses a series of dilemmas or situations for veteran storytelling, each encircling the issue of 'voice'. First, is the burden of contending with *expected stories*. When veterans are invited to tell stories – for example, to a reporter or politician, or perhaps a doctor or pensions adviser – they are expected to speak in recognisable terms. Their experiences are claimed by others as representative of familiar universal 'truths' about war, suffering or heroism. Speaking of the injured veteran, Wool writes that 'He is rendered sacrificial because others claim his pain, his death, his loss in their own name. He is their sacrificial victim; *there is little he can do to be otherwise.*'[3] Because veterans are such strongly symbolic figures, their stories easily serve the meanings others wish to attribute to them, either to exploit a sense of scandal or, conversely, for national glory. Concurrently, as I discussed in Chapter 4, the state imposes its own expectations, calling on veterans to become ambassadors for the military experience and to eschew notions of 'brokenness' by avoiding the wrong kind of story. Faced with these webs of expectations, veterans may prefer not to tell stories, or perhaps to tell familiar stories they know will placate the listener's demands.[4] The result may be inauthentic, heavily curated, or at least censored and sanitised versions of veterans' stories coming to dominate public representations of veteranhood.[5] Consequently, a cultural politics of veterans' narratives must keep asking *whose* voice is active in the telling and retelling of veterans' stories, how are veterans' voices being positioned, and how might they resist or refuse these positionings?

Secondly, is the challenge of formulating stories that remain, in certain respects, unshareable. Stories can be or seem unshareable for different reasons. One reason is that, as McLoughlin writes, war experience *itself* remains 'incomprehensible, unassimilable, and (hence) unshareable'.[6] Under such circumstances, efforts towards narration impose a sense of order which experience itself refuses.[7] The burden of telling stories when experience feels incomprehensible is clear: if veterans are unable to fathom their own experiences, what chance would a listener stand? Narration brings consternation, and the kind of pitying responses veterans detest. 'The onlooker', McLoughlin continues, 'may feel sadness or sorrow, yes, but not empathy, sympathy or imaginative involvement'.[8] It is this denial of imaginative involvement which, above all, stifles engaged and critical dialogue. Another reason is that storytelling sometimes poses too great a risk. Some stories leave their tellers vulnerable to rebuke, censure or 'damaged identities'.[9] Stories of military sexual violence, for example, can prove especially difficult to verbalise. As I discussed in Chapter 2, it can take many years for a veteran – whether male, female or non-binary – to feel 'ready' to tell a story of sexual violence. And this is not to suggest that, even then, they will feel 'safe' in telling this story. Transforming the conditions of sexual violence storytelling, such as by decentring the perpetrators and by holding the military accountable for providing justice, thus constitutes a collective priority.[10]

Thirdly, is the difficulty of articulating counter-narratives that contest the dominant representations of 'veteranhood' and reject the expected stories. Examples include trauma narratives which emphasise communal healing and reject the isolating tendencies of institutional narratives, or anti-war narratives which harness the potential of veteran dissent and activism.[11] Stories which depart from the expected may not always take the form of a counter-narrative, for counter-narratives tend to possess a more deliberate or coordinated quality. Indeed, the act of *countering* suggests not only intention but work, effort and collective struggle. Countering involves what Plummer refers to as 'Narrative mobilization and community making'; that is, the moment when personal stories become 'overtly and explicitly political'.[12] Counter-narratives are difficult and can be burdensome – emotionally, and in other ways – for the teller. They require support from communities and allies. And they take hold in stages. Plummer describes how narratives must first overcome the void of silences and move towards initial imagination and vocalisation. Storytellers need to take up their voice and allow stories of resistance to adopt the mantle of identity before they can become public and political. As I have emphasised throughout this book, narrative power is integral to this process. A cultural politics of veterans' narratives thereby seeks to understand how people develop the confidence to tell stories which cut apart the established narratives and how they can mobilise forms of power that support their ability to do so.

Narratives as Knowledge Practices

The five underpinning principles introduced in Chapter 1 collectively endow veterans' narratives with the capacities of 'knowledge practices', which is to say that they claim and enact war knowledges with performative and ideological effects. To function as knowledge practices means that veterans' narratives articulate particular versions of 'war', 'military', 'state' and 'nation'; they bring these things into being, give them form, and ascribe them the weight of tradition or of institutional authority. Narratives as knowledge practices constitute the social realities they describe,[13] and on this basis they make certain actions, policies or even wholesale formations of militarism, thinkable, possible and natural. They situate our understanding of the morality and politics of war and military life and are therefore profoundly influential. It is useful here, again, to distinguish between 'veterans' narratives' and the stories that veterans themselves tell about war and their military experience, for these are two different kinds of narrative, practising different kinds of knowledge. Veterans' narratives (narratives *about* veterans) tend to serve power by organising and circulating a knowledge of the veteran which supports the goals and ambitions of the state. Examples include the institutionalised state narratives of trauma (Chapter 7), transition (Chapter 4), and liberal progress (Chapter 5). These are knowledges 'from above': hegemony-seeking knowledge practices which 'minorize', in Foucault's terms,[14] other subjects of knowledge and experience. Veterans' narratives as knowledge practices mask and/or subjugate the stories veterans themselves tell of their experience by classifying them as subjective, partial or non-representative. In effect, they *deny* veterans' experiences without ever appearing to do so, making their stories easier to ignore when they do not align with the authoritative truths claimed by the state.

One final example worth considering regards the debate over veterans' suicide. In recent years, several large cohort studies have examined the rate and risk of suicide among veterans compared with the civilian public.[15] Such studies consistently report that veterans are at no overall greater risk of suicide compared with the general population. They also report that younger veterans who served for shorter periods of time may be at increased risk compared with age-matched civilian peers,[16] but that this difference can be largely attributed to postal code (i.e., social deprivation, rather than military service).[17] The narrative reality these studies establish is one in which the military constitutes no greater threat to life than civilian society, whereby the military may even constitute a *protective* environment.[18] Veterans – and by implication, the military which produced them – are robust and resilient, and media reports of veteran suicide are exaggerated. The narrative is useful to the state because, as Ross McGarry argues, it creates distance between the problem of suicide and the military institution.[19] As a performative political action – a knowledge practice – it masks the *character* of veteran suicide behind the detached 'nomothetic gaze'[20] of the state and deflects moral responsibility. Stories 'from below', such as the one told by the bereaved parents of Nathan Hunt on the 'Declassified' podcast are, to paraphrase again from the government-sponsored *Veterans Transition Review*, placed 'in their proper context'.[21]

The stories veterans tell of their own experiences likewise function as knowledge practices, but in different ways from the hegemony-seeking state narratives. The knowledge they claim is that of the 'flesh witness' – one who has experienced war and the military through his or her body and can deliver first-hand knowledge or 'ground truth'. This is not to suggest that veterans' stories are unmediated; the military has its own culture of storytelling with codes such as respect, modesty (and, of course, rank), which condition how stories can be expressed. But rather, that veterans can speak of war from having lived it, and this furnishes the 'truth-telling' capacity of their stories with a great deal of cultural capital. As a result, veterans' stories are difficult to refute overtly. Instead, they must be deftly managed, as I have argued above and throughout, so that their capacities to act in subversive or antagonistic ways as knowledge practices are stifled. Veterans' stories speak around, aside, apart from, sometimes in tune with, and sometimes *back to* the state and media narratives, offering their own versions of the wars they fought and suggestions for how others should respond.

Only a close reading of veterans' stories will suffice to come to terms with what these stories are actually saying about war and militarised violence. A casual reading poses the risk of allowing their stories to act presumptively, which, as I have argued, is too often how they do act. For all the reasons veterans tell stories – as McLoughlin posits in this conclusion's epigraph – the effects they have on cultural politics are too often based on the presumed understanding of veterans created by society's caricatured representations of them.[22] Their stories act on the basis of packaged forms – the narrative 'skins' that our public culture wraps their stories up in. As a result, our knowledge of war and its many legacies is often simply skin deep. I argue that we need to reject the packaged assumptions of what veterans' stories are and, to paraphrase Frank, allow their stories *room to breathe*. I do not wish to suggest – naively – that to know veterans' stories better (as I have called for) would necessarily help to mobilise opposition to militarism. Indeed, some veterans' voices are among those most fervently supportive of war – or, at least, the military. Veterans' stories might also reinforce racist, sexist, or colonising ideologies, thus normalising oppression. Some stories might need to be challenged, or even denounced. All of this, though, depends on a more thorough and critical appreciation of veterans' stories, something a cultural politics of veterans' narratives both enables and demands.

Notes

1. McLoughlin, *Veteran Poetics*, p. 148.
2. Plummer, 'Narrative power, sexual stories and the politics of storytelling', p. 290.
3. Wool, *After War*, p. 112 (my emphasis).
4. See, for example, Wool, *After War*; Wool, 'On movement'. Writing in an American context, Wool suggests that in some respects the easiest response to the culture of platonic 'gratitude' whereby soldiers are ritually thanked for their service is to quietly accept the affirmations of ill-informed but well-intentioned others, and to avoid the burden of educating them by telling their stories.
5. On the issue of state and self-censorship in veterans' narratives (memoirs), see Woodward and Jenkings, *Bringing War to Book*.
6. McLoughlin, *Veteran Poetics*, p. 185.
7. Edkins, *Trauma and the Memory of Politics*.
8. McLoughlin, *Veteran Poetics*, p. 234.
9. Nelson, *Damaged Identities, Narrative Repair*.
10. MacKenzie, *Good Soldiers Don't Rape*.
11. Schrader, *Fight to Live, Live to Fight*; Glenton, *Veteranhood*.
12. Plummer, 'Narrative power, sexual stories and the politics of storytelling', p. 284 (original emphasis).
13. Manchanda, *Imagining Afghanistan*, p. 64.
14. Foucault, *Society Must be Defended*, p. 10.
15. Bergman, Mackay and Pell, 'Suicide among Scottish military veterans'; Rodway et al., 'Suicide after leaving the UK armed forces 1996–2018'; Kapur et al., 'Suicide after leaving the UK Armed Forces'.
16. Rodway et al., 'Suicide after leaving the UK armed forces'.
17. Bergman, Mackay and Pell, 'Suicide among Scottish military veterans'.
18. Kapur et al., 'Suicide after leaving the UK Armed Forces'.
19. McGarry, 'Demystifying the "victimized state"'.
20. Ibid., p. 76.
21. Ashcroft, *Veterans Transition Review*, p. 25.
22. Parry and Pitchford-Hyde, '"We may have bad days . . . that doesn't make us killers"'; Parry, 'Representing public service and post-militariness in *Bodyguard* (BBC, 2018)'.

REFERENCES

Åhäll, L. (2019). 'Feeling everyday IR: embodied, affective, militarising movement as choreography of war'. *Cooperation and Conflict* 54(2), 149–66.
Ahmed, S. (2014). *The Cultural Politics of Emotions*. Edinburgh: Edinburgh University Press.
Albertson, K. (2019). 'Relational legacies impacting on veteran transition from military to civilian life: trajectories of acquisition, loss, and reformulation of a sense of belonging'. *Illness, Crisis & Loss* 27(4), 255–73.
Alcoff, L. (1991). 'The problem of speaking for others'. *Cultural Critique* 20, 5–32.
Allen, D. (2020). *Forewarned: Cockups, Conspiracy and Misogyny in the British Army (1983–2020)*. London: Cranthorpe Millner.
Allport, A. (2009). *Demobbed: Coming Home after the Second World War*. New Haven, CT: Yale University Press.
Anderson, B. (1983). *Imagined Communities: Reflections On the Origin and Spread of Nationalism*. London: Verso.
Andrews, M. (2014). *Narrative Imagination and Everyday Life*. Oxford: Oxford University Press.
Andrews, M., Squire, C. and Tamboukou, M. (2013). *Doing Narrative Research*. Thousand Oaks, CA: Sage.
Arias, L. (2017). *Minefield/Campo Minado*. London: Oberon.
Armour, C., McGlinchey, E. and Ross, J. (2021). 'The health and wellbeing of armed forces veterans in Northern Ireland'. Available at: 20210422-NIVHWS-MHWB-Survey-Report-FINAL.pdf (pcdn.co), last accessed 31 October 2023.
Ashcroft, M. (2014). *Veterans Transition Review*. Available at: vtrreport.pdf (veteranstransition.co.uk), last accessed 30 October 2023.

Ashplant, T., Dawson, G. and Roper, M. (2004). *Commemorating War: The Politics of Memory*. London: Routledge.

Atherton, S. (2021). 'Protecting those who protect us: women in the Armed Forces from recruitment to civilian life', House of Commons. Available at: Women in the Armed Forces: From Recruitment to Civilian Life (parliament.uk), last accessed 30 October 2023.

Badenoch, K. (2020). 'Black History Month'. The full text of the speech is available via Hansard government records, available at: Black History Month - Hansard - UK Parliament, last accessed 31 October 2023.

Baines, G. (2014). *South Africa's 'Border War': Contested Narratives and Conflicting Memories*. London: Bloomsbury.

Baker, C. (ed.). (2020). *Making War on Bodies: Militarisation, Aesthetics and Embodiment in International Politics*. Edinburgh: Edinburgh University Press.

Barker, S. (2021). 'Veterans forced to food banks after being told they don't qualify for DWP support'. *Daily Mirror*. Available at: Veterans forced to food banks after being told they don't qualify for DWP support - Mirror Online, last accessed 31 October 2023.

Barthwal-Datta, M., Krystalli, R. and Shepherd, L. (2022). 'Narrative in politics and the politics of narrative'. In P. Dawson and M. Mäkelä (eds), *Routledge Companion to Narrative Theory*. New York: Routledge, 465–78.

Basham, V. (2013). *War, Identity and the Liberal State: Everyday Experiences of the Geopolitical in the Armed Forces*. London: Routledge.

Basham, V. (2016). 'Gender, race, militarism and remembrance: the everyday geopolitics of the poppy'. *Gender, Place & Culture* 23(6), 883–96.

Basham, V. (2018). 'Liberal militarism as insecurity, desire and ambivalence: gender, race and the everyday geopolitics of war'. *Security Dialogue* 49(1/2), 32–43.

BBC News (2019). 'New troops "not getting help for mental health"'. Available at: New troops 'not getting help for mental health' - BBC News, last accessed 31 October 2023.

Beneiot-Montagut, R. (2011). 'Ethnography goes online: towards a user-centred methodology to research interpersonal communication on the internet'. *Qualitative Research* 11(6), 716–35.

Berezin, M (2002). 'Secure states: towards a political sociology of emotion'. *Sociological Review* 50, 33–52.

Bergman, B., Mackay, D. and Pell, J. (2022). 'Suicide among Scottish military veterans: follow-up and trends'. *Occupational and Environmental Medicine* 79, 88–93.

Berman, M., Jonides, J. and Kaplan, S. (2008). 'The cognitive benefits of interacting with nature'. *Psychological Science* 19, 1207–12.

Booth, R. (2019). 'Red poppy to be used to remember civilian victims for first time'. *The Guardian*. Available at: https://www.theguardian.com/uk-news/2019/oct/15/red-poppy-used-remember-civilian-victims-for-first-time?CMP=share_btn_tw, last accessed 30 October 2023.

Bourdieu P. (1990). *The Logic of Practice*. Cambridge: Polity Press.

Bourke, J. (1994). *Dismembering the Male: Men's Bodies, Britain and the Great War*. London: Reaktion.

Bourke, J. (2001). *The Second World War: A People's History*. Oxford: Oxford University Press.

Bourke, J. (2004). 'Remembering war'. *Journal of Contemporary History* 39(4), 473–85.

Bourke, J. (2013). 'Bodily pain, combat and the politics of memoirs: between the American Civil War and the war in Vietnam'. *Histoire Sociale* 46(91), 43–61.

Bourke, J. (2014). *Wounding the World: How Military Violence and War-play Invade Our Lives*. London: Virago.

British Army (2018). 'Sexual harassment report'. Available at: Army sexual harassment report 2018 (publishing.service.gov.uk), last accessed 30 October 2023.

British Army (2018). 'Values and standards of the British Army'. Available at: https://www.army.mod.uk/media/5219/20180910-values_standards_2018_final.pdf, last accessed 31 October 2023.

British Army (2021). 'Army veteran Jessica Masterman MBE on her successful transition to Amazon UK'. Available at: Army Veteran to Amazon UK Program Manager | The British Army (mod.uk), last accessed 31 October 2023.

Bruner, J. (1990). *Acts of Meaning*. Cambridge, MA: Harvard University Press.

Bruner, J. (1991). 'The narrative construction of reality'. *Critical Inquiry* 18(1), 1–21.

Bulmer, S. and Eichler, M. (2017). 'Unmaking militarized masculinity: veterans and the project of military-to-civilian transition'. *Critical Military Studies* 3(2), 161–81.

Bulmer, S. and Jackson, D. (2016). '"You do not live in my skin": embodiment, voice, and the veteran'. *Critical Military Studies* 2(1/2), 25–40.

Bunkall, A. (2019). 'Top military charities sitting on £277m – while veterans struggle'. *Sky News*. Available at: Top military charities sitting on £277m - while veterans struggle | UK News | Sky News, last accessed 31 October 2023.

Burdett, H., Woodhead, C., Iversen, A. C., Wessely, S., Dandeker, C. and Fear, N. T. (2013). "Are you a veteran? Understanding of the term "veteran" among UK ex-service personnel: a research note. *Armed Forces & Society* 39(4), 751–9.

Burdett, H., MacManus, D., Fear, N., Rona, R. and Greenberg, N. (2018). 'Veterans and benefits: relationships between social demographics, Service characteristics and mental health with unemployment and disability benefit usage by GB ex-Service personnel', available at: Veterans and benefits (pcdn.co), last accessed 31 October 2023.

Burkitt, I. (2014). *Emotions and Social Relations*. Thousand Oaks, CA: Sage.

Butler, J. (2020). *The Force of non-Violence*. London: Verso.

Caddick, N. (2021). 'Life, embodiment and (post)war stories: studying narrative in critical military studies'. *Critical Military Studies* 7(2), 155–72.

Caddick, N. (2021). 'Poetic encounters with war's "others"'. *Critical Military Studies* 7(3), 355–9.

Caddick, N., Cooper, L., Godier-McBard, L. and Fossey, M. (2021). 'Hierarchies of wounding: media framings of "combat" and "non-combat" injury'. *Media, War & Conflict* 14(4), 503–21.

Caddick, N. and Fossey, M. (2023). 'Should we give military families a break? A call for research on military family holidays'. *BMJ Military Health* 169(3), 269–70.

Caddick, N., Godier, L., Sanchez-Vasquez, A., Fossey, M., Ivory, C. and Down, S. (2018). 'Evaluation of the Ministry of Defence Spouse Employment Support Trial'. Research report commissioned by Forces in Mind Trust, UK.

Caddick, N., Smith, B. and Phoenix, C. (2015). 'The effects of surfing and the natural environment on the well-being of combat veterans'. *Qualitative Health Research* 25, 76–86.

Caddick, N., Smith, B. and Phoenix, C. (2015). 'Male combat veterans' narratives of PTSD, masculinity, and health'. *Sociology of Health and Illness* 37, 97–111.

Caso, F. (2020). 'The political aesthetics of the body of the soldier in pain'. In C. Baker (ed.), *Making War on Bodies: Militarisation, Aesthetics and Embodiment in International Politics*. Edinburgh: Edinburgh University Press, pp. 54–73.

Catignani, S. and Basham, V. (2021). 'The gendered politics of researching military policy in the age of the "knowledge economy"'. *Review of International Studies* 47(2), 211–30.

Chisholm, A. (2015). 'From warriors of empire to martial contractors: reimagining Gurkhas in private security'. In M. Eichler (ed.), *Gender and Private Security in Global Politics*. Oxford: Oxford University Press, 95–113.

Chouliaraki, L. (2014). 'From war memoirs to milblogs: language change in the witnessing of war, 1914–2014'. *Discourse & Society* 25(5), 600–18.

Clarke, P., Glenton, J., Hoh, M. and Sharrocks, W. (2019). 'The good, the bad and the rebels'. *Critical Military Studies* 5(4), 387–91.

Cockburn, C. and Enloe, C. (2012). 'Militarism, patriarchy and peace movements: Cynthia Cockburn and Cynthia Enloe in conversation. *International Feminist Journal of Politics* 14(4), 550–7.

Cohen, D. (2001). *The War Come Home: Disabled Veterans in Britain and Germany, 1914–1939*. Berkeley: University of California Press.

Cole, S., Robson, A. and Doherty, R. (2020). 'Armed forces charities: an overview and analysis'. Available at: https://s31949.pcdn.co/wp-content/uploads/Sector-Insight-Armed-Forces-Charities-web.pdf, last accessed 31 October 2023.

Cooper, L., Caddick, N., Godier, L., Cooper, A. and Fossey, M. (2018). 'Transition from the military into civilian life: an exploration of cultural competence'. *Armed Forces and Society* 44(1), 156–77.

Corley, L. (2017). 'Epistemological interference and the trope of the veteran'. *Journal of Veterans Studies* 2(1), 69–78.

Cree, A. (2020). 'Sovereign wives? An emotional politics of precarity and resistance in the UK's military wives choir'. *International Political Sociology* 3, 304–22.

Cree, A. and Caddick, N. (2020). 'Unconquerable heroes: Invictus, redemption, and the cultural politics of narrative'. *Journal of War and Culture Studies* 13(3), 258–78.

Cromby, J. (2015). *Feeling Bodies: Embodying Psychology*. Basingstoke: Palgrave Macmillan.

Crossley, N. (2012). *Towards Relational Sociology*. London: Routledge.

Csikszentmihalyi, M. (2011). *Flow: The Psychology of Optimal Experience*. New York: HarperCollins.

Dannatt, R. (2010). *Leading From the Front*. London: Corgi.

Dannatt, R. (2021). 'The West has squandered its early success in Afghanistan'. *The Telegraph*. Available at: The West has squandered its early success in Afghanistan (telegraph.co.uk), last accessed 13 October 2022.

Darda, J. (2018). 'Military whiteness'. *Critical Inquiry* 45, 76–96.

Darda, J. (2019). 'Like a refugee: veterans, Vietnam, and the making of a false equivalence'. *American Quarterly* 71(1), 83–104.

Dawson, G. (1994). *Soldier Heroes: British Adventure, Empire and the Imagining of Masculinities*. London: Routledge.

Dawson, G. (2016). 'The theory of popular memory and the contested memories of the Second World War in Britain'. In K. Hoffmann, H. Mehrtens and S. Wenk (eds), *Myths, Gender and the Military Conquest of Air and Sea*. Oldenburg: BIS Verlag.

Dietrich, Z., Joye, S. and Garcia, J. (2015). 'Natural medicine: wilderness experience outcomes for combat veterans'. *Journal of Experiential Education* 38(4), 394–406.

Dixon, P. (2018). *Warrior Nation: War, Militarisation and British Democracy*. London: Forces Watch.

Docherty, L. (2007). *Desert of Death*. London: Faber & Faber.

Dodds, C. D. and Kiernan, M. D. (2019). 'Hidden veterans: a review of the literature on women veterans in contemporary society'. *Illness, Crisis & Loss* 27, 293–310.

Dorling, D. and Tomlinson, S. (2019). *Rule Britannia: Brexit and the End of Empire*. London: Biteback.

Duncombe, C. (2019). 'The politics of Twitter: emotions and the power of social media'. *International Political Sociology* 13, 409–29.

Dyvik, S. (2016). '"Valhalla rising": gender, embodiment and experience in military memoirs'. *Security Dialogue* 47(2), 133–50.

Dyvik, S. (2016). 'Of bats and bodies: methods for reading and writing embodiment'. *Critical Military Studies* 2(1/2), 56–69.

Dwyer, P. (2018). 'Making sense of the muddle: war memoirs and the culture of remembering'. In P. Dwyer (ed.), *War Stories: The War Memoir in History and Literature*. London: Berghahn, pp. 1–26.

Edgerton D. (2006). *Warfare State: Britain, 1920–1970*. Cambridge: Cambridge University Press.

Edkins, J. (2003). *Trauma and the Memory of Politics*. Cambridge: Cambridge University Press.

Edwards, P. and Wright, T. (2019). 'No man's land: research study to explore the experience and needs of women veterans in the UK'. Available at: https://static1.squarespace.com/static/5829ccde2e69cf19589499ac/t/5d6d386d21083d00012a670a/1567438965062/No+Mans+Land+Final+TW+1.pdf, last accessed 30 October 2023.

Eichler, M. (2012). *Militarizing Men: Gender, Conscription, and War in post-Soviet Russia*. Stanford: Stanford University Press.

Eichler, M. (2017). 'Add female veterans and stir? A feminist perspective of gendering veterans research'. *Armed Forces & Society* 43(4), 674–94.

Elliott, M. and Ormrod, M. (n.d.). 'No limits', available at: https://www.youtube.com/watch?v=BoZd08Pkiu4, last accessed 30 November 2023.

Enloe, C. (2000) *Maneuvers: The International Politics of Militarizing Women's Lives*. Berkeley: University of California Press.

Enloe, C. (2007). *Globalization and Militarism: Feminists Make the Link*. Lanham, MD: Rowman & Littlefield.

Enloe, C. (2010). *Nimo's War, Emma's War: Making Feminist Sense of the Iraq War*. Berkeley: University of California Press.

Fairclough, N. (1992). 'Discourse and text: linguistic and intertextual analysis within discourse analysis'. *Discourse & Society* 3(2), 193–217.

Fell, A. (2018). *Women as Veterans in Britain and France after the First World War*. Cambridge: Cambridge University Press.

Forces in Mind Trust (2018). 'Activity Report 2017'. Available at: https://s31949.pcdn.co/wp-content/uploads/20180622-FiMT-Report-2017-v.7Final.pdf, last accessed 31 October 2023.

Forces in Mind Trust (2020). 'Impact Report 2019'. Available at: https://s31949.pcdn.co/wp-content/uploads/20200717-FiMT-Electronic-Impact-Report-2019.pdf, last accessed 31 October 2023.

Forces in Mind Trust (2020). '2020 impact report'. Available at: FiMT-Impact-Report-2020-Electronic.pdf (pcdn.co), last accessed 31 October 2023.

Forces Net (2020). 'Life after service'. Available at: Life after service (forces.net), last accessed 31 October 2023.

Foucault, M. (2003). *Society Must be Defended*. London: Penguin.

Fussell, P. (1975). *The Great War and Modern Memory*. Oxford: Oxford University Press.

Frank, A. W. (2006). 'Health stories as connectors and subjectifiers'. *Health: An Interdisciplinary Journal* 10(4), 421–40.

Frank, A. W. (2010). *Letting Stories Breathe: A Socio-Narratology*. Chicago: University of Chicago Press.

Frank, A. W. (2012). 'Practicing dialogical narrative analysis'. In J. A. Holstein and J. F. Gubrium (eds), *Varieties of Narrative Analysis*. Thousand Oaks, CA: Sage, 33–52.

Frank, A. (2016). 'Knowing other people's stories: empathy, illness, and identity'. *Concentric: Literary and Cultural Studies* 42(2), 151–65.

Freeman, M. (2010). *Hindsight: The Promise and Peril of Looking Backward*. Oxford: Oxford University Press.

Gallagher, B. (2016). 'Burdens of proof: veteran frauds, PTSD pussies, and the spectre of the welfare queen'. *Critical Military Studies* 2(3), 139–54.

Gbadegesin, V. (2020). 'Gender ideology and identity in humorous social media memes'. *Digital Scholarship in the Humanities* 35(3), 529–46.

Gentleman, A. (2020). 'British army veteran faces £27,000 NHS hospital bill'. *The Guardian*. Available at: https://www.theguardian.com/uk-news/2020/may/18/british-army-veteran-faces-27000-nhs-hospital-bill?CMP=Share_iOSApp_Other, last accessed 30 October 2023.

Gergen, K. (2009). *Relational Being: Beyond Self and Community*. Oxford: Oxford University Press.

Gilbert, J. (2020). *Twenty-first Century Socialism*. Cambridge: Polity Press.

Gilroy, P. (2004). *After Empire: Melancholia or Convivial Culture?* London: Routledge.

Giroux, H. (2000). 'Public pedagogy as cultural politics: Stuart Hall and the crisis of culture'. *Cultural Studies* 14(2), 341–60.

Glenton, J. (2013). *Soldier Box: Why I Won't Return to the War on Terror*. London: Verso.

Glenton, J. (2021). *Veteranhood: Rage and Hope in British ex-Military Life*. London: Repeater.

Godier, L., Caddick, N., Kiernan, M. and Fossey, M. (2018). 'Transition support for vulnerable Service leavers in the U.K.: providing care for early Service leavers'. *Military Behavioural Health* 6(1), 13–21.

Godier-McBard, L., Caddick, N. and Fossey, M. (2020). 'Confident, valued and supported: examining the benefits of employment support for military spouses'. *Military Psychology* 32(3), 273–86.

Godier-McBard, L., Gillin, N. and Fossey, M. (2021). 'We also served: the health and well-being of female veterans in the UK'. Available at: https://www.centreformilitarywomensresearch.com/wp-content/uploads/2022/11/WeAlsoServed_Electronic.pdf, last accessed 31 October 2023.

Godier-McBard, L., Gillin, N. and Fossey, M. (2022). '"Treat everyone like they're a man": stakeholder perspectives on the provision of health and social care support for female veterans in the UK'. *Health and Social Care in the Community* 30, 3966–76.

Godier-McBard, L., Wood, A., Kohomange, M., Cable, G. and Fossey, M. (2023). 'Barriers and facilitators to mental healthcare for women veterans: a scoping review'. *Journal of Mental Health* 32(5), 951–61.

Goodley, H. (2012). *An Officer and a Gentlewoman: The Making of a Female British Army Officer*. London: Constable, pp. 169–70.

Gray, H. (2016). 'Researching from the spaces in between? The politics of accountability in studying the British military'. *Critical Military Studies* 2(1/2), 70–83.

Gray, H. (2016). 'Domestic abuse and the public/private divide in the British military'. *Gender, Place & Culture* 23(6), 912–25.

Green, C. (2017). *Spin Zhira (Old Man in Helmand)*. London: OMiH.

Green, G., Emslie, C., O'Neill, D., Hunt, K. and Walker, S. (2010). 'Exploring the ambiguities of masculinity in accounts of emotional distress in the military among young ex-servicemen'. *Social Science and Medicine* 71, 1480–8.

Gubrium, J. and Holstein, J. (2009). *Analyzing Narrative Reality*. Thousand Oaks, CA: Sage.

Halkiopoulos, S., Makinson, L. and Heal, J. (2018). 'Improving transition out of the Armed Forces': engaging families through behavioural insights'. Available at: https://www.fim-trust.org/wp-content/uploads/improving-transition-armed-forces-engaging-families-behavioural-insights.pdf, last accessed 31 October 2023.

Hall, S. (2011). 'The neoliberal revolution'. *Cultural Studies* 25(6), 705–28.

Hall, S. (2016). *Cultural Studies 1983: A Theoretical History*. Durham, NC: Duke University Press.

Harari, Y. (2008). *The Ultimate Experience: Battlefield Revelations and the Making of Modern War Culture, 1450–2000*. Basingstoke: Palgrave Macmillan.

Harel-Shalev, A. (2021). '"A room of one's own(?)" in battlespace: women soldiers in war rooms'. *Critical Military Studies* 7(1), 42–60.

Harel-Shalev, A. and Daphna-Tekoah, S. (2016). 'Bringing women's voices back in: conducting narrative analysis in IR'. *International Studies Review* 18(2), 171–94.

Harman, S. (2019). *Seeing Politics: Film, Visual Method, and International Relations*. Montreal: McGill-Queens University Press.

Hast, S. (2020). 'Synching the martial body: poetic encounters with Finnish cadets'. *Critical Military Studies* 8(4), 385–408.

Havlick, D., Cerveny, L. and Derrien, M. (2021). 'Therapeutic landscapes, outdoor programs for veterans, and public lands'. *Social Science & Medicine* 268, 1–9.

Hawkins, B., Townsend, J. and Garst, B. (2016). 'Nature-based recreational therapy for military service members: a strengths approach'. *Therapeutic Recreation Journal* 1(1), 55–74.

Herman, A. and Yarwood, R. (2015). 'From warfare to welfare: veterans, military charities and the blurred spatiality of post-service welfare in the United Kingdom'. *Environment and Planning A* 47, 2628–44.

Herriott, C., Wood, A., Gillin, N., Fossey, M. and Godier-McBard, L. (2023). 'Sexual offences committed by members of the armed forces: is the service justice system fit for purpose? *Criminology & Criminal Justice*. https://doi.org/10.1177/17488958231153353.

Higate, P. (2023). 'Proud to "fly a desk" and wear a medal? Interrogations of military pride through the eyes of the RAF veteran'. *Critical Military Studies* 9(1), 5–23.

Higate, P. and Cameron, A. (2006). 'Reflexivity and researching the military'. *Armed Forces & Society* 32(2), 219–33.

Higate, P., Dawes, A., Edmunds, T., Jenkings, N. and Woodward, R. (2021). 'Militarization, stigma, and resistance: negotiating military reservist identity in the civilian workplace'. *Critical Military Studies* 7(2), 173–91.

Hirsh, A. (2018). *Brit(ish): On Race, Identity and Belonging.* London: Penguin.

HM Government (2018). 'The strategy for our veterans: valued, contributing, supported'. Available at: Strategy for our veterans - GOV.UK (www.gov.uk), last accessed 30 October 2023.

HM Government. (2019). 'PM creates new Office for Veterans Affairs to provide lifelong support to military personnel'. Available at: https://www.gov.uk/government/news/pm-creates-new-office-for-veterans-affairs-to-provide-lifelong-support-to-military-personnel, last accessed 30 October 2023.

HM Government (2021). 'Defence response to the 'Women in the Armed Forces' report'. Available at: Defence response to the 'Women in the Armed Forces' Report - GOV.UK (www.gov.uk), last accessed 30 October 2023.

HM Government (2022). 'Tackling sexual offending in Defence'. Available at: 20220718_Sex_Offending_Strategy.pdf (publishing.service.gov.uk), last accessed 30 October 2023.

HM Government (2022). 'Veterans' Strategy Action Plan 2022–2024'. Available at: https://assets.publishing.service.gov.uk/government/

uploads/system/uploads/attachment_data/file/1047675/Veterans-Strategy-Action-Plan-2022-2024.pdf, last accessed 31 October 2023.

Holland, J. (2015). 'Constructing crises and articulating affect after 9/11'. In L. Åhäll and T. Gregory (eds), *Emotions, Politics and War*. London: Routledge, pp. 167–81.

Holyfield, L., Cobb, M., Herford, S., and Ogle, K. (2019). 'Masculinity under attack: melodramatic resistance to women in combat'. *Critical Military Studies* 5(2), 168–88.

Howarth, C., Doherty, R. and Cole, S. (2021). 'Armed forces charities' financial support'. Available at: https://s31949.pcdn.co/wp-content/uploads/Focus-On-Finance-FINAL-PDF.pdf, last accessed 31 October 2023.

Howell, A. (2012). 'The demise of PTSD: from governing through trauma to governing resilience'. *Alternatives: Global, Local, Political* 37(3), 214–26.

Howell, A. (2018). 'Forget "militarization": race, disability and the "martial politics" of the police and of the university'. *International Feminist Journal of Politics* 20(2), 117–36.

Hunt, R. and Robbins, I. (1998). 'Telling stories of the war: ageing veterans coping with their memories through narrative'. *Oral History* 26(2), 57–64.

Huxford, G. (2016). The Korean War never happened: forgetting a conflict in British society and culture. *Twentieth Century British History* 27(2), 195–219.

Huxford, G., Alcade, A., Baines, G., Burtin, O. and Edele, M. (2019). Writing veterans' history: a conversation on the twentieth century. *War and Society* 38(2), 115–38.

Hyde, A. (2016). 'The present tense of Afghanistan: accounting for space, time and gender in processes of militarisation'. *Gender, Place and Culture* 23(6), 857–68.

Ingham, S. (2014). *The Military Covenant: Its Impact on Civil–Military Relations in Britain*. London: Routledge.

Jenkings et al. (2011). 'Military occupations: methodological approaches and the military–academy research nexus'. *Sociology Compass* 5(1), 37–51.

Jude, S. (2020). 'Breaking the silence: embodiment, militarisation and military dissent in the Israel/Palestine conflict'. In C. Baker (ed.), *Making War on Bodies: Militarisation, Aesthetics and Embodiment in International Politics*. Edinburgh: Edinburgh University Press, pp. 97–120.

Kapur, N., While, D., Blatchley, N., Bray, I. and Harrison, K. (2009). 'Suicide after leaving the UK Armed Forces: a cohort study. *PLoS Medicine* 6(3), 1–9.

Kienzler, H. (2008). 'Debating war-trauma and post-traumatic stress disorder in an interdisciplinary arena'. *Social Science & Medicine* 67, 218–27.

Kleinreesink, L. (2014). 'On Military Memoirs: Soldier-authors, Publishers, Plots and Motives', doctoral thesis, Erasmus University, Rotterdam.

Kleinreesink, L. and Soeters, J. (2016). 'Truth and (self)censorship in military memoirs'. *Current Sociology* 64(3), 373–91.

Kronsell, A. and Svedberg, E. (2012). *Making Gender, Making War: Violence, Military and Peacekeeping Practices*. London: Routledge.

Ledwidge, F. (2013). *Investment in Blood: The True Cost of Britain's Afghan War*. New Haven, CT: Yale University Press.

Leigh, D. (2023). 'From savages to snowflakes: race and the enemies of free speech'. *Review of International Studies* 49(4), 763–79.

Lembcke, J. (2015). *PTSD: Diagnosis and Identity in post-Empire America*. Lanham, MD: Lexington Books.

Levitt, H. M., Surace, F. I., Wu, M. B., Chapin, B., Hargrove, J. G., Herbitter, C., Lu, E. C., Maroney, M. R. and Hochman, A. L. (2022). 'The meaning of scientific objectivity and subjectivity: from the perspective of methodologists'. *Psychological Methods* 27(4), 589–605.

Lister, R. (1997). 'Citizenship: towards a feminist synthesis'. *Feminist Review* 57, 28–48.

Long, E. (2022). 'Maximising operational effectiveness: exploring stigma, militarism, and the normative connections to military partners' support-seeking'. *Sociology* 56(3), 538–55.

Lyon, P. (2013). 'Continuities and discontinuities: 'investigating British poetry anthologies of the Second World War'. *Journal of War & Culture Studies* 6(3), 201–14.

MacKenzie, M. (2023). *Good Soldiers Don't Rape: The Stories We Tell about Military Sexual Violence*. Cambridge: Cambridge University Press.

MacLeish, K. (2013). *Making War at Fort Hood: Life and Uncertainty in a Military Community*. Princeton, NJ: Princeton University Press.

MacLeish, K. (2020). 'Churn: Mobilization–demobilization and the fungibility of American military life'. *Security Dialogue* 51(2/3), 194–210.

Manchanda, N. (2020). *Imagining Afghanistan: The History and Politics of Imperial Knowledge*. Cambridge: Cambridge University Press.

Mattingly, C. (2010). *The Paradox of Hope: Journeys Through a Clinical Borderland*. Berkeley: University of California Press.

Mattingly, C. (2014). *Moral Laboratories: Family Peril and the Struggle for a Good Life*. Oakland: University of California Press.

McCartney, H. (2011). 'Hero, victim or villain? The public image of the British soldier and its implications for defense policy'. *Defense & Security Analysis* 27(1), 43–54.

McGarry, R. (2017). 'Demystifying the "victimised state": a civil–military crisis in waiting?' *Illness, Crisis & Loss* 25(1), 63–84.

McGarry, R. (2021). 'Visualizing liminal military landscape: a small scale study of Armed Forces Day in the United Kingdom'. *Critical Military Studies* 8(3), 273–98.

McGarvey, D. (2017). *Poverty Safari: Understanding the Anger of Britain's Underclass*. London: Picador.

McLoughlin, K. (2018). *Veteran Poetics: British Literature in the Age of Mass Warfare, 1790–2015*. Cambridge: Cambridge University Press.

McSorely, K. (2013). *War and the Body: Militarisation, Practice and Experience*. London: Routledge.

Mercer, J. (2017). *We Were Warriors: One soldier's Story of Brutal Combat*. London: Sidgwick & Jackson.

Messner, M. (2018). *Guys Like Me: Five Wars, Five Veterans for Peace*. New Brunswick, NJ: Rutgers University Press.

Millar, K. (2023). *Support the Troops: Military Obligation, Gender, and the Making of Political Community*. Oxford: Oxford University Press.

Millar, K and Tidy, J. (2017). 'Combat as a moving target: masculinities, the heroic soldier myth, and normative martial violence'. *Critical Military Studies* 3(2), 142–60.

Ministry of Defence (2019). 'Annual population survey: UK armed forces veterans residing in Great Britain, 2017'. Available at: https://assets.publishing.service.gov.uk/government/uploads/system/uploads/attachment_data/file/774937/20190128_-_APS_2017_Statistical_Bulletin_-_OS.pdf, last accessed 30 October 2023.

Ministry of Defence (2020). 'Unacceptable behaviours: Progress review 2020'. Available at: Unacceptable behaviours-progress review 2020 (publishing.service.gov.uk), last accessed 7 November 2023.

Molendijk, T., Kramer, E. and Verweij, D. (2016). 'Conflicting notions on violence and PTSD in the military: institutional and personal narratives of combat-related illness'. *Culture, Medicine & Psychiatry* 40, 338–60.

Nelson, H. L. (2001). *Damaged Identities, Narrative Repair*. New York: Cornell University Press.

Nguyen, V. T. (2016). *Nothing Ever Dies: Vietnam and the Memory of War*. Cambridge, MA: Harvard University Press.

Noakes, L. (2006). *Women in the British Army: War and the Gentle Sex, 1907–1948*. London: Routledge.

Office for Veterans Affairs (2020). Veterans' Office marks one year since establishment. Available at: Veterans' Office marks one year since establishment - GOV.UK (www.gov.uk), last accessed 30 October 2023.

Olusoga, D. (2014). *The World's War: Forgotten Soldiers of Empire*. London: Head of Zeus.

Omar, Q. A. (2013). *A Fort of Nine Towers*. London: Picador.

de Orellana, P. and Michelsen, N. (2019). 'Reactionary internationalism: the philosophy of the New Right'. *Review of International Studies* 45(5), 748–67.

Ormrod, M. (2009). *Man Down*. London: Bantam.

O'Toole, F. (2018). *Heroic Failure: Brexit and the Politics of Pain*. London: Head of Zeus.

Parashar, S. (2013). 'What wars and "war bodies" know about international relations'. *Cambridge Review of International Affairs* 26(4), 615–30.

Pearson, C. and Caddick, N. (2018). 'Meeting the needs of Commonwealth personnel and families: A map of service provision'. Research report commissioned by Forces in Mind Trust, UK.

Parry, K. (2022). 'Representing public service and post-militariness in *Bodyguard* (BBC, 2018)'. *New Review of Film and Television Studies* 20(2), 169–93.

Parry, K. and Pitchford-Hyde, J. (2022). '"We may have bad days . . . that doesn't make us killers": how military veterans perceive contemporary British media representations of military and post-military life'. *Media, War & Conflict* 16(3), 440–58.

Peace Pledge Union. (n.d.) 'Remembrance and white poppies'. Available at: https://www.ppu.org.uk/remembrance-white-poppies, last accessed 30 October 2023.

Pividori, C. (2014). 'Of heroes, ghosts, and witnesses: the construction of masculine identity in the war poets' narratives'. *Journal of War & Culture Studies* 7(2), 162–78.

Plummer, K. (1995). *Telling Sexual Stories: Power, Change and Social Worlds*. London: Routledge

Plummer, K. (2016). 'Narrative power, sexual stories and the politics of storytelling'. In I. Goodson, A. Antikainen, P. Sikes and M. Andrews (eds), *The Routledge International Handbook on Narrative and Life History*. London: Routledge, pp. 280–92.

Plummer, K. (2019). *Narrative Power*. Cambridge: Polity Press.

Polkinghorne, D. (1988). *Narrative Knowing and the Human Sciences*. New York: SUNY Press.

Pozo, A. and Walker, C. (2014). 'UK armed forces charities: an overview and analysis', Report commissioned by Forces in Mind Trust. Available at: Sector Insight - Armed Forces Charities (dsc.org.uk), last accessed 31 October 2023.

Purdy, M. (2019). 'Paternalism and prosthesis: life for disabled veterans and their families on a post-war settlement'. In D. Swift and O. Wilkinson (eds), *Veterans of the First World War: Ex-Servicemen and ex-Servicewomen in post-War Britain and Ireland*. Abingdon: Routledge, pp. 142–57.

Qureshi, A. (2020). *I Refuse to Condemn*. Manchester: Manchester University Press.

Reed, M. and Fazey, I. (2021). 'Impact culture: transforming how universities tackle twenty-first-century challenges'. *Frontiers in Sustainability* 2, 1–18.

Riessman, C. (2008). *Narrative Methods for the Human Sciences*. Thousand Oaks, CA: Sage.

Rodway, C., Ibrahim, S., Westhead, J., Bojanić, L., Turnbull, P., Applby, L., Bacon, A., Dale, H., Harrison, K. and Kapur, N. (2023). 'Suicide after leaving the UK armed forces 1996–2018: a cohort study'. *PLoS Medicine*, 20(8), e1004273. https://doi.org/10.1371/journal.pmed.1004273.

Rose, N. and Miller, P. (1992). 'Political power beyond the state: problematics of government'. *British Journal of Sociology* 43(2), 173–205.

Roselle, L., Miskimmon, A. and O'Loughlin, B. (2014). 'Strategic narrative: a new means to understand soft power'. *Media, War & Conflict* 7(1), 70–84.

Rossdale, C. (2019). *Resisting Militarism: Direct Action and the Politics of Subversion*. Edinburgh: Edinburgh University Press.

Royal British Legion. (n.d.). 'What is Remembrance?' Available at: https://www.britishlegion.org.uk/get-involved/remembrance/about-remembrance, last accessed 30 October 2023.

Royal British Legion (2014). 'A UK household survey of the ex-service community'. Available at: A UK household survey of the ex-Service community (rblcdn.co.uk), last accessed 30 October 2023.

Sabbagh, D. (2019). 'Thousands of military veterans "let down by medical discharge failures"'. *The Guardian*. Available at: Thousands of military veterans 'let down by medical discharge failures' | Military | The Guardian, last accessed 31 October 2023.

Said, E. (1978). *Orientalism*. London: Penguin.

Said, E. (1994). *Culture and Imperialism*. London: Vintage.

Said, E. (1994). *Representations of the Intellectual*. New York: Vintage.

Sasson-Levy, O. (2002). 'Constructing identities at the margins: masculinities and citizenship in the Israeli Army'. *Sociological Quarterly* 43(3), 357–83.

Schiff, B. (2017). *A New Narrative for Psychology*. Oxford: Oxford University Press.

Schiller, N. (1997). 'Cultural politics and the politics of culture'. *Identities: Global Studies in Culture and Power* 4(1), 1–7.

Schrader, B. (2019). *Fight to Live, Live to Fight: Veteran Activism after War*. Albany: SUNY Press.

Scott, G. (2021). 'Johnson should apologise to troops and families over Afghanistan, says Tory MP'. *The Evening Standard*. Available at: Johnson should apologise to troops and families over Afghanistan, says Tory MP | Evening Standard, last accessed 31 October 2023.

Scullion, L., Dwyer, P., Jones, K., Martin, P. and Hynes, C. (2019). 'Sanctions, support and service leavers: social security benefits and transitions from military to civilian life'. Available at: https://www.fim-trust.org/wp-content/uploads/sanctions-support-service-leavers-final-report.pdf, last accessed 31 October 2023.

Shay, J. (1994). *Achilles in Vietnam: Combat Trauma and the Undoing of Character*. New York: Scribner.

Shilling, C. (2012). *The Body and Social Theory*, 3rd edn. Thousand Oaks, CA: Sage.

Smith, B. and Sparkes, A. (2008). 'Contrasting perspectives on narrating selves and identities: an invitation to dialogue'. *Qualitative Research* 8(1), 5–35.

Smith, H. L. (2017). *Don't Let My Past Be Your Future*. London: Constable.

Smith, S. and Watson, J. (2010). *Reading Autobiography: A Guide for Interpreting Life Narratives*. Minneapolis: University of Minnesota Press.

Soloman, T. (2015). 'Embodiment, emotions, and materialism in international relations'. In L. Åhäll and T. Gregory (eds), *Emotions, Politics and War*. London: Routledge.

Somers, M. (1994). 'The narrative constitution of identity: a relational and network approach'. *Theory & Society* 23(5), 605–49.

Somers, M. (2008). *Genealogies of Citizenship: Markets, Statelessness, and the Right to Have Rights*. Cambridge: Cambridge University Press.

Sparkes, A. and Smith, B. (2008). 'Narrative constructionist research'. In J. Holstein and J. Gubrium (eds), *Handbook of Constructionist Research*. New York: Guilford Press, pp. 295–314.

SSAFA (2016). 'The new frontline: voices of veterans in need'. Available at: the-new-frontline-ssafa-research-report.pdf, last accessed 31 October 2023.

SSAFA (2018). 'The Nation's Duty: Challenging Society's Disservice to a New Generation of Veterans'. Available at: the-nations-duty-ssafa-research-report.pdf, last accessed 31 October 2023.

Stahl, R. (2009). 'Why we "support the troops": rhetorical evolutions'. *Rhetoric & Public Affairs* 12(4), 533–70.

Stavrianakis, A. (2009). 'In arm's way: arms company and military involvement in education in the UK'. *ACME* 8(3): 505–20.

Stewart, S. (2023). 'I'm not a victim: I'm a survivor', *The Sunday Post*. Available at: RAF veteran reveals rape as she calls for change in forces (sundaypost.com), last accessed 30 October 2023.

Strand, S. (2021). 'Inventing the Swedish (war) veteran'. *Critical Military Studies* 7(1), 23–41.

Swift, D. (2017). *For Class and Country: The Patriotic Left and the First World War*. Liverpool: Liverpool University Press.

Swift, D. and Wilkinson, O. (eds). (2019). *Veterans of the First World War: Ex-servicemen and ex-Servicewomen in post-War Britain and Ireland*. Abingdon: Routledge.

Sylvester, C. (2011). *Experiencing War*. London: Routledge.

Sylvester, C. (2013). *War as Experience: Contributions from International Relations and Feminist Analysis*. London: Routledge.

Thomson, L., McKenzie, C. and Vaughan, B. (2022). 'Evaluation of the Poppy Factory's NHS-embedded employment support pilot for veterans. Available at: TPF-Final-Report-.pdf (pcdn.co), last accessed 31 October 2023.

Tidy, J. (2016). 'The gender politics of "ground truth" in the military dissent movement: the power and limits of authenticity claims regarding war'. *International Political Sociology* 10, 99–114.

Tidy, J. (2018). 'Fatherhood, gender, and interventions in the geopolitical: analyzing paternal peace, masculinities, and war'. *International Political Sociology* 12(1), 2–18.

Tidy, J. (2019). 'War craft: the embodied politics of making war'. *Security Dialogue* 50(3): 220–38.

Ware, V. (2010). 'Whiteness in the glare of war'. *Ethnicities* 10(3), 313–30.

Ware, V. (2012). *Military Migrants: Fighting for YOUR Country*. London: Palgrave Macmillan.

Wasinksi, C. (2019). 'When the war machine produces its enemies: making sense of the Afghan situation through British airpower'. *Critical Military Studies* 5(4), 341–58.

Wessely, S. (2005). 'Risk, psychiatry and the military'. *British Journal of Psychiatry* 186, 459–66.

West, H. and Antrobus, S. (2023). '"Deeply odd": women veterans as critical feminist scholars'. *Critical Military Studies* 9(1), 24–39.

Wheaton, B. (2007). 'Identity, politics, and the beach: environmental activism in Surfers Against Sewage'. *Leisure Studies* 26(3), 279–302.

Whelan, J. (2014). *Going Crazy in the Green Machine: The Story of Trauma and PTSD among Canada's Veterans*. Victoria, BC: Friesen Press.

Wibben, A. (2011). *Feminist Security Studies: A Narrative Approach*. Abingdon: Routledge.

Wieskamp, V. (2019). '"I'm going out there and I'm telling my story": victimhood and empowerment in narratives of military sexual violence'. *Western Journal of Communication* 83(2), 133–50.

Wigston, M. (2019). 'Report on inappropriate behaviours'. Available at: Wigston review (publishing.service.gov.uk), last accessed 30 October 2023.

Wilkinson, O. (2019). 'Ex-prisoners of war, 1914–18: veteran association, assimilation and disassociation after the First World War'. In D. Swift and O. Wilkinson (eds), *Veterans of the First World War: Ex-Servicemen and ex-Servicewomen in post-War Britain and Ireland*. Abingdon: Routledge, pp. 172–90.

Woodward, R. and Jenkings, K. (2012). '"This place isn't worth the left boot of one of our boys": geopolitics, militarism and memoirs of the Afghanistan war'. *Political Geography* 31, 495–508.

Woodward, R. and Jenkings, K. (2018). *Bringing War to Book: Writing and Producing the Military Memoir*. London: Palgrave Macmillan.

Woodward, R., Dawes, A., Edmunds, T., Higate, P. and Jenkings, K. (2020). 'The possibilities and limits of impact and engagement in research on military institutions'. *Area* 52, 505–13.

Woodward, R., Winter, T. and Jenkings, N. (2009). 'Heroic anxieties: the figure of the British soldier in contemporary print media'. *Journal of War & Culture Studies* 2(2), 211–23.

Wool, Z. (2013). 'On movement: the matter of US soldiers' being after combat'. *Ethnos* 78(3), 403–33.

Wool, Z. (2015). *After War: The Weight of Life at Walter Reed*. Durham, NC: Duke University Press.

Young, A. (1997). *The Harmony of Illusions: Inventing Post-Traumatic Stress Disorder*. Princeton, NJ: Princeton University Press.

INDEX

academic, 115–20, 126, 128–30, 132
activism, 172, 180
affect, 82, 90, 173
Afghanistan, 6, 12, 14–15, 22, 31–2, 38, 45, 52, 108, 120, 135–54
aggression, 157–8, 162, 164–5, 171
Alcade, A., 47
alienation, 13, 49, 63, 105–7, 109–10
Allen, D., 35–7, 71
amateurism, 132
ambiguity, 46, 48, 52
Andrews, M., 25, 30, 33, 111
Antrobus, S., 53–4
anxiety, 63, 120, 158, 164
Arias, L., 18
Armed Forces Covenant Fund Trust, 127
army, 6, 35–7, 55, 60, 71, 95–6, 101, 105, 138–40, 142, 146, 157, 163, 169
Ashcroft, M., 68n, 97–101, 125
Ashplant, T., 26, 34
Atherton, S., 59–62
audience, 37, 39
autobiography, 26, 56, 136, 139, 159; *see also* memoir

Badenoch, K., 75
Bakhtin, M., 137–8
banter, 85–7, 170, 172
Basham, V., 5–6, 34, 141
betrayal, 45, 49, 83–5, 97, 109–10, 143, 169, 173
Black Lives Matter, 75, 85–6, 88
Blair, T., 140

body, 21–5, 41n, 49, 158–9, 162–4, 171, 174; *see also* embodiment
Bolland, H., 57–8
Bourdieu, P., 129
Bourke, J., 49
British Forces Broadcasting Service, 101
Bulmer, S., 63, 107, 110
Butler, J., 70, 88–90

Cameron, D., 97
care, 126–9, 168, 170, 172
Cenotaph, 114
censorship, 136
character, 12, 30, 45, 47, 69–72, 76–82, 84, 89–90, 94n, 109–11, 140, 148
charity, 96–7, 103, 105, 107–8, 121, 124–9, 157, 160, 162, 172
citizenship, 56, 79–81, 89
 super-citizens, 64, 69–91
civilian, 6, 8, 11, 32, 54–6, 63, 72–3, 77, 90, 95–6, 98, 100, 103, 106–11, 139, 166, 178
civvy street, 3
class, 73, 89, 91n
Coates, M., 75–6, 80, 102–3
colonialism, 7–8, 52, 81, 85, 92n
combat, 5, 7, 54, 56–7, 74, 77–8, 174
commemoration, 32–4, 51–3, 65
Commonwealth, 55
compassion, 15, 159, 162–3, 168–9, 172; *see also* care
Cree, A., 108
Crick, A., 76

cultural capital, 8, 36, 38, 142, 182
cultural politics
  academic intersection with, 116–18, 129–33
  and Afghanistan, 152–4
  contested, 75, 95
  core principles of, 21–38
  critical project, 4, 64–5, 70–1, 90–1, 177–9, 183
  definition, 8–9
  divisive, 19
  key questions of, 19, 28, 32, 37–8
  occurring in narrative, 7–12
  trauma as integral to, 158–9, 170–2

Dannatt, R., 138–42, 146, 148–9, 152–3
Darda, J., 86
declassified podcast, 13, 75–81, 84, 90, 102–3, 182
democracy, 32, 56, 85, 119, 124, 144–5, 148
depoliticised, 3, 117, 119, 126, 129–30, 132, 152, 173; *see also* narrative politics
diagnosis, 158–62, 166; *see also* post-traumatic stress disorder
dialogue, 18–21, 30, 38, 51–2, 64–5, 70, 137–8, 151–2, 154, 178
disavowal, 145–6
disillusionment, 49, 73, 83, 96, 142, 147
dissent, 148, 180
Dixon, P., 37, 83
Duncombe, C., 81–2

Edkins, J., 169, 176n
Eichler, M., 107, 110
embodiment, 22, 25, 87, 171, 175n
emotion, 5, 13, 22–3, 45, 81–4, 93n, 108–9, 115, 164–5
  emotional scripts, 35, 108–9, 165
empathy, 126, 145; *see also* narrative empathy
empire, 6, 53, 75, 85; *see also* imperialism
employment, 54, 98, 100, 106–7, 114, 117
Enloe, C., 90
ethics of recognition, 19, 34

Facebook, 82
Fairclough, N., 137
Falklands/Malvinas War, 18–19, 30–1, 52, 141
Fazey, I., 131
Fell, A., 50
female *see* women
feminism, 21, 54, 79, 81, 86
First World War, 49–50, 53
flesh witnesses, 135, 161, 182
Forces in Mind Trust, 14, 114, 118–26, 132
Foucault, M., 181
Frank, A., 9–10, 12, 20, 24, 28, 38, 65, 69, 77, 94n, 109, 136, 138, 140, 152, 159, 182
functionalist, 118, 120–1, 133n
Fussel, P., 49

Gbadegesin, V., 82
Gee, D., 73
gendered, 12, 23, 29, 34, 50, 53–4, 58–9, 74, 86, 90, 106–7, 124, 135, 168–70, 172
genre, 25, 38–9, 47, 70, 138
Gilroy, P., 50, 52
Glenton, J., 73, 146–9, 153
Goodley, H., 27
Gray, H., 134n
Green, C., 142–7, 149, 153
grievability, 70, 90
ground truth, 135, 182
Gurkhas, 87

Hall, S., 91n
Harari, Y., 161
Harmer, 78
healing, 158–9, 168–72, 174, 176n, 180
Helmand Province, 142–4, 146
Herman, A., 126
heroes, 45, 55, 63–4, 70, 77, 147–8, 152, 159
Herriott, L., 62
heteroglossia, 137–8, 152
Higate, P., 56, 73
Hirsch, A., 81
history, 45, 47–53, 63, 75, 85

Howell, A., 3, 160-1
humanitarianism, 5, 46, 48, 149, 151
Huxford, G., 53

imagination, 24, 30-2, 42n, 137, 179-80; *see also* stories
impact, 14, 114-16, 119-21, 124, 127-8, 130-1
imperialism, 46, 53, 85, 136-7, 146, 149, 152; *see also* empire
Ingham, S., 48
inherent morality, 30, 139; *see also* stories
institutional gaslighting, 59-60; *see also* narrative gaslighting
interpretive openness, 30, 151, 153; *see also* stories
Invictus Games, 1-2, 22-3, 54, 64, 76
Iraq, 52, 57, 108
Islam, M., 77-8

Jackson, D., 63
Jenkings, K., 136
Johnson, B., 44-5, 75, 109

Kabul, 149-50
knowledge, 117, 132
   knowledge economy, 120
Korean War, 52-3

McGarry, R., 63, 99, 133-4n, 181-2
MacKenzie, M., 59-62, 68n
MacLeish, K., 162, 175n
McLoughlin, K., 47-8, 177, 179, 182
Manchanda, N., 42n, 137, 154
marginalisation, 5, 7, 45, 48-50, 52-6, 63-4, 110-11, 131-2
martial politics, 3, 117
masculinity, 23, 29, 34, 53-4, 56, 58, 74, 77, 86, 107, 147-8, 153, 168-70, 172
Masterman, J., 95
materiality, 159
medicalisation, 161, 173
memes, 82-8, 92n
memoir, 14, 22, 26, 135-54
memory, 51-3, 162
Mercer, J., 12, 44-5, 76, 102, 107

migrant, 55, 64, 81, 88-9
militarism, 3, 6, 10-11, 19-20, 28, 46, 50, 56, 62, 73, 83, 89, 137, 149, 154, 181
   academy, 14, 114-33
   anti-militarism, 14, 118, 131
   British, 4, 6, 16, 38, 45-6, 52, 62-4, 97, 123, 135, 146, 148, 158, 163
   failure of, 14-15, 135-54
   liberal, 27, 37, 46, 123-4, 141, 148, 153
   militarist terms of reference, 5, 13, 46-7, 64, 70, 79, 90
   vectors of, 136
military sexual trauma, 57, 67n; *see also* sexual violence
Mill, J. S., 142
Millar, K., 23
mimetic logic, 24
Minefield/Campo Minado, 18-19, 30-1
Ministry of Defence, 4, 53, 57, 60-1, 98-9, 101, 107, 114-16, 119-23, 159
misogyny, 35-7, 62, 71, 82
Molendijk, T., 161
monarchy, 73-4, 81, 92n
moral injury, 160-1
multiculturalism, 83, 86

narrative
   agency, 25, 28, 153
   analysis, 20, 38, 40n
   archetypal, 13-14, 63, 96, 110-11
   context, 38-39, 137
   counter-narrative, 26-9, 104, 180
   definition, 9
   disenfranchisement, 13, 49, 96, 103-10, 127
   empathy, 21, 65, 90, 175
   gaslighting, 106
   institutional, 15, 158-62, 171, 173-4, 180
   intertextual, 135-54
   knowledge practices, 180-3
   liberal progress, 14, 97, 116, 119-26
   macro, 25, 28, 37
   politics, 7-8, 21, 25, 114-33; *see also* politics of storytelling

narrative (*cont.*)
  power, 13, 21, 29, 35–8, 97, 102, 104, 110, 116, 180
  public, 5, 25–6, 59, 63–4
  relational and historical, 32–5, 137
  resources, 49
  state transition, 13, 97–104, 109, 121, 123–4, 127
nation, 45, 48, 52–3, 56, 63–4, 72, 74, 78, 83, 116
nationalism, 4, 35, 51, 83, 85–6, 89
nature, 162, 171, 174, 176n
neoliberal, 14, 46, 89, 100, 116, 121, 125, 130
Nguyen, V., 19, 34, 51–2
Northern Ireland, 52
Nugee, R., 116

objectivity, 121, 126, 132
Office for Veterans' Affairs, 12, 44, 98, 101–2, 120
Olusoga, D., 50
Omar, Q. A., 31–2, 138, 149–153
operational effectiveness, 125
orientalist, 113n, 145, 151
Ormrod, M., 21–2, 24, 26

pandemic, 74–6
Parashar, S., 21–22
pathology, 160–1
patriotism, 11, 19, 45, 50, 53, 56, 63–5, 73, 85, 87, 132, 173, 178
Peace Pledge Union, 34
Plummer, K., 7, 12, 21, 36–7, 97, 102, 116, 177, 180
point of view, 30; *see also* stories
policy, 119–20, 122, 124–32
  policymakers, 116, 120, 124, 160
politics of storytelling, 12, 21, 45, 59, 61
post-traumatic growth, 76
post-traumatic stress disorder, 3, 15, 29, 56–7, 157–62, 166, 169–74; *see also* trauma
Prince Harry, 1–3, 7, 23, 76
professional, 131–2
psychiatry, 159–60, 174

Queen Elizabeth II, 87

racialised, 50, 55, 85, 87, 153
racism, 75, 82, 85–6, 89–90, 183
Ratucaucau, T., 55–6
recovery, 165; *see also* healing
Reed, M., 131
refugees, 71, 75, 81, 85, 88–9, 93–4n, 150
Remembrance, 9, 32, 34, 64, 66n, 74
research, 115–20, 132, 159–60
  funding of, 14, 115–21, 125–7, 130–1
  Research Excellence Framework, 118, 127, 131
respect, 5, 11, 13, 52, 64–5, 69–70, 78, 90, 177–8
retention, 115, 117
Richardson, W., 105
Rossdale, C., 46, 118
Royal Air Force, 57, 101
Royal British Legion, 32–3, 66n, 68n
Royal Marine, 22
Royal Navy, 166

Said, E., 113n, 131–2, 137
Schiff, B., 24
Schiller, N., 9
Schrader, B., 27, 73, 172
Second World War, 32–3, 46, 50–4
service, 56, 64, 70, 73, 79–80, 84–5, 90–1, 108, 110, 116, 178
Service Justice System, 57–8, 62
sexism, 36–7, 71, 90
sexual violence, 12, 45, 57–62, 67n, 68n, 174, 180
Shay, J., 171, 174–5
Smith, S., 136
social media, 8, 13, 52, 71, 81–2, 85, 92–3n, 108
socio-narratology, 20–1, 69, 159
soldier, 24, 86, 99, 138–40, 143
Soloman, T., 41n
Somers, M., 79–80, 87–8
spouses, 114–17, 121
SSAFA, 51, 96, 105–7
state, 4, 22, 26, 49, 62, 96, 98–100, 102–3, 106, 109–10, 127, 142, 181–2
stigma, 61, 105, 109, 173

stories
    actors, 12, 19–21, 28–32, 37, 41n
    capacities of, 10, 29–32, 69, 159–60
    contested, 95–7, 102–10
    contextual, 16n, 20
    definition, 9
    dilemmas of storytelling, 179–80
    'good', 19, 30–1, 69, 103, 109
    shareable, 61, 68n, 179–80
    out of control, 20
Strand, S., 100
structures of feeling, 73, 91n
suicide, 76, 166, 181–2
support, 119–20, 126, 129–30
surfing, 15, 157–75
    description of, 163–4, 167
    flow, 167
    Surfers Against Sewage, 172
Swift, D., 49
symptoms, 57, 161–2, 171; *see also* post-traumatic stress disorder

Taliban, 22, 31, 120, 135, 138, 145, 147, 149–52
Thatcher, M., 141
Tidy, J., 23, 91n
transition, 13, 63, 95–111, 122–3, 126
trauma, 15, 29, 57, 78, 126, 157–75, 180
    as political, 160–1, 171–5
    clinical trauma discourse, 158, 160, 175n
    communalisation of, 171–2
    contested trauma stories, 160–1
    culture of, 160
    unlearning of, 164–5, 170–1
    valorisation of, 173
trouble, 159–60; *see also* stories
trust, 162, 168–9, 171, 174
truth-telling, 29, 32, 182; *see also* stories
Twitter, 81–2, 92n, 108, 118
Tytherleigh, E., 78

values, 3, 9, 11, 13, 19, 23, 29–30, 32, 39, 64, 69, 72, 75–9, 92n, 178
    values talk, 78, 178

veterans
    anti-war, 147–9
    broken, 96, 159, 179
    critical, 73
    culture, 72–5
    definition, 5
    entrepreneurial, 97, 101, 104, 110
    history, 12, 47–53
    identity, 5, 12, 53, 72, 82–3, 96, 107–10
    political figures, 4
    veteranness, 5, 14, 71, 96, 100–3, 107, 109–11
Veterans and Families Institute, 115
Veterans Strategy, 62, 101, 103
Veterans Transition Review, 68n, 97–103, 182
victimhood, 61–2, 64, 161
Vietnam War, 159
violence, 54, 56–7, 64, 85, 90, 115, 130, 151, 153, 157–8, 162, 169
voice, 20, 109–10, 179–80
    reclaiming of, 57, 61

War on Terror, 52, 149
Ware, V., 55–6
Watson, J., 136
Wessely, S., 160
West, H., 53–4
whiteness, 53, 55, 86, 172
Wibben, A., 7, 173
Wieskamp, V., 61
Wigston, M., 58–60, 62
Wiseman, D., 75
women, 35–7, 50, 53–4, 58–62, 70–1, 77, 103, 106–7, 115
Wood, B., 75
Wood, L., 76, 78
Woodward, R., 136
Wool, Z., 162, 175n, 179, 183n
Wren, J., 51–2
Wylie, J., 69, 78

Yarwood, R., 126

EU Authorised Representative:
Easy Access System Europe Mustamäe tee 50, 10621 Tallinn, Estonia
gpsr.requests@easproject.com

Printed and bound by CPI Group (UK) Ltd, Croydon, CR0 4YY
02/03/2026
02063697-0003